PSYCHOLOGY AND LAW:
TRUTHFULNESS ACCURACY AND
CREDIBILITY

One Week Loan

One
Week
Loan

PSYCHOLOGY AND LAW: TRUTHFULNESS ACCURACY AND CREDIBILITY

Amina Memon, Aldert Vrij and Ray Bull

McGraw-Hill Publishing Company

London · New York · St Louis · San Francisco · Auckland · Bogotá · Caracas
Lisbon · Madrid · Mexico · Milan · Montreal · New Delhi · Panama · Paris
San Juan · Sao Paulo · Singapore · Sydney · Tokyo · Toronto

Published by
McGraw-Hill Publishing Company
Shoppenhangers Road, Maidenhead, Berkshire, SL6 2QL, England
Telephone 01628 502500
Facsimile 01628 770224

The LOC data for this book has been applied for and may be obtained from the
Library of Congress, Washington, D.C.

A catalogue record for this book is available from the British Library.

Further information on this and other McGraw-Hill titles is to be found at
http://www.mcgraw-hill.co.uk

McGraw-Hill

A Division of The McGraw-Hill Companies

Typeset by Mackreth Media Services, Hemel Hempstead

Printed and bound in Great Britain at the University Press, Cambridge
Printed on permanent paper in compliance with ISO Standard 9706

CONTENTS

PART 2 ■ ACCURACY

The last 20 years has seen an explosion of research in the psychology and law field. The area that has grown more than any other is research on perceptions of credibility and accuracy of participants in the legal system. Psychologists have asked questions that have direct relevance in the legal arena such as what factors influence the accuracy of eyewitness reports? Psychologists have also conducted research to address such questions as: are there reliable indicators of deception? Does facial appearance predict criminality? Most recently, the debate concerning the reliability and validity of evidence based upon recovered memories has been addressed by legal professionals in North America and Europe. The controversy surrounding recovered memories relies on knowledge about psychological mechanisms underlying forgetting and this knowledge is likely to determine whether or not testimony based on a recovered memory is admissible in court.

In putting together the chapters for this book we have drawn upon material we have used in an advanced undergraduate psychology option (Psychology and Law) that we jointly taught at the universities of Portsmouth and Southampton. The topics selected reflect our own areas of expertise in the field of legal psychology as well as issues that have been of particular interest to our students on the psychology and law course. We do not aim to provide a complete coverage of the area but instead to focus our attention on the pre-trial or investigative phase of the legal process. The emphasis of this text is on the application of psychological research in the legal context and our text is mainly directed towards undergraduate and graduate students taking options in legal psychology, forensic psychology, criminology and law. Much of the material is new data and we review numerous research projects that have been conducted in the last 5–10 years. The aim of our text is to provide an up-to-date and balanced review of the North American and European literature on the topic.

When physical evidence is lacking or ambiguous, as is often the case in investigations, there are two things that the criminal justice system relies upon: (1) perceived credibility of the participants (offenders, victims and witnesses), and (2) accuracy of evidence. The first part of the book provides a detailed discussion of credibility issues. Current research on statement validity analysis is reviewed. A full description of the latter is provided in the opening chapter. Chapter 2 examines nonverbal communication and credibility. It explores whether or not there are nonverbal differences between truth tellers and liars, observers' beliefs about nonverbal indicators and the extent to which lay-persons and experts can detect deception. Facial appearance and criminality is the topic for Chapter 3 which among other things examines evidence on prisoners' recidivism rates of surgery designed to improve facial appearance. The detection of physiological activity in liars through the use of the polygraph is explored in the final chapter in the credibility section. This chapter examines the nature of the assumed relationship between physiological measures and credibility by evaluating the polygraph.

Credibility is one factor that is likely to influence decision making in the legal context. However, perceived credibility and accuracy do not always correspond. The opening chapter in Part II reviews psychological factors known to influence the accuracy of eyewitness testimony and sets the scene for the remainder of the book. In this chapter we compare accurate versus inaccurate witnesses; factors that influence encoding and retrieval of information (such as the characteristics of the testing procedure) and how this knowledge can be used in giving evidence on eyewitness issues in court.

Accuracy of details relies upon co-operation from witnesses. Suspects are not always willing to talk. Chapter 6 focuses on interviews with suspects and examines the conditions under which confessions are elicited and how this may influence accuracy. Chapter 7 provides us with some poignant examples of the impact of recovered memories in the legal context. Evidence from experimental and clinical studies of memory are reviewed and there is a discussion of the legal implications of the recovered memory debate.

There are two chapters on interviewing, each of which focuses on current research and practices with respect to investigative interviews with adult and child witnesses (Chapters 8 and 9, respectively). The final chapter examines the role of psychologists who may serve as experts to the courts. This chapter draws upon material considered in earlier chapters in order to discuss the role of psychological research in the courts and the rules governing the admissibility of expert evidence.

ACKNOWLEDGEMENTS

The preparation of this manuscript was undertaken while Amina Memon was on leave from Southampton University, UK and during her time as visiting professor at University of Texas at Dallas and Southern Methodist University. Aldert Vrij and Ray Bull are at Portsmouth University, UK. The original idea for this text came from Professor Peter Robinson of Bristol University and was encouraged by our students and colleagues in the field of psychology and law. We are grateful to the following experts for providing us with comments on various chapters in the book: Doug Brandon, Tony Gale, Dan Shuman, John Pearse, Julie Cherryman, Frans Winkel, Gisli Gudjonsson and Eberhard Höfer.

PART 1

Perceived Credibility

VERBAL COMMUNICATION AND CREDIBILITY: STATEMENT VALIDITY ASSESSMENT

Aldert Vrij and Lucy Akehurst

INTRODUCTION

In 1954 the Supreme Court of West Germany summoned a small number of experts to a hearing. The Court wanted to assess to what extent psychologists could help in determining the credibility of child witnesses' testimonies (particularly in trials for sexual offences). The forensic psychologist Udo Undeutsch reported the case of a 14-year-old alleged victim of rape which he had investigated. The five Justices of the Senate "were impressed by the demonstration and convinced themselves that in assessing the truthfulness of the testimony of a child or juvenile witness an expert psychologist conducting an out-of-court examination has other and better resources than the persons acting as fact finders within the formal atmosphere of a courtroom trial" (Undeutsch, 1989, p. 104). Subsequently a ruling was made by the German Supreme Court in 1955 that required the use of psychological interviews and assessments of credibility in virtually all contested cases of child sexual abuse. This led to numerous cases in which psychologists were called on as experts (Arntzen (1982) estimated that by 1982 expert testimony had been offered in more than 40 000 cases) and also to the development, in West Germany and Sweden, of various interview procedures and content criteria to assess the credibility of statements made by alleged victims of sexual abuse (Arntzen, 1983; Trankell, 1972; Undeutsch, 1967, 1982). Based on their work, Steller and Köhnken (1989) have compiled a list of such assessment criteria and have described a procedure for evaluating the veracity of a statement. This is now known as Statement Validity Assessment or SVA.

STATEMENT VALIDITY ASSESSMENT (SVA)

SVA consists of three major elements (Raskin and Esplin, 1991b, p. 268):

1. A structured interview
2. A Criteria-Based Content Analysis (CBCA) that systematically assesses the contents and qualities of the obtained statement
3. Integration of the CBCA with information derived from a set of questions (Validity Checklist) that combine the results of the content analysis with other relevant information and factors derived from an analysis of the interview.

The structured interview

The first phase, the interview, is an open-ended investigative interview based on psychological principles designed to obtain as much information as possible from the child in free narrative style (see Bull (1992, 1995) and Chapter 9 of this volume for a detailed description of this type of interview). An SVA interview is not a therapy session (it is not meant to 'help' the child to cope with his or her emotional problems) or an interrogation (the interviewer will never exert any kind of psychological or physical pressure to obtain information). SVA interviews are always audiotape recorded. Videotape recording, however, is preferred because any possible biasing effects of the interviewer can then be identified more easily (Honts, 1994; Lamb, Sternberg and Esplin, 1994; Yuille, 1988). The interview is normally transcribed afterwards and these transcriptions are used for the Criteria-Based Content Analysis. It is preferable that the content analysis takes place on the basis of the transcription and not on the basis of the videotape, because the nonverbal content of the videotape may have a disturbing influence on the raters (see Chapter 2 of this volume).

The Criteria-Based Content Analysis

The second phase of SVA is the systematic assessment of the credibility of the statement given during the interview, the so-called Criteria-Based Content Analysis (CBCA). Table 1.1 provides an overview of the 19 criteria used in the assessment. Trained evaluators examine the statement and judge the presence or absence of each of the 19 criteria, usually

TABLE 1.1 *Content criteria for statement analysis*

General characteristics
  1. Logical structure
  2. Unstructured production
  3. Quantity of details

Specific contents
  4. Contextual embedding
  5. Descriptions of interactions
  6. Reproduction of conversation
  7. Unexpected complications during the incident
  8. Unusual details
  9. Superfluous details
 10. Accurately reported details misunderstood
 11. Related external associations
 12. Accounts of subjective mental state
 13. Attribution of perpetrator's mental state

Motivation-related contents
 14. Spontaneous corrections
 15. Admitting lack of memory
 16. Raising doubts about one's own testimony
 17. Self-deprecation
 18. Pardoning the perpetrator

Offence-specific elements
 19. Details characteristic of the offence

---

on a 3-point scale where '0' is assigned if the criterion is absent, '1' if the criterion is present and '2' if the criterion is strongly present. CBCA is not a 'verbal lie detector', that is it is not searching for 'lie symptoms'. CBCA focuses on the presence of specific semantic content characteristics. The presence of each criterion in the statement enhances the quality of the statement and strengthens the hypothesis that the account is based on genuine personal experience. The absence of a criterion does not necessarily mean that the statement is fabricated (Yuille, 1988).

General characteristics

The general characteristics of the statement include criteria which refer to the statement as a whole.

  1. *Logical structure.* Logical structure is present if the statement essentially makes sense, that is if the statement is coherent and logical and the different segments fit together, that is different segments are not inconsistent or discrepant.
  2. *Unstructured production.* Unstructured production is present if the information is scattered throughout the statement instead of mentioned in a structured, coherent and chronological order. The incoherent and unorganized manner of presentation is, for instance caused by digressions or spontaneous shifts of focus. However, the statement

as a whole should not include inconsistencies (criterion 1). Winkel, Vrij, Koppelaar and van der Steen (1991) found that emotionally disturbed adults rape victims tend to speak in very unstructured and incoherent ways.

3. *Quantity of details.* This criterion requires that the statement must be rich in detail, that is specific descriptions of place, time, persons, objects and events should be present, for instance peculiar details about the place where the alleged crime occurred.

Specific contents

Specific contents refer to particular passages in the statement and are meant to reveal the concreteness and vividness of the statement.

4. *Contextual embedding.* Contextual embedding is present if the events are placed in time and location, and when the actions are connected with other daily activities and/or customs. For example, 'Mr S. would ask me to come over and play after school 'cause Mrs S. had to go clean people's houses then... We had to take off our clothes and put on bathrobes 'cause our clothes might get dirty and my mom would be mad at me.'[1]

5. *Descriptions of interactions.* This criterion is fulfilled if the statement contains information about interactions involving at least the accused and witness, and if this information consists of three parts, i.e. an action of actor A leads to a reaction of actor B which leads to a reaction of actor A again. For example, 'I said no and he pulled me anyway and I tried to run' would fulfil this criterion because the three necessary elements are present.

6. *Reproduction of speech.* Reproduction of speech is present if speech, or parts of the conversation, is reported in its original form and if the different speakers are recognizable in the reproduced dialogues. This criterion is not satisfied by a report about the content of a dialogue; it is only satisfied when there is a virtual replication of the utterances of at least one person. Thus, 'I said "please stop" to him' fulfils this criterion but 'Then we talked about sports' would not.

7. *Unexpected complications during the incident.* This criterion is present if there are elements incorporated in the event which are somewhat unexpected. For instance an unforeseen interruption of the event, such as 'He stopped when they knocked on the door to bring us our pizza'.

8. *Unusual details.* Unusual details refer to details of persons, objects, or events which are unusual and/or unique but meaningful in the context, such as a child who gives a description of a tattoo on the alleged perpetrator's backside.

9. *Superfluous details.* Superfluous details are present if the witness describes details in connection with the allegations which are not essential for the accusation, such as a child who says that the adult tried to get rid of the cat which entered the bedroom because he (the adult) is allergic to cats.

10. *Accurately reported details misunderstood.* This criterion is fulfilled if the witness speaks of details that lie beyond the horizon of the comprehension of the witness, for instance a child that describes the adult's sexual behaviour but attributes it to a sneeze or to pain. Gordon, Schroeder and Abams (1990) and Volbert and van der Zanden (1996) found that children younger than 8-years-old hardly have any knowledge about sexual behaviour.

11. *Related external associations*. A related external association is present when the witness reports conversation that is not part of the alleged offences but refers to other similar events, for instance 'He talked about the women he had done it with and the differences between them'.
12. *Accounts of subjective mental state*. This criterion is present when the witness describes feelings or thoughts experienced at the time of the incident, as well as reports of cognitions, such as thinking about how to escape while the event was in progress. For instance 'I said that in a kind of a shaky voice 'cause I got so scared'.
13. *Attribution of perpetrator's mental state*. This criterion is present if the witness describes the perpetrator's feelings, thoughts or motives during the incident. For instance 'I told him to stop and he wouldn't, 'cause he didn't hear me 'cause he was dreaming'.

Motivation-related contents

Motivation-related contents refer to the way the statement is presented by the witness. Similar to 'specific contents', it refers to specific passages of the statement.

14. *Spontaneous corrections*. This criterion is fulfilled if corrections are spontaneously offered or information is spontaneously added to material previously provided in the statement (spontaneous means without any interference by the interviewer). For instance 'Then he pulled the dining room table out and, no, actually then he talked about sexual things again...' (correction) or 'Then he pulled the dining room table out and...the colour of the table was brown, he pulled it out in a specific manner, only with the help of two fingers' (addition).
15. *Admitting lack of memory*. This criterion is present if a witness admits lack of memory by either saying 'I don't know' or 'I don't remember' or by giving a more extensive answer. For example: 'I forgot all about this except for the part when we were in the car'.
16. *Raising doubts about one's own testimony*. This criterion is present if the witness expresses concern that some part of the statement seems incorrect or unbelievable. For example 'You know, this thing is so weird and Mr L. is so nice that I thought nobody would ever believe me'.
17. *Self-deprecation*. Self-deprecation is present if the witness mentions personally unfavourable, self-incriminating details, for example 'And I was scared to tell 'cause I shouldn't have been at his house'.
18. *Pardoning the perpetrator*. Pardoning the perpetrator is present if the witness tends to favour the alleged perpetrator in terms of making excuses for the alleged perpetrator or failing to blame the alleged perpetrator. For example 'I know he didn't want to hurt me. He was just really drunk and he looked really sad the next day, and is he going to jail?'.

Offence-specific elements

Offence-specific elements relate the statement to the particular crime. It differs from category two, i.e. specific contents, because it is not related to the general vividness of the statement *per se* but only in its relation to the particular crime.

19. *Details characteristic of the offence*. This criterion is present if a witness describes

events in a manner in which professionals know that certain crimes occur. For instance the progression of events in an incestuous relationship would be expected to differ from the dynamics surrounding a single-incident stranger assault, that is the first type of crime usually includes less violence and less resistance by the victim than the latter type of crime.

CBCA is based on the hypothesis, originally stated by Undeutsch (1967), that a statement derived from memory of an actual experience differs in content and quality from a statement based on invention or fantasy. This is known as the Undeutsch Hypothesis (Steller, 1989). The Undeutsch Hypothesis implicitly assumes that only a person who actually experienced an event is likely to incorporate certain types of content into a statement (this is referred to by Köhnken (1996) as the cognitive component of the Undeutsch Hypothesis). More precisely, the cognitive component refers to the question: 'Would a child be able to make up an allegation with qualities such as those described by the criteria?' (Steller, 1989, p. 138). It is assumed that persons who invent an event are more unlikely to speak in as concrete and vivid a way as those who actually experienced the event, possibly due to less knowledge about the event, or due to a lack of imagination to make up certain vivid details.

The Undeutsch Hypothesis further assumes that persons who fabricate a story are also unlikely to say things that might easily be interpreted by others as making up a story (this is referred to by Köhnken (1996) as the motivational component of the Undeutsch Hypothesis). Hence, the motivational component refers to the question: 'Would somebody mention details that tend to be unfavourable to him or herself if the person were fabricating an account?' (Steller, 1989, p. 138). For instance if liars believe that adding corrections, admitting lack of memory, and raising doubts about one's own memory will undermine their perceived credibility, they may avoid these aspects. Witnesses who invent stories with the aim of damaging someone else are not likely to state that it was at least partly their fault that the incident occurred.

A combination of these cognitive and motivational components may explain the general characteristics of the statement. Individuals who fabricate a statement might be of the opinion that inconsistencies will make their story seem less convincing, and therefore prefer to tell their story in such a way that makes it easy to remember what they have said previously, that is in a chronological, structured way without mentioning too many details.

The Validity Checklist

CBCA itself is not sufficient to form a definite conclusion concerning the validity of the allegations. A victim may have, for a variety of reasons, provided a statement lacking most of the criteria, and sometimes fabricated statements contain several criteria. In order to organize and standardize the final assessment, a Validity Checklist has been developed (Steller, 1989; Steller and Boychuk, 1992). The Validity Checklist is presented in Table 1.2. By systematically addressing each of the topics, the evaluator can explore and consider alternative interpretations of the CBCA outcomes. A negative response by the evaluator to each topic is consistent with the outcome adopted on the basis of the CBCA.

TABLE 1.2 *Validity checklist*

Psychological characteristics
1. Inappropriateness of language and knowledge
2. Inappropriateness of affect
3. Susceptibility to suggestion

Interview characteristics
4. Suggestive, leading or coercive questioning
5. Overall inadequacy of the interview

Motivation
6. Questionable motives to report
7. Questionable context of the original disclosure or report
8. Pressures to report falsely

Investigative questions
9. Inconsistency with the laws of nature
10. Inconsistency with other statements
11. Inconsistency with other evidence

Each affirmative response raises a question about the appropriateness of the CBCA outcome. After considering the elements of the Validity Checklist and all of the available information, the evaluator will make a conclusion about the likely validity of the statement.

Psychological characteristics

The first category of topics deals with individual characteristics of the interviewee.

1. *Inappropriateness of language and knowledge.* This issue refers to whether the witness' use of language and display of knowledge was beyond the normal capacity for a person of his or her age and beyond what the witness may have learned from the incident. When this occurs, it may indicate the influence of other people in preparing the statement.
2. *Inappropriateness of affect.* This issue refers to whether the affect displayed by the witness (usually via nonverbal behaviour) is unlikely to occur given the witness' experiences and the circumstances under which the interview takes place. For example, if a girl reports details of her abuse, without showing any sign of emotion, the story is less trustworthy than in the case of a clear display of emotions.
3. *Susceptibility to suggestion.* This issue refers to whether the witness demonstrated any susceptibility to suggestion during the interview. Yuille (1988) and Landry and Brigham (1992) recommend asking the witness, at the end of the interview, a few leading questions about peripheral information in order to assess the witness' susceptibility to suggestion.

Interview characteristics

Interview characteristics (items 4 and 5) refer to the interviewer's style or manner while conducting the interview. The interview should be conducted following the psychological principles designed to obtain as much information as possible from the witness in free narrative style. This issue will be further addressed in Chapter 9 of this volume.

Motivation

This section explores the motives of the witness in reporting the incident.

6. *Questionable motives to report.* This issue refers to whether the witness possibly has questionable motives to report. This applies, for example to the relationship between the witness and the accused and to the possible consequences of the accusation for all individuals involved. Relevant in this context is a possible custody/access dispute or divorce process between the child's parents. For example it is possible that one of the parties in a conflict or a custody dispute could coach the child to make an incriminating statement about the other party in order to win the dispute.

7. *Questionable context of the original disclosure or report.* This issue refers to the origin and history of the statement, in particular the context of the first report. Possible questionable elements in the context of the original disclosure of the accusation are explored. For example whether the first report was voluntary and who asked the child to report (boyfriend, girlfriend, parents, teacher and so on).

8. *Pressures to report falsely.* This issue deals with the question of whether there are indications that others suggested, coached, pressured, or coerced the witness to make a false report.

Investigative questions

The fourth category deals with the statement in its relation to the type of crime and previous statements. Raskin and Esplin (1991b) moved criterion 19 of the CBCA list into this section on the grounds that it is not related to the general vividness of the statement *per se* but to the particular crime.

9. *Inconsistency with the laws of nature.* This issue refers to the possibility the described events are unrealistic.

10. *Inconsistency with other statements.* This issue refers to the possibility that major elements of the statement are inconsistent or contradicted by another statement made by the witness or by another witness.

11. *Inconsistency with other evidence.* This issue refers to the possibility that major elements in the statement are contradicted by reliable physical evidence or other concrete evidence.

OBJECTIVE VERBAL CHARACTERISTICS OF TRUTH TELLING

A literature review of CBCA studies

SVA is widely used nowadays in Germany in criminal cases in order to assess children's statements concerning alleged sexual abuse. Undeutsch (1982, 1984) has conducted about 1500 statement analyses, the majority of them in cases of sexual offences against children or juveniles. Ninety per cent of these statements were diagnosed by him as truthful, and in

95 per cent of these diagnosed truthful cases the accused was convicted by the court. 'Not one of those convicted defendants has ever been shown to have been innocent by the later discovery of conflicting evidence' (Undeutsch, 1982, p. 50). SVA is well established in German courts, prosecutors and defence lawyers very rarely challenge the reliability or validity of the test, although they are allowed to do this (Köhnken, 1997, personal communication). Prosecution and defence are also allowed to challenge or discredit the SVA evidence, for instance by finding weak spots in the expert witnesses' reasoning, by cross-examining the expert in court or by hiring another expert to advise them about the quality of the expertise (Köhnken, 1997, personal communication). It sometimes occurs that two experts come to a different conclusion, for instance because one expert believes that the other did not appropriately take into account the origin of the statements, i.e. type of questioning, suggestibility and so on. Moreover, the courts do not always follow the results of the assessment (Köhnken, 1997, personal communication). In Germany, there does not yet exist a formal way of becoming an expert. To date 'you become an expert when you are nominated as such by court'. This will probably change in the future as the German Psychology and Law Society is currently developing an official education program to allow psychologists to become SVA experts (Köhnken, 1997, personal communication).

The opinion in North American countries (Canada and the USA) about using SVA in court is divided. Some experts/researchers are in favour of presenting the results of SVA as evidence in court (see for instance Raskin and Esplin, 1991b; Honts, 1994; Yuille, 1988), others are more sceptical (see for instance Boychuk, 1991; Wells and Loftus, 1991). The results of SVA are presented as evidence through expert testimony in some North American courts, but it is considerably less common than in Germany. The main value of SVA in North America seems to lie in its utility for gathering information, guiding investigations, making administrative decisions, and exercising prosecutorial discretion (Raskin and Esplin, 1991b).

Although SVA has been used in German criminal trial cases for over 40 years, surprisingly little scientific research has been conducted so far in order to obtain evidence for the validity of CBCA-based assessments. One approach would be to examine the technique under controlled laboratory conditions. In such a situation participants would be asked to tell the truth or to fabricate an account, and their statements would be assessed afterwards by evaluators utilizing the CBCA technique. The major advantage of this approach is that the scientist has control over the situation and knows with certainty which participants are lying and which participants are telling the truth. Undeutsch (1984) believes that laboratory experiments would be of little use, 'especially for the evaluation of a technique whose aim is to seize the qualities of genuine experience of emotionally affecting events' (p. 63). Laboratory experiments will, according to Undeutsch, inevitably lack ecological validity and realism. He suggests that field studies should be conducted instead to assess the validity of the technique.

However, field studies have limitations as well. Perhaps the greatest problem concerns the criterion against which one measures the accuracy of the technique. It is virtually impossible, in most criminal cases, to get to the 'basic reality', to establish some sort of *ground truth* (Raskin, 1982). In other words it is often impossible to know for sure which people are telling the truth and which people are lying. Confessions of the alleged perpetrators are usually used as external criteria. As argued by Steller and Köhnken (1989), there are, however, some particular problems associated with the use of this external criterion. In Germany 'Statement analyses by psychological experts are usually obtained if no other incriminating or exonerating evidence is available. If, under such conditions, an incriminating statement is judged as truthful, the chances for the defendant to obtain an acquittal decrease dramatically... and, if there is no chance of avoiding a guilty verdict, it may be a beneficial strategy to confess to a crime not committed, since this is usually considered as repentance by the court and results in a reduction of the penalty... . On the other hand, there is no reason for the defendant to confess to a crime if the expert witness has judged the major witnesses' statement to be deceptive. As a result, the probability of a confession may be influenced by the diagnosis itself, and the attempt to validate this diagnosis by the confession is clearly circular' (p. 239).[2] (Chapter 6 of this volume deals with the issue of confessions).

Eleven studies utilizing CBCA assessments appear to have been published to date, three field studies and eight experimental studies.[3] The results are presented in Table 1.3.

Field studies
A scientifically credible field study should fulfil four criteria (Lykken, 1988):

TABLE 1.3 *Objective (actual) relationship between verbal characteristics and truth-telling*

	Criteria																		
	1	2	3	4	5	6	7	8	9	10	11	12	13	14	15	16	17	18	19
Field studies utilizing CBCA list																			
Boychuk (1991)	>	>	>	>	>	>	>	>	>	−	>	>	−	>	−	−	−	>	−
Esplin *et al.* (1988)	>	>	>	>	>	>	>	>	>	−	>	>	>	>	>	>	−	−	>	>
Lamb *et al.* (in press)	−	>	>	>	>	>	−	>	−	−	−	−	−	−	−				
Experimental studies utilizing CBCA list																			
Akehurst (1997)*	−	>	>	−	−	−	−	>	−	−		−	−	>	−	>			
Höfer *et al.* (1996)*	>	−	>	>	−	>	>	−	−		>	−	−						
Köhnken *et al.* (1995)*	−	>	>		−	−	−	−	−	−		−	−	>	−				
Landry *et al.* (1992)*	<		>	>	>	>	−	>	>		>	<	>	>	>	−			
Porter *et al.* (1996)*	>	−	>	−	−	−	−	−	−	−	−	−	−	>	−	−	−	−	−
Steller *et al.* (1988)	>		>	>	−	−	>	>	>	>	>	>	>	−	−	−		<	−
Winkel *et al.* (1995)	>	>	>	>	>			−			>			−	−	−			
Zaparniuk (1995)*	−	>	−	−	−	−	−	−	−	−	−	−	−	−	−	−	−	−	−

Note: The signs refer to the actual verbal characteristic–truth-telling relationship (> = increase in the frequency of the verbal characteristic during truth-telling, < = decrease in the frequency of the verbal characteristic during truth telling, − = no difference found between the frequency during fabricated and truthful statements, blank = frequency is not investigated).
* used adult statements.
Porter *et al.* (1996) used statements of suspects.

1. Selection of a representative sample of cases
2. Administration under real-life circumstances
3. Having the statements independently scored by at least two evaluators who were blind to case disposition (that is who were unaware of the ground truth), and
4. Comparison of these scores with ground truth established by some criterion that is independent of the CBCA findings.

Only the study conducted by Lamb, Sternberg, Esplin, Hershkowitz, Orbach, and Hovav (in press) fulfilled these four scientific criteria. This implies that at present only one CBCA study that fulfils scientific criteria is available. The findings of the other two studies (Boychuck, 1991; Esplin, Bochuck and Raskin, 1988) should be interpreted with caution. The first CBCA study ever presented was Esplin, Boychuk and Raskin's (1988) field study (also described by Raskin and Esplin (1991a)). They analysed the witness statements, in sexual abuse cases, of 40 children (aged 3 to 15 years). Twenty of these cases were 'confirmed'. The confirmations were based on (a) perpetrators' confessions to the allegations and (b) definite physical evidence. The other 20 cases were classified as doubtful based on (a) persistent denial by the accused, (b) lack of corroborating evidence, (c) recantation by the child, (d) polygraph results indicating that the accused was truthful in denying the allegation, or (e) judicial dismissal of the case. The transcribed statements were evaluated by one rater who had received training in CBCA and who was blind to the group membership (confirmed or doubtful) of the cases. If a criterion was not present in the statement, it received a score of 0; if it was present, it received a score of 1, and if it was strongly present it received a score of 2. Hence, total CBCA scores were possible in a range of 0 to 38. The results were striking. The confirmed cases received a mean CBCA score of 24.8, the doubtful statements received a mean score of 3.6. Moreover, the distributions of scores of the confirmed and doubtful groups did not show a single overlap: the highest score in the doubtful group was 10 (one child received that score, three children obtained a score of 0), the lowest score in the confirmed group was 16 (one child obtained that score, the highest score was 34). By assessing differences between the two groups on each criterion, differences between the doubtful and confirmed groups emerged for 17 out of 19 criteria (all in the expected direction, that is the criteria were more often present in the confirmed cases than in the doubtful cases, see Table 1.3).

Wells and Loftus (1991) refer to Esplin *et al.*'s findings as 'among the most impressive we have ever encountered in a psychological study' (p. 169). They give alternative explanations for the outcomes. First, the differences between the two groups could be caused by age differences between these groups. Indeed, the children in the 'confirmed' group were slightly older (9.1 years) than the children in the 'doubtful' group (6.9 years). Secondly, it might be the case that the children in the 'doubtful' group were less convincing than the children in the 'confirmed' group. 'They might be unconvincing, even though sexual abuse occurred, for any number of reasons. For example these children might have deficiencies in logical reasoning, they might have been frightened to the extent that they could not process peripheral detail, they might have poor verbal skills, and so on. Because they are unconvincing witnesses, prosecutors might be unlikely to press charges (lack of prosecution), judges might feel that conviction is unlikely (judicial dismissal), and defense attorneys might be unlikely to advise their clients to admit to the charges (no confessions and persistent denial by the accused)' (p. 169). Thirdly, perhaps the cases selected in this study were extreme cases and less striking outcomes may appear when more uncertain cases are assessed.

Boychuk (1991) addressed some of these criticisms in her study. She controlled for age differences, used three raters who were blind to case disposition and included in her sample (apart from 'confirmed' and 'doubtful' groups) a third group, namely a 'likely abused' group. The 'likely abused' were those without medical evidence but with confessions by the accused or criminal sanctions from a Superior Court. Unfortunately, in all of her analyses (including the one presented in Table 1.3) she combined the confirmed group and the likely abused group. By assessing differences between the two groups on each criterion, Boychuk found less significant differences than Esplin and colleagues (see Table 1.3) but all differences found were in the expected direction, that is the criteria were more often present in the confirmed cases than in the doubtful cases.

Lamb et al. (in press) analysed the plausibility of the statements of 98 alleged victims of child sexual abuse (aged 4 to 12 years). Based upon independent evidence (such as medical evidence, confessions, polygraph examinations) the statements of 76 children were classified as likely plausible, the statements of 13 children as unlikely plausible and the remaining nine statements as questionable (the questionable category was excluded from the analyses). They found fewer significant differences than Boychuk and Esplin et al. (although not all criteria were included in the assessment), however, again all differences were in the expected direction, i.e. the criteria were more often present in the likely plausible group than in the unlikely plausible group. Like Esplin et al., they also calculated the mean CBCA scores of their two groups. Significantly more criteria were present in the confirmed cases (6.74) than in the doubtful cases (4.85) (only 14 criteria were used, hence, 14 was the maximum score), however, this difference is much smaller than the difference found by Esplin et al.

A fourth (unpublished) field study has been conducted by Craig (1995) in which he examined statements of children aged 3 to 16. He also found a relatively small difference between his confirmed cases (7.2) and his doubtful cases (5.7). Only mean CBCA scores were reported in this study. Again, only 14 criteria were used.

Perhaps as important as the criteria's ability to discriminate, is their frequency of occurrence in statements. A criterion that discriminates highly between truthful and fabricated statements is only useful when it occurs often in statements. Esplin et al.'s study showed that criteria 10, 11, and 16 seldomly occurred in the statements. Lamb et al. found that criteria 9 and 11 seldomly, and criterion 1 almost always, occurred in the statements. Finally, Boychuk found that particularly criteria 10, 13, and 17 seldomly occurred in the statements. However, the frequency of a criterion may depend in part on the age of the witness, which will be discussed later.

Experimental studies

Of course, it is easier to conduct experimental studies that fulfil scientific criteria than it is field studies. The problem with experimental studies, however, is their ecological validity. It is difficult to assess whether the findings are applicable to real-life settings.

The eight experiments utilizing CBCA scores used different experimental settings, and the participants included both children and adults (it is a pity that only a few studies have been conducted with children, as the method was developed to assess statements of children). Fewer differences between truthful and fabricated statements were found in the experimental studies compared to the field studies. Almost all the significant findings, however, were in the expected direction, which means that the criteria were more often present in truthful statements than in fabricated statements (see Table 1.3). One of the incidental exceptions occurred in Landry and Brigham's (1992) study (using statements of adults) where logical structure and attribution of another's mental state were cited more often in the fabricated statements than in the truthful statements. They give, as an explanation for these unexpected findings, the possibility that the participants 'were trying very hard to make their false story seem believable and one fairly obvious way would be to make certain that a logical structure exists' (p. 674).

Many other studies particularly focus on differences between truthful and fabricated accounts concerning consistency (criterion 1), number of details (criterion 3) and contextual embedding (criterion 4). Generally, these studies provide further evidence for the Undeutsch Hypothesis. Most studies found that truth telling is associated with consistencies (see DePaulo, Stone and Lassiter (1985) for a literature review), many details (see for instance Jones and McGraw, 1987; Jones and McQuinston, 1989; Köhnken and Wegener, 1982; Lindsay and Johnston, 1987) and contextual embeddings (see for instance Alonso-Quecuty, 1991; Johnson and Raye, 1981; Johnson and Foley, 1984; Johnson, Foley, Suengas and Raye, 1988). However, there are studies with contradictory findings concerning number of details (for instance Neisser, 1981).

Although not many studies have been published to date concerning the relationship between CBCA scores and truth telling, the pattern which emerges from Table 1.3 is rather clear and shows, in general, support for the Undeutsch Hypothesis. When we make a distinction between the four categories of the CBCA criteria it can be seen that 'motivation-related contents' (criteria 14 to 18) received the weakest support (three out of these five criteria (criteria 16, 17, and 18) received only limited support). Criterion 17, for instance (self-deprecation) has not so far received support at all. Offence-specific elements, the fourth category, is hardly ever investigated in experiments because this criterion is usually not relevant in an experimental context. The lack of support for most of the motivation-related contents is perhaps due to the limitations of experimental studies, in which it is very difficult to stimulate 'high motivation'. Obviously, the motivation to make an honest impression in experiments is not comparable with the motivation to make an honest impression by genuine victims or false accusers in the field. Raskin and Esplin (1991b) also argued for caution with respect to the 'motivated-related content' variables, 'This category includes some criteria that one could argue might be provided by a witness who has fabricated an allegation and is experiencing some ambivalence about having done so. This could be addressed in the form of concerns about actual untruthfulness and lack of knowledge, or blaming oneself and pardoning the accused because the allegations are not true. Furthermore, these criteria may be different from the other criteria in that they require inferences about witnesses' motivations, which is not the same as making inferences about the characteristics of reports derived from the memory of an experience' (p. 284).

Accuracy rates and the CBCA assessments

To what extent are evaluators who use assessments based on the list of CBCA criteria able to correctly classify truth tellers as truth tellers and liars as liars? Research indicates that evaluators who are familiar with CBCA obtain higher accuracy rates than evaluators who are not familiar with CBCA (Landry and Brigham, 1992; Steller, Wellershaus, and Wolf (1988) presented in Steller, 1989). This suggests that utilizing CBCA improves the accuracy of evaluating the truthfulness of statements. Raskin and Esplin (1991b) pointed out that, in order to learn to use this method effectively, a training program lasting two or three days is advisable. However, research indicated that 45 to 90 minutes of training is sufficient to enable college students to improve their accuracy in differentiating between truthful and fabricated statements given by children (Steller, 1989) and by adults (Landry and Brigham, 1992). Horowitz (1991) stated that the three criteria that constitute the General Characteristics (criteria 1, 2 and 3) are difficult to teach new coders. Perhaps this is because they are less specific than the other criteria.

Results concerning the accuracy rates of evaluators familiar with CBCA are presented in Table 1.4.

The results are mixed. Esplin *et al.* (1988) (analysing statements of children aged 4 to 15 years) achieved a 100 per cent accuracy rate in their study (a perfect classification of each

TABLE 1.4 *Accuracy rates of classifying truths and lies when using the CBCA scoring method*

	Truth	Lie	Total
Field studies			
Esplin *et al.* (1988) (children)	100%	100%	100%
Experimental studies			
Akehurst (1997) (adults)	73%	67%	70%
Höfer *et al.* (1996) (adults)			71%
Köhnken *et al.* (1995) (adults)	88%	82%	85%
Landry *et al.* (1982) (adults)	75%	35%	55%
Porter *et al.* (1996) (adults)			78%
Sporer (1996) (adults)	70%	60%	65%
Steller *et al.* (1988) (children)	78%	62%	70%
Yuille (1988) (children)	91%	74%	83%
Zaparniuk *et al.* (1995) (adults)	80%	77%	78%

statement), and Landry and Brigham (1992) obtained an accuracy rate of 55 per cent (50 per cent is the level of chance). Other studies obtained accuracy rates between these two extremes, varying from 65 per cent (Sporer, 1996) to 85 per cent (Köhnken, Schimossek, Aschermann and Höfer, 1995). The findings do not reveal differences in accuracy rates when assessing statements of children and adults. A distinction between 'detecting truths' and 'detecting lies' provides some evidence for a 'truth bias', i.e. CBCA is more successful in detecting truths than in detecting lies. Steller (1989) considered this outcome consistent with the theoretical basis of the assessment technique, 'CBCA is a truth verifying rather than a lie detection method. Future research should be directed towards adding "lie criteria" to the content criteria of CBCA' (p. 149). This focus on searching for supportive evidence instead of trying to detect lies may partly be influenced by the (German judiciary) assumption that '90 per cent of credibility assessments in criminal cases of alleged sexual abuse are based on experienced events' (Steller and Wellershaus, 1996; Undeutsch, 1984). The development of a 'lie detector' instrument seems therefore less useful, because fabricated statements occur relatively rarely.

Complications in using CBCA

Reliability of criterion ratings
The first issue to address is how 'objective' a CBCA-based assessment is, that is to what extent do different evaluators obtain the same outcome when assessing the same statements? This, of course, is an important issue. As Wells and Loftus (1991) stated: 'If CBCA is a technique that is being advocated for wider use, and this seems to be the intent of its developers, then we must have studies that assess variance across evaluators' (p. 170). Studies in which overall interrater-agreement rates were reported obtained quite high but never perfect interrater-agreement rates (Anson, Golding, and Gully (1993): .72; Boychuk (1991), .86; Höfer, Akehurst, and Metzger (1996): .78; Steller et al. (1988): .75). (These studies report the proportion agreement rates for the presence of criteria). More studies have reported interrater-agreement rates per criterion, which are sometimes quite low. Höfer et al. (1996) for instance had to exclude three criteria (out of 15 used) from further analysis due to no significant interrater-agreements. Anson et al. (1993) argued that their low interrater-agreement rates per criterion could be caused by the fact that they provided their raters with videotapes which could have affected the reliability of the recorded judgements, particularly as the CBCA system is designed for use with transcripts (see Chapter 2 concerning how videotapes can disturb judgements). We may conclude that CBCA is a satisfactorily reliable assessment technique as long as transcripts are used, although some improvements could still be made. On the basis of their literature review, Horowitz, Lamb, Esplin, Boychuk, Krispin, and Reiter-Lavery (in press) concluded that especially criterion 8 (unusual details), criterion 9 (superfluous details), criterion 11 (related external associations), criterion 14 (spontaneous corrections), and criterion 15 (admitting lack of memory) need to be defined more clearly.

Number of criteria employed and weighting of the criteria
At present there are no formalized decision rules for determining cut-off scores to differentiate between truthful and deceptive statements on the basis of the amount or

strength of the content criteria that are present. In fact, such a formalized decision is almost impossible to develop because a decision in applied settings is never made upon the CBCA score, the circumstances (as described in the Validity Checklist) are taken into account as well. In practice, in German judicial procedure there is a rule of thumb that at least three reality criteria must be given in order to classify a testimony as credible (Steller and Köhnken, 1989). According to Yuille (cited in Horowitz, 1991) statements can be classified as truthful if they meet the first five criteria plus any two of the remaining criteria. Another decision rule, proposed by Raskin and Steller (cited in Zaparniuk et al., 1995), is that a credible statement is indicated by the presence of criteria 1 to 3, plus any four of the remaining criteria. Craig (1995) argued that statements containing more than five criteria are likely to be valid. A factor that makes this 'number of criteria issue' even more complicated is that not all experts use all 19 criteria when assessing statements.

Steller and Köhnken noted that these rules of thumb are misleading, because they do not take into account that some criteria may be of more value in assessing truthfulness than others. 'It should be pointed out that the various reality criteria have different values for assessing the veracity of a statement. For example accurately reported but misunderstood details (criterion 10) and reports of offence-specific elements (criterion 19) are apparently of more significance than relatively simple descriptions of interactions (criterion 4) or contextual embeddings (criterion 5)' (pp. 231–232). There is also disagreement among CBCA experts about the weight of criteria. For example Raskin and Esplin (1991b) argued that criterion 4 and criterion 5 are especially important. They further argued for the elimination of criterion 19 (details characteristic of the offence) and placed it in the third portion of the Validity Checklist. They found this item more characteristic of investigative interviews as a whole, rather than a verbal content criterion addressed in the CBCA. Yuille (1988) predicts that criterion 19 will be of less value in the future. He argues that the offender in sexual abuse cases is usually a trusted, known adult who attempts to bribe or coerce the child into secrecy about the abuse. 'These features are not, at present, common knowledge. Thus, an account which includes details which are contrary to popular beliefs enhances credibility. The current trend toward improving the awareness of both children and adults about the typical pattern of sexual abuse (through primary prevention training programs in schools and day care centres) may render this criterion of less value in the future' (p. 258).

Another way perhaps to determine the weighting of the criteria is to assess, via laboratory studies and field studies, the power of each criterion in discriminating between fabricated and truthful accounts. As can be seen in Table 1.3, criterion 3 (quantity of details) and criterion 4 (contextual embedding) have been shown to be particularly successful in discriminating between truthful and fabricated accounts and therefore perhaps deserve a high weighting. On the other hand, criteria 10, 13 and several motivation-related content criteria (criteria 16, 17 and 18) have only received limited support so far and therefore perhaps deserve little weighting.

When is a criterion fullfilled?
Many factors can influence the account of witnesses, such as type of crime, age of the child, interviewer style, the number of times the child was interviewed, and whether or not during

the interview memory enhancement techniques such as the Cognitive Interview were used (see Chapter 8 of this volume for a detailed description of this technique).

- *Type of crime.* Obviously, a relatively simple sexual incident will result in fewer reported details than an account of complex and repeated sexual acts (Raskin and Esplin, 1991a).

- *Age of the child.* As the cognitive abilities of a witness increase more details are likely to occur. Boychuk (1991) argued that children under eight years old can only view the world from their own perspective. She compared the CBCA scores of statements of children of different age groups and found that criterion 5 (descriptions of interactions) and criterion 15 (admitting lack of memory) were more often present in statements of older children (between 8 and 16 years old) than in statements of younger children (between 4 and 7 years old). She also found that younger children were unable to manifest criterion 13 (accounts of a perpetrator's mental state). Craig (1995) found that the number of criteria present in the statements was significantly greater for older children (age 10–16) than for younger children (age 3–9). Lamb *et al.* (in press) and Lamers-Winkelman (1995) found a significant positive correlation between age and the number of criteria present in the statements.

- *Interviewer style.* Lamb, Hershkowitz, Sternberg, Esplin, Hovav, Manor and Yudilevitch (in press) and Sternberg, Lamb, Hershkowitz, Esplin, Redlich and Sunshine (in press) investigated the number of details reported by 4–12-year-old children as a function of the interviewer style. They found that open-ended invitations yielded more detailed responses than directive utterances, regardless of age (see also Lamb, Esplin, and Sternberg, 1995).

- *Number of interviews.* Boychuk (1991) compared CBCA scores of children who were once, twice, three times or at least four times interviewed. No major differences were found between children who were once, twice or three times interviewed, the interviews of the children who were at least four times interviewed, however, contained less richness than the statements of the other children. Boychuk gives as a possible explanation for her findings, 'the child may be tired of talking to professionals about a subject that may have caused distress' (p. 70). Yuille and Cutshall (1989) and Goodman and Schwartz-Kenney (1992) found that children provide more details in a second interview compared with a first interview. In all, these findings suggest that only a limited number of interviews (up to three interviews) are appropriate.

- *Cognitive interview.* Köhnken, Schimossek, Aschermann, and Höfer (1995) and Steller and Wellershaus (1996) interviewed participants with either the Cognitive Interview (CI) technique or a standardized interview technique in order to examine the impact of CI on CBCA scores. Both studies found more richness in the statements in the Cognitive Interview conditions.

As all the factors mentioned above influence the child witness' report, their impact must be taken into account when assessing the credibility of the report, preferably via a checklist procedure. This raises questions of (1) What is the exact nature of the impact of each of these factors on the accounts and (2) are there still unidentified factors which affect the accounts? Both questions are difficult to answer. First, you can never find out whether all relevant factors are taken into account. Secondly, the exact impact of a specific factor on an individual report can never be determined, it can only be *estimated*. By definition these aspects weaken the strength of the assessment technique.

An assessment technique for children's statements only?

CBCA was developed in order to evaluate statements from children who were alleged victims (most commonly of sexual abuse). However, the theory underlying the CBCA, the Undeutsch Hypothesis, is not necessarily restricted either to children or to victims. Thus, perhaps the technique is applicable in evaluating adults' statements as well, and it is perhaps also possible to evaluate witnesses' or suspects' statements with the technique. Many authors still describe CBCA as a technique solely to evaluate statements of children in sexual abuse cases (Honts, 1994; Horowitz *et al.*, 1996; Raskin and Esplin, 1991b; Yuille, 1988). However, especially Köhnken and colleagues (Steller and Köhnken, 1989; Köhnken *et al.*, 1995) advocated the use of the technique in evaluating suspects' and witnesses' statements as well. Porter and Yuille (1996) used suspects' statements in their study. Their findings (also reported in Porter and Yuille (1995)) are in line with the Undeutsch Hypothesis (see Table 1.3): truthful accounts were rated as more coherent (criterion 1), and contained more details (criterion 3) compared to the deceptive accounts. Moreover, honest suspects more frequently admitted lack of memory than deceptive suspects. Recent studies of Landry and Brigham (1992) and Köhnken *et al.* (1995) showed that some criteria successfully discriminated between adults' (who were witnesses) fabricated and truthful accounts (see Table 1.3). It seems reasonable though to suggest that not all criteria are applicable in assessing adults' statements, for instance criterion 10 (accurately reporting details misunderstood) seems unlikely to occur in adults' statements. On the other hand, perhaps other, new, criteria may be developed for assessing adults' statements.

However, some questions still need to be addressed in future research, such as: (1) whether adults' accounts must include *more criteria* to be assessed truthful than children's accounts and, if so, how many more criteria should be included; and (2) whether *more information/details* must be given to fulfil a criterion in an adult's statement compared to a child's statement and, if so, how many more details should be included.

Combining CBCA with Reality Monitoring

Recently, Alonso-Quecuty (1992) and Porter and Yuille (1995) have suggested supplementing the CBCA criteria with Reality Monitoring criteria (Johnson and Raye, 1981). Johnson and Raye (1981) addressed how memories for past perceptions of actual events can be distinguished from memories for fictitious events, using a model called 'Reality Monitoring' (RM). This model states that memories of actual events are associated with more contextual information (similar to criterion 4 of the CBCA list), and more sensorial information (e.g. 'it was a small blue noisy car') whereas memories for fictitious events, which are the result of cognitive processes, are accompanied by more references to cognitive operations (e.g. 'I remember seeing the car and thinking how nice the small blue car was, but can still hear the terrible noise the car made'). In line with this suggestion, Alonso-Quecuty (1991, 1996) and Schooler, Gerhard and Loftus (1986) found that participants gave more sensorial details in actual event memories compared to fabricated event memories.

To our knowledge Sporer (1996) and Höfer, Akehurst and Metzger (1996) are the only researchers to have combined CBCA and RM assessments in one study. Sporer's experiment showed a beneficial effect of RM criteria on accuracy rates: The accuracy rate on the basis of CBCA score was 65 per cent (70 per cent for truthful accounts and 60 per cent for false accounts) whereas the accuracy rate for the combined CBCA/RM assessments was 79 per cent (83 per cent for truthful accounts and 75 per cent for false accounts). The Höfer *et al.* (1996) study showed no beneficial effect of combining the two assessment techniques.

Other studies give the impression that there are certain restrictions in the use of the reality monitoring criteria. Johnson *et al.* (1988), for instance found more and larger effects regarding recent memories than childhood memories. Similarly, Alonso-Quecuty (1992) found that descriptions of lies contained more information about cognitive operations than descriptions of true stories, but only when participants were asked to recall the experienced or fabricated event immediately. Delayed false statements contained less information about cognitive operations than delayed true statements. Manzanero and Diges (1996) found the expected differences between true and fabricated accounts only when they gave their participants no opportunity to prepare their accounts. Manzanero and Diges (1996) explained their findings and Alonso-Quecuty's (1992) findings by saying that if people talk or think about an event, external memories (memories of experienced events) become more internal and internal memories (memories about fictitious events) become more external. 'When real memories are prepared there is a greater involvement of cognitive processes, which produces internalisation of these events. In the case of imagination, preparation mainly produces an enrichment of the scene' (p. 61). This conclusion suggests that RM characteristics only occur in immediate, spontaneous recalls.

Finally, Lindsay and Johnson (1987) and Ceci and Bruck (1995) pointed out that children do not differentiate ongoing fact and fantasy as clearly as adults do (see also Chapters 7 and 9). Hence, their memories of these two kinds of experiences might not differ from one another in the way adults' memories do.

AN ASSESSMENT OF THE VALIDITY CHECKLIST

Research into the effectiveness of the Validity Checklist has not been carried out to date. For example in the CBCA field studies which were mentioned earlier, validity checks of the CBCA ratings were not reported (or perhaps not carried out). Validity checks in experimental CBCA studies are never carried out and are, in fact, unnecessary, as the circumstances are usually standardized in these types of study.

On the basis of existing research, one may question the justification of some of the Validity Checklist criteria, namely 'inappropriateness of affect' (criterion 2), 'susceptibility to suggestion' (criterion 3) and 'inconsistency with other statements' (criterion 10). Criterion 2 stated that if someone reports details of abuse without showing any sign of emotion, the story is less trustworthy than in the case of a clear display of emotions. In our view, this is a difficult point, as not all people react emotionally in a similar way when informing others about negative experiences. Vrij and Fischer (1995) for instance found that some victims show their distress clearly whereas other victims present themselves with controlled emotion. A field study of Littmann and Szewczyk (1983) also found that showing distress (eg 'howling') during an interview was not a valid predictor of the validity of the statement.

Criterion 3 deals with susceptibility to suggestion. Yuille (1988) and Landry and Brigham (1992) recommend asking the witness, at the end of the interview a few leading questions about peripheral information in order to assess the witness' susceptibility to suggestion. This, however, might be inappropriate, given Goodman, Rudy, Bottoms and Aman's (1990) finding that children show more resistance to suggestibility for central parts than peripheral parts of the event and Davies' (1991) finding that children are more resistant to suggestibility for stressful events than for events which are less stressful.

Criterion 10 deals with inconsistencies between statements of different witnesses and with inconsistencies between different statements of the same witness. The latter topic is, in our view, problematic. Research has shown (Moston, 1987; Poole and White, 1991) that contradictory statements by one child, in two different interviews, does not always mean that the statement is fabricated. This could be the result of question repetition. Young children especially may give two different answers to the same question, because they might think 'if the same question is asked for the second time, the first answer must have been wrong'. Thus, inconsistent or contradictory statements may be elicited by the interviewer. In judging inconsistencies or contradictions, this interviewer factor should therefore be taken into account.

SUBJECTIVE VERBAL CHARACTERISTICS OF TRUTH TELLING

Which verbal characteristics make a story more or less credible to observers who are not familiar with the CBCA literature? Very little research has been conducted so far addressing this issue. To our knowledge only one study has been published (Akehurst, Köhnken, Vrij and Bull, 1996) addressing observers' beliefs about most of the 19 CBCA criteria. In this study, participants were provided with a list of CBCA criteria and were asked whether they believed that the frequency of occurrence of these criteria increases or decreases during fabrication compared to truth telling or does not differ between truth telling and fabrication. The study was conducted in the UK and included lay persons and police officers as participants. The findings showed that lay persons and police officers did have similar beliefs. Moreover, the correct relationship, an increase in these criteria during truth telling, was only mentioned three times. Observers believed that a truthful account compared to a fabricated account has a more logical structure (criterion 1), incorporates more details (criterion 3), and includes more attributions of the perpetrator's mental state (criterion 13) (see Table 1.5).

TABLE 1.5 *Subjective (perceived) relationship between verbal characteristics and truth-telling*

	Criteria																		
	1	2	3	4	5	6	7	8	9	10	11	12	13	14	15	16	17	18	19
Akehurst *et al.* (1996)	>	<	>	–	–	<	<	<	<			<	>	<	<	<	–		

Note: The signs refer to people's beliefs about verbal characteristics of truthful statements. (> = a believed increase in the frequency of the verbal characteristic during truth-telling, < = a believed decrease in the frequency of the verbal characteristic during truth-telling, – = no believed association of the verbal characteristic with truth-telling, blank = believed association was not investigated.)

On the other hand, an incorrect relationship, that is a decrease in these criteria during truth telling, was mentioned seven times. Observers believed that truthful accounts compared to fabricated accounts were more structured (criterion 2), included fewer reproductions of conversation (criterion 6), fewer unexpected complications (criterion 7), fewer superfluous details (criterion 9), fewer accounts of the witness' own mental state (criterion 12), fewer spontaneous corrections (criterion 14), fewer admissions of lack of memory (criterion 15) and fewer doubts about one's own testimony (criterion 16). Particularly, the outcomes concerning the motivation-related contents (criteria 14, 15 and 16) were not surprising as this is exactly what CBCA evaluators want to test with these criteria. It is very unlikely that people include these sorts of details on purpose in their accounts, because they believe it probably makes the account less convincing, hence, the presence of such details may be interpreted as signs of credibility. These outcomes suggest (although it is a very tentative conclusion due to the small amount of studies conducted in this area) that the CBCA criteria are not in line with common sense nor are they popular beliefs, which makes them probably more useful. For instance somebody who fabricates a story and wants to be convincing will probably tell a story in the way he or she believes a convincing/reliable story should be told, in other words, will give an account according to these popular beliefs. The fact that these beliefs differ from real contents of truthful accounts, make fabricated accounts easier to detect for the CBCA assessor.

Further studies have not actually included the list of CBCA criteria but focused more on the relationship between perceived credibility and number of details. Most studies found that many details make a reliable impression (Bell and Loftus, 1988, 1989; Conte, Sorenson, Fogarty and Rosa, 1991; Wells and Leippe, 1981). For instance Bell and Loftus (1989) and Wells and Leippe (1981) found that subject jurors tended to believe witnesses who recalled more trivial and irrelevant details about a crime than those who remembered only central information. Freedman, Adam, Davey, and Koegl (1996), however, found that this relationship depends on the context. When observers have the suspicion that somebody is lying, maximum impact is incurred by an intermediate level of detail. Too many details in these circumstances could easily give observers impressions such as 'the person was trying too hard to be convincing', 'the person was being defensive' or 'the person was making up some of the material'. Also Coolbear (1992) mentioned that too much detail evokes suspicion, because it suggests that the child has been given the story.

Coolbear (1992) investigated to what extent professionals (not familiar with SVA) actually use the Validity Checklist criteria in assessing the credibility of allegations. She held structured interviews about the methods used to assess the credibility of allegations with 51 professionals (from legal professions and human services) who had experience with child sexual abuse allegations. The most common response was that the use of childlike language was an indicator of truthfulness (item 1 on the Checklist), also, emotional congruence with the nature of the material covered by the child (item 2 of the Checklist) was mentioned as indicative of a truthful story. Finally, many participants stated that they would proceed cautiously with a sexual abuse allegation if they knew that there was a custody/access dispute or divorce process between the child's parents (items 6 to 8).

CONCLUSION

The findings presented in this chapter give some support for the Undeutsch Hypothesis, that is they give some support for the idea that 'a statement derived from memory of an actual experience differs in content and quality from a statement based on invention or fantasy'. However, the fact that not many studies have been conducted so far, in order to test the Undeutsch Hypothesis, makes this conclusion a tentative one. In our view, there are at present several restrictions and reservations in using the CBCA/SVA instrument in court cases.

- Accuracy rates in laboratory studies (the only type of study in which someone can be certain about the ground truth) ranges between 55 and 85 per cent. However, a distinction between lie detection and truth detection showed that especially the accuracy rates in lie detection are rather low (most researchers find an accuracy rate between 60 and 75 per cent, but even lower accuracy rates have been found). A 75 per cent accuracy rate in lie detection means that 25 per cent of the fabricated statements were incorrectly classified as truthful. These percentages of incorrect classifications are very high, especially given the seriousness of the error. In real life the CBCA method is usually used to assess the statements of witnesses or victims. Such an error would therefore imply that somebody who is actually innocent would be falsely accused of a crime because the witness' fabricated statement was incorrectly classified as truthful. False incrimination of 25 per cent of innocent suspects is unacceptable, especially in the context of Western legal systems which are founded on the ideal that it is better to acquit 10 guilty people than to convict one person who is innocent. Hence, achieving higher accuracy rates is essential. Combining CBCA with Reality Monitoring, for instance may be worth while, especially because Reality Monitoring offers an elaborated theoretical framework for understanding the function and working of human memory, and, as Höfer *et al.* (1996) argue, interviewees' statements have a lot to do with memories.

- Interrater-agreement ratings between CBCA-evaluators are usually satisfactorily high but never perfect. This means that two different evaluators usually interpret the same statement slightly differently. This makes it, in our view, essential that in applied settings at least two evaluators evaluate a statement in order to make the evaluation less subjective (the current German practice is that only one expert evaluates a statement).

■ Apart from the age of the interviewee, other factors may influence the quality of the statement as well. We have already mentioned type of crime, interviewer style, the number of times the interviewee was interviewed, and whether or not some memory enhancement techniques were used during the interview. Numerous other factors may be relevant as well, such as preferred speech style, memory, and social skills of the interviewee, whether or not the interviewee is socially anxious, whether or not the interviewee has learning disabilities and so on. Even external circumstances which influence people's accuracy in recalling witnessed events may influence the quality of statements (see Chapter 5 for an overview of external factors on eyewitness testimony). To date, little is known regarding how and to what extent these factors influence the effectiveness of CBCA assessments. One might say that the effectiveness of CBCA has mainly been investigated in 'a vacuum', that is under relatively simplistic circumstances (e.g. well-controlled experiments). Real life is, of course, much more complicated. In our view, studies must be conducted under more realistic circumstances as well in order to make a well-considered judgement about the effectiveness of the technique. Such a judgement is required before the technique can be advocated for use in the judicial process.

Our pessimistic view about the usefulness of SVA in court has recently been supported by Lamb *et al.* (in press). They conclude, on the basis of the field study they have conducted, that:

> Although the results are consistent with Raskin and Esplin's prediction that more CBCA criteria should be present in accounts that are independently deemed credible than in accounts of incidents that appear unlikely to have happened, the level of precision clearly remains too poor to permit the designation of CBCA as a reliable and valid test suitable for the courtroom (p. 16).

Apart from these criticisms, CBCA evaluators appear to be able to detect truths and lies above the level of chance. We therefore believe that CBCA assessments may be useful in police investigations, for example to determine whether it is useful or not to put more effort into interviewing suspects in particular cases.

Further research into SVA

■ Although SVA has been developed to assess the veracity of statements of children, only a few studies have been conducted with children to date. More research with children is therefore needed.

■ The effectiveness of CBCA/SVA has only been studied in a judicial context so far. As the technique is a method of investigating reports based on memory, it would seem to have relevance for a range of other situations. It might, for example be applied to the question of accuracy in repressed memories (see Chapter 7), or to the assessment of client recollections during some forms of therapy. Research is needed to clarify the potential of this approach to the evaluation of testimony.

■ An issue which is not widely addressed so far in CBCA-related literature is to what extent people are able to mislead evaluators, that is, are people who are lying able to give an account which includes enough CBCA criteria to make a reliable impression on CBCA evaluators? It seems plausible to assume that some CBCA criteria are easier to manipulate by deceivers than others. For instance motivation-related contents, such as admitting lack of memory, raising doubts about one's own memory and self-deprecation are probably easier to include in a fabricated account than 'reproductions of conversations', 'unexpected complications', 'unusual details' or 'superfluous details'. The difficulty with these latter criteria does not occur when actually fabricating them but more with remembering them once they have been included in a fabricated statement. Adequate memory about these fabricated details is important to avoid inconsistencies in the statement and to avoid forgetting these details in a subsequent interview. We cannot rule out the possibility that somebody who prepares his or her fabricated statement carefully is able to include and remember all the fabricated details, although it is doubtful that very young children are able to do this since they probably lack the necessary cognitive skills. The issue of misleading the CBCA evaluators seems therefore a question particularly relevant in assessing statements of older children and adults. Further research is required to test these assumptions.

NOTES

1. The examples are derived from Boychuk (1991), Raskin and Esplin (1991b), Steller and Boychuk (1992), and Yuille (1988).
2. See Horowitz, Lamb, Esplin, Boychuk, Krispin and Reiter-Lavery (1996) for a discussion about establishing ground truth in studies of child sexual abuse.
3. Another study was conducted by Lamers-Winkelman (1995). She analysed 97 sexual abuse statements made by children. This study is not presented in Scheme 1 because her sample did not include a 'doubtful cases' category. She compared 'confirmed' cases with 'very likely abused' cases and found one difference: children in the confirmed group made more attributions of the accused's mental state (criterion 13) than children in the very likely abused group. Lamers-Winkelman and Buffing (1996) provide an English version of some of the results.

REFERENCES

Akehurst, L. (1997). Deception and its detection in children and adults via verbal and nonverbal cues (PhD thesis) University of Portsmouth; Psychology Department.

Akehurst, L., Köhnken, G., Vrij, A. and Bull, R. (1996). Lay persons' and police officers' beliefs regarding deceptive behaviour. *Applied Cognitive Psychology*, **10**, 461–471.

Alonso-Quecuty, M.L. (1991). Post-event information and reality monitoring: when the witness cannot be honest. Paper presented at the First Spanish and British Meeting on Psychology, Law and Crime in Pamplona, Spain.

Alonso-Quecuty, M.L. (1992). Deception detection and reality monitoring: a new answer to an old question? In F. Lösel, D. Bender and T. Bliesener (eds), *Psychology and Law: International Perspectives* (pp. 328–332). Berlin, Germany: Walter de Gruyter.

Alonso-Quecuty, M.L. (1996). Detecting fact from fallacy in child and adult witness accounts. In G. Davies, S. Lloyd-Bostock, M. McMurran and C. Wilson (eds), *Psychology, Law and Criminal Justice: International Developments in Research and Practice* (pp. 74–80). Berlin, Germany: Walter de Gruyter.

Anson, D.A., Golding, S.L. and Gully, K.J. (1993). Child sexual abuse allegations: reliability of criteria-based content analysis. *Law and Human Behavior*, **17**, 331–341.

Arntzen, F. (1982). Die Situation der Forensischen Aussagenpsychologie in der Bundesrepublik Deutschland (Forensic psychology in West Germany: state of the art). In A. Trankell (ed.), *Reconstructing the Past: The Role of Psychologists in Criminal Trials* (pp. 107–120). Deventer, The Netherlands: Kluwer.

Arntzen, F. (1983). *Psychologie der Zeugenaussage: Systematik der Glaubwür-digkeitsmerkmale* (Psychology of Witness Statements). München, Germany: C.H. Beck.

Bell, B.E. and Loftus, E.F. (1988). Degree of detail of eyewitness testimony and mock juror judgments. *Journal of Applied Social Psychology*, **18**, 1171–1192.

Bell, B.E. and Loftus, E.F. (1989). Trivial persuasion in the courtroom: the power of (a few) minor details. *Journal of Personality and Social Psychology*, **56**, 669–679.

Boychuk, T. (1991). Criteria-Based Content Analysis of children's statements about sexual abuse: A field–based validation study. Unpublished doctoral dissertation, Arizona State University.

Bull, R. (1992). Obtaining evidence expertly: the reliability of interviews with child witnesses. *Expert Evidence: The International Digest of Human Behavior Science and Law*, **1**, 3–36.

Bull, R. (1995). Innovative techniques for the questioning of child witnesses, especially those who are young and those with learning disability. In M. Zaragoza *et al.* (eds), *Memory and Testimony in the Child Witness* (pp. 179–195). Thousand Oaks, CA: Sage.

Ceci, S.J. and Bruck, M. (1995). *Jeopardy in the Courtroom*. Washington, DC: American Psychological Association.

Conte, J.R., Sorenson, E., Fogarty, L. and Rosa, J.D. (1991). Evaluating children's reports of sexual abuse: results from a survey of professionals. *Journal of Orthopsychiatry*, **61**, 428–437.

Coolbear, J.L. (1992). Credibility of young children in sexual abuse cases: assessment strategies of legal and human service professionals. *Canadian Psychology*, **33**, 151–164.

Craig, R.A. (1995). Effects of interviewer behaviour on children's statements of sexual abuse. Unpublished manuscript.

Davies, G. (1991). Research on children's testimony: Implications for interviewing practice. In C.R. Hollin and K. Howells (eds), *Clinical Approaches to Sex Offenders and their Victims*. New York: John Wiley and Sons.

DePaulo, B.M., Stone, J.I. and Lassiter, G.D. (1985). Deceiving and detecting deceit. In B.R. Schlenker (ed.), *The Self and Social Life* (pp. 323–370). New York: McGraw-Hill.

Esplin, P.W., Boychuk, T. and Raskin, D.C. (1988, June). A field validity study of Criteria-Based Content Analysis of children's statements in sexual abuse cases. Paper presented at the NATO Advanced Study Institute on Credibility Assessment in Maratea, Italy.

Freedman, J.L., Adam, E.K., Davey, S.A. and Koegl, C.J. (1996). The impact of a statement: more detail does not always help. *Legal and Criminological Psychology*, **1**, 117–130.

Goodman, G.S., Rudy, L., Bottoms, B. and Aman, C. (1990). Children's concerns and memory: issues of ecological validity in the study of children's eyewitness testimony. In R. Fivush and J. Hudson (eds), *Knowing and Remembering in Young Children* (pp. 249–284). New York: Cambridge University Press.

Goodman, G.S. and Schwartz-Kenney (1992). Why knowing a child's age is not enough: influences of cognitive, social and emotional factors on children's testimony. In H. Dent and R. Flin (eds), *Children as Witnesses* (pp. 15–32). Chichester, UK: John Wiley and Sons.

Gordon, B.N., Schroeder, C.S. and Abrams, J.M. (1990). Age and social class differences in children's knowledge of sexuality. *Journal of Clinical Child Psychology*, **19**, 33–43.

Höfer, E. and Akehurst, L. and Metzger, G. (1996, August). Reality monitoring: a chance for further development of CBCA? Paper presented at the annual meeting of the European Association on Psychology and Law in Siena, Italy.

Honts, C.R. (1994). Assessing children's credibility: scientific and legal issues in 1994. *North Dakota Law Review*, **70**, 879–903.

Horowitz, S.W. (1991). Empirical support for statement validity assessment. *Behavioral Assessment*, **13**, 293–313.

Horowitz, S.W., Lamb, M.E., Esplin, P.W., Boychuk, T.D., Krispin, O. and Reiter-Lavery, L. (in press). Reliabilty of Criteria-Based Content Analysis of child witness statements. *Legal and Criminological Psychology*.

Horowitz, S.W., Lamb, M.E., Esplin, P.W., Boychuk, T.D., Reiter-Lavery, L. and Krispin, O. (1996). Establishing ground truth in studies of child sexual abuse. *Expert Evidence*, **4**, 42–52.

Johnson, M.K. and Foley, M.A. (1984). Differentiating fact from fantasy: the reliability of children's memory. *Journal of Social Issues*, **40**, 33–50.

Johnson, M.K., Foley, M.A., Suengas, A.G. and Raye, C.L. (1988). Phenomenal characteristics of memories for perceived and imagined autobiographical events. *Journal of Experimental Psychology: General*, **117**, 371–376.

Johnson, M.K. and Raye, C.L. (1981). Reality monitoring. *Psychological Review*, **88**, 67–85.

Jones, D.P.H. and McGraw, J.M. (1987). Reliable and fictitious accounts of sexual abuse to children. *Journal of Interpersonal Violence*, **2**, 27–45.

Jones, D.P.H. and McQuinston, M. (1989). *Interviewing the Sexually Abused Child*. London: Gaskell.

Köhnken, G. (1996). Social psychology and the law. In G.R. Semin and K. Fiedler (eds), *Applied Social Psychology* (pp. 257–282). London: Sage.

Köhnken, G., Schimossek, E., Aschermann, E. and Höfer, E. (1995). The cognitive interview and the assessment of the credibility of adults' statements. *Journal of Applied Psychology*, **80**, 671–684.

Köhnken, G. and Wegener, H. (1982). Zur Glaubwürdigkeit von Zeugenaussagen: Experimentelle Uberprüfung ausgewählter Glaubwürdigkeitskriterien (Credibility of witness statements: experimental examination of selected reality criteria). *Zeitschrift für Experimentelle und Angewandte Psychologie*, **29**, 92–111.

Lamb, M.E., Esplin, P.W. and Sternberg, K.J. (1995). Making children into competent witnesses: reactions to the Amicus Brief in re Michaels. *Psychology, Public Policy and Law*, **1**, 438–449.

Lamb, M.E., Hershkowitz, I., Sternberg, K.J., Esplin, P.W., Hovav, M., Manor, M. and Yudilevitch, L. (in press). Effects of investigative utterance types on Israeli children's responses. *International Journal of Behavioral Development*.

Lamb, M.E., Sternberg, K.J. and Esplin, P.W. (1994). Factors influencing the reliability and validity of statements made by young victims of sexual maltreatment. *Journal of Applied Developmental Psychology*, **15**, 255–280.

Lamb, M.E., Sternberg, K.J. and Esplin, P.W. Hershkowitz, I., Orbach, Y. and Hovav, M. (in press). Criterion-Based Content Analysis: a field validation study. *Child Abuse and Neglect*.

Lamers-Winkelman, F. (1995). *Seksueel misbruik van jonge kinderen: Een onderzoek naar signalen en signaleren, en naar ondervragen en vertellen inzake seksueel misbruik.* Amsterdam, The Netherlands: VU Uitgeverij.

Lamers-Winkelman, F. and Buffing, F. (1996). Children's testimony in the Netherlands: a study of Statement Validity Analysis. In B.L. Bottoms and G.S. Goodman (1996). *International Perspectives on Child Abuse and Children's Testimony*. Thousand Oaks, CA: Sage Publications.

Landry, K. and Brigham, J.C. (1992). The effect of training in Criteria-Based Content Analysis on the ability to detect deception in adults. *Law and Human Behavior*, **16**, 663–675.

Lindsay, D.S. and Johnson, M.K. (1987). Reality monitoring and suggestibility: children's ability to discriminate among memories from different sources. In S.J. Ceci, M.P. Toglia and D.F. Ross (eds), *Children's Eyewitness Memory* (pp. 92–121). New York: Springer Verlag.

Littmann, E. and Szewczyk, H. (1983). Zu einigen Kriterien und Ergebnissen forensisch-psychologischer Glaubwürdigkeitsbegutachtung von sexuell misbrauchten Kindern und Jugendlichen. *Forensia*, **4**, 55–72.

Lykken, D.T. (1988). The case against polygraph testing. In A. Gale (ed.), *The Polygraph Test: Lies, Truth and Science* (pp. 111–126). London: Sage.

Manzanero, A.L. and Diges, M. (1996). Effects of preparation on internal and external memories. In G. Davies, S. Lloyd-Bostock, M. McMurran and C. Wilson (eds), *Psychology, Law and Criminal Justice: International Developments in Research and Practice* (pp. 56–63). Berlin, Germany: Walter de Gruyter.

Moston, S. (1987). The suggestibility of children in interview studies. *Child Language*, **7**, 67–78.

Neisser, U. (1981). John Dean's memory: a case study. *Cognition*, **9**, 1–22.

Poole, D.A. and White, L.T. (1991). Effects of question repetition and retention interval on the eyewitness testimony of children and adults. *Developmental Psychology*, **27**, 975–986.

Porter, S. and Yuille, J.C. (1995). Credibility assessment of criminal suspects through statement analysis. *Psychology, Crime and Law*, **1**, 319–331.

Porter, S. and Yuille, J.C. (1996). The language of deceit: an investigation of the verbal clues to deception in the interrogation context. *Law and Human Behavior*, **20**, 443–459.

Raskin, D.C. (1982). The scientific basis of polygraph techniques and their uses in the judicial process. In A. Trankell (ed.), *Reconstructing the Past* (pp. 319–371). Deventer, The Netherlands: Kluwer.

Raskin, D.C. and Esplin, P.W. (1991a). Assessment of children's statements of sexual abuse. In J. Doris (ed.), *The Suggestibility of Children's Recollections* (pp. 153–165). Washington DC: American Psychological Association.

Raskin, D.C. and Esplin, P.W. (1991b). Statement Validity Assessment: interview procedures and content analysis of children's statements of sexual abuse. *Behavioral Assessment*, **13**, 265–291.

Schooler, J.W., Gerhard, D. and Loftus, E.F. (1986). Qualities of the unreal. *Journal of Experimental Psychology: Learning, Memory and Cognition*, **12**, 171–181.

Sporer, S.L. (1996, February). The less traveled road to truth: verbal cues in deception detection in accounts of fabricated and self-experienced events. Paper presented at the biennial meeting of American Psychology-Law Society in Hilton Head, South Carolina.

Steller, M. (1989). Recent developments in statement analysis. In J.C. Yuille (1989), *Credibility Assessment* (pp. 135–154). Deventer, The Netherlands: Kluwer.

Steller, M. and Boychuk, T. (1992). Children as witnesses in sexual abuse cases: investigative interview and assessment techniques. In H. Dent and R. Flin (eds), *Children as Witnesses* (pp. 47–73). New York: John Wiley and Sons.

Steller, M. and Köhnken, G. (1989). Criteria-Based Content Analysis. In D.C. Raskin (ed.), *Psychological Methods in Criminal Investigation and Evidence* (pp. 217–245). New York: Springer Verlag.

Steller, M. and Wellershaus, P. (1996). Information enhancement and credibility assessment of child statements: the impact of the cognitive interview on criteria-based content analysis. In G. Davies, S. Lloyd-Bostock, M. McMurran and C. Wilson (eds), *Psychology, Law and Criminal Justice: International Developments in Research and Practice* (pp. 118–127). Berlin, Germany: de Gruyter.

Steller, M., Wellershaus, P. and Wolf, T. (1988, June). Empirical validation of Criteria-Based Content Analysis. Paper presented at the NATO Advanced Study Institute on Credibility Assessment in Maratea, Italy.

Sternberg, K.J., Lamb, M.E., Hershkowitz, I., Esplin, P.W., Redlich, A. and Sunshine, N. (in press). The relationship between investigative utterance types and the informativeness of child witnesses. *Journal of Applied Developmental Psychology*.

Trankell, A. (1972). *Reliability of Evidence*. Stockholm, Sweden: Beckmans.

Undeutsch, U. (1967). Beurteilung der Glaubhaftigkeit von Aussagen (Evaluation of statement credibility). In U. Undeutsch (ed.), *Handbuch der Psychologie Vol. 11: Forensische Psychologie* (pp. 26–181). Göttingen, Germany: Hogrefe.

Undeutsch, U. (1982). Statement reality analysis. In A. Trankell (ed.), *Reconstructing the Past: The Role of Psychologists in Criminal Trials* (pp. 27–56). Deventer, The Netherlands: Kluwer.

Undeutsch, U. (1984). Courtroom evaluation of eyewitness testimony. *International Review of Applied Psychology*, **33**, 51–67.

Undeutsch, U. (1989). The development of statement reality analysis. In J.C. Yuille (ed.), *Credibility Assessment* (pp. 101–121). Dordrecht, The Netherlands: Kluwer.

Volbert, R. and van der Zanden, R. (1996). Sexual knowledge and behavior of children up to 12 years: what is age appropriate? In G. Davies, S. Lloyd-Bostock, M. McMurran and C. Wilson (eds), *Psychology, Law* and *Criminal Justice: International Developments in Research and Practice* (pp. 198–216). Berlin, Germany: de Gruyter.

Vrij, A. and Fischer, A. (1995). The expression of emotions in simulated rape interviews. *Journal of Police and Criminal Psychology*, **10**, 64–67.

Wells, G.L. and Leippe, M.R. (1981). How do triers of fact infer accuracy of eyewitness identification? Using memory of peripheral details can be misleading. *Journal of Applied Psychology*, **66**, 682–687.

Wells, G.L. and Loftus, E.F. (1991). Commentary: is this child fabricating? Reactions to a new assessment technique. In J. Doris (ed.), *The Suggestibility of Children's Recollections* (pp. 168–171). Washington DC: American Psychological Association.

Winkel, F.W., Vrij, A., Koppelaar, L. and van der Steen, J. (1991). Reducing secondary victimisation risks and skilled police intervention: enhancing the quality of police rape victim encounters through training programmes. *Journal of Police and Criminal Psychology*, **7**, 2–11.

Winkel, F.W. and Vrij, A. (1995). Verklaringen van kinderen in interviews: een experimenteel onderzoek naar de diagnostische waarde van Criteria Based Content Analysis. *Tijdschrift voor Ontwikkelingspsychologie*, **22**, 61–74.

Yuille, J.C. (1988). The systematic assessment of children's testimony. *Canadian Psychology*, **29**, 247–262.

Yuile, J.C. and Cutshall, J. (1989). Analysis of statements of victims, witnesses and suspects. In J.C. Yuille (ed.), *Credibility Assessment* (pp. 175–191). Dordrecht, The Netherlands, Kluwer.

Zaparniuk, J., Yuille, J.C. and Taylor, S. (1995). Assessing the credibility of true and false statements. *International Journal of Law and Psychiatry*, **18**, 343–352.

CHAPTER 2

NONVERBAL COMMUNICATION AND CREDIBILITY

Aldert Vrij

INTRODUCTION

The importance of nonverbal behaviour in credibility assessments

Example 1—A man is seen by a police officer trying to break a bicycle lock with a screwdriver. The man might have lost his key or be trying to steal the bike. The officer asks the man whether the bike belongs to him. The man replies with a simple 'Yes'. How can the police officer know whether this is a truthful statement?

Example 2—A suspect brought in for questioning appears very cooperative and is very talkative during his interview with the police. He denies committing the offense in question. There is no concrete evidence that the police may use, so they have to rely on the interpretation of the man's statements. How can the police officer know whether the man is guilty of the offence?

Assessing the credibility of what people say is an important part of policing. Examples 1 and 2 provide simple illustrations. Relying on the characteristics of verbal behaviour (discussed in Chapter 1) has at least two limitations. First, you can only analyse verbal characteristics when a reasonable amount of spoken words are available. Hence, situations such as those described in the first example are not suitable for verbal credibility assessments. Secondly, verbal credibility assessments are only possible on the basis of written transcripts, which are not immediately available. This implies that situations which require immediate decisions (for instance customs officers at airports who have to decide whether or not to search the luggage of passengers) are not appropriate for verbal assessments either. In such circumstances, the only available source of information for credibility assessment is nonverbal behaviour. This chapter examines research into the relationship between nonverbal behaviour and the assessment of credibility. Naturally, credibility assessments on the basis of nonverbal behaviour have a different, less official, status than credibility assessments on the basis of verbal characteristics. For instance nonverbal credibility assessments can never be used as evidence in court. Nevertheless, it would be very useful if accurate assessments about someone's credibility could be made on the basis of nonverbal behaviour. It would be a useful tool for customs officers to decide whose luggage will be searched. In the first example, the officer would have a better basis on which to decide whether to take further action and so on.

People sometimes give mixed messages, that is, their behaviour does not seem to match their speech content. In the first example, it is possible that the body movements of the man increased as soon as he noticed the police officer and that he answered 'yes' with a high-pitched and weak voice. In the second situation, the suspect may have avoided looking the interviewer in the eyes when asked to explain where he was when the crime was committed. In both cases, the verbal content reveals nothing unusual but their behaviour suggests that they feel uncomfortable. Research has shown that, if verbal and nonverbal behaviour do not match, nonverbal behaviour is usually a more valid indicator of someone's true emotional state than verbal communication. Hence, in both examples, police officers would have a very good reason to assume that both men felt uncomfortable and it would therefore be worth while to further investigate the situation and to try to find out why both men suddenly felt uncomfortable.

The reason why nonverbal behaviour gives the most insight into someone's emotional state is that individuals are less able to control aspects of their nonverbal behaviour than their verbal communication (DePaulo and Kirkendol, 1989; Ekman, 1985; Ekman and Friesen, 1974). For instance suppose that the man in the first example is trying to steal the bike, it is easy for him to say 'yes' when the right answer is 'no'. It is more difficult to say this in a *convincing manner*. DePaulo and Kirkendol (1989) give three reasons why it is harder to control nonverbal behaviour.

■ There are certain automatic links between emotions and nonverbal behaviours. When people suddenly become afraid, their bodies jerk backwards and their faces contort in a certain way almost automatically. However, there are not certain things people automatically say when they are afraid. Hence, when people want to control their behaviour in emotionally involving deceptive situations, they have to somehow override these automatic nonverbal links, whereas they don't have to bother about automatic verbal links.

■ People are generally not entirely aware of their nonverbal style of presentation. For instance they don't know exactly what hand movements and how many hand movements they normally make, which makes it very difficult to control such movements efficiently, that is, it is very difficult to show normal behaviour on purpose, if people do not know how they normally behave.

■ Even if people know how they usually behave, it is not clear whether they actually could change their behaviour, because they are not very well practised in controlling their behaviour. People have to be very good at acting in order to control their behaviour successfully and most people are not very good actors.

In short, nonverbal behaviour might be a useful source of information in detecting deception. However, two questions are important: (1) Are there systematic nonverbal differences between liars and truth tellers? and (2) Are observers aware of these cues and are they able to detect deception using these cues? The first question refers to *objective* or *actual* indicators of deception, namely nonverbal behaviours which have been found to be associated with deception. The second question refers to *subjective* or *perceived* indicators of deception, namely nonverbal behaviours that observers associate with deception, regardless of whether such behaviour is a manifestation of actual deception. Both types of indicators will be discussed in this chapter. Box 2.1 provides an overview and descriptions of the behaviours to be discussed.

BOX 2.1
Overview and descriptions of the nonverbal behaviours used in this chapter

Vocal characteristics
1. *Ah-speech disturbances*: use of the word 'ah'
2. *Non-ah speech disturbances*: word and/or sentence repetition, sentence change, sentence incompletions, slips of the tongue and so forth
3. *Pitch of voice*: changes in pitch of voice, such as rise in pitch or fall in pitch
4. *Speech rate*: number of spoken words in a certain period of time
5. *Latency period*: period of silence between question and answer

Facial characteristics
6. *Gaze*: looking at the face of the conversation partner
7. *Smile*: smiling and laughing

Movements
8. *Self manipulations*: scratching the head, wrists, and so forth
9. *Arm and hand movements*: functional hand and arm movements designed to modify and/or supplement what is being said verbally (gestures) or nonfunctional hand and arm movements including subtle movements of hands, fingers and so forth (hand/finger movements)
10. *Leg and foot movements*: movements of feet and legs
11. *Head movements*: head nods and head shakes
12. *Trunk movements*: movements of the trunk (usually accompanied with head movements)
13. *Shifting position*: movements made to change the sitting position (usually accompanied with trunk and foot/leg movements)

OBJECTIVE (ACTUAL) INDICATORS OF DECEPTION

Theoretical reasons for the existence of objective indicators of deception

Liars may experience three different processes during deception, namely emotional, cognitive and controlling processes (DePaulo, Stone and Lassiter, 1985; Köhnken, 1989; Zuckerman, DePaulo and Rosenthal, 1981a). Each process emphasizes a different aspect of deception and deceptive behaviour. We will therefore call them approaches.

The emotional approach (Ekman, 1985; Knapp, Hart and Dennis, 1974; Köhnken, 1989; Riggio and Friedman, 1983) proposes that deception can result in three different types of emotion, namely guilt, fear or excitement. Suppose that the man in the first example is actually trying to steal the bike. He might feel guilty while trying to deceive the police officer (he might have been taught by his parents or teachers that it is wrong to deceive police officers). Or he might be afraid, because he is worried that the police officer will find out that he is trying to steal the bike. Or he might become very excited because he has the opportunity to fool a police officer. These three emotions might affect his behaviour. Guilt might result in gaze aversion because he doesn't dare to look the police officer straight in the eye while telling this wicked lie. Fear and excitement might result in signs of stress, such as an increase in movements, speech disturbances or a higher pitched voice. Of course, the man in the second example may experience the same emotions for similar reasons.

The cognitive approach (Burgoon, Kelly, Newton and Keely-Dyreson, 1989; Ekman and Friesen, 1972; Goldman-Eisler, 1968; Köhnken, 1989) emphasizes that deception is a cognitively complex task. It is presumably more difficult to fabricate a plausible and convincing lie that is consistent with everything the observer knows or might find out than it is to tell the truth. In the second example, if the police officer asks the man several questions about his alibi, he must immediately give plausible answers. This is easier to do if he can speak the truth, than when he has to lie. Evidence has suggested that people engaged in cognitively complex tasks make more speech disturbances, speak slower and wait longer before giving an answer (Goldman-Eisler, 1968). They also make fewer hand and arm movements (Ekman and Friesen, 1972). The decrease in hand and arm movements is based on the fact that a greater cognitive load results in a neglect of body language, reducing overall animation (Ekman and Friesen, 1972).

The attempted control approach (DePaulo, 1988, 1992; DePaulo and Kirkendol, 1989; Ekman, 1989; Köhnken, 1990) emphasizes that liars tend to control their behaviour, in order both to avoid giving possible nonverbal indicators of their deception and to enhance the credibility of the impression they make on others. Thus, according to the control approach, the men in both examples will try to behave as 'normally' as possible. But this is not easy. They have to suppress their tendency to show the emotions they experience and, they must know how to behave normally. The control approach predicts some behaviours will, despite their efforts, give the lie away, most likely those behaviours which are the most difficult to control. Theoretically, the face should be easier to control than the body (Ekman, 1985). This reasoning refers to gaze aversion and smiling and excludes microexpressions of emotions which are much more difficult to control, as will be discussed later. The great communicative potential of the face means that people are practised at using and therefore controlling it. The body, on the other hand, is a channel that may not be as salient in communication and is less often attended to and reacted to by others. Hence, when controlling their behaviour, liars may exhibit a pattern of behaving that will appear planned, rehearsed and lacking in spontaneity. For example liars may believe that movements will give their lies away and will therefore move very deliberately and tend to avoid those movements which are not strictly essential. This will result in an unusual degree of rigidity and inhibition, because people normally make movements which are not essential. Like the face, the voice has a great sending capacity, is salient and is a channel that other persons comment on. Therefore, it should be a controllable channel as well. In fact, however, for reasons that are not entirely clear, tone of voice is much more difficult for senders to control than are facial expressions (Ekman, 1981).

The three approaches therefore predict different behaviours. For example the emotional approach predicts an increase in movements (nervous behaviour), whereas both the attempted control approach and the cognitive approach predict a decrease in movements during deception (although the reasoning is different: the attempted control approach predicts a decrease in movements caused by overcontrol, whereas the cognitive approach predicts a decrease in movements as a result of simply neglecting the use of body language). The emotional and cognitive approach predict an increase in speech disturbances due to nervousness and cognitive load, respectively, whereas the control approach predicts that liars will attempt to suppress those speech disturbances.

Which behaviours do liars usually show? The next paragraphs provide the answer. Before describing these objective indicators of deception, two comments have to be made. The approaches only suggest that the presence of signs of emotions, cognitive load and overcontrol may be indicative of deception. None of these approaches claim that the presence of these signs *necessarily* indicate deception. For instance truth tellers may also show signs of nervous behaviour. It is possible that the men in the two examples will show nervous behaviour, *even when they are telling the truth*. The men in both examples may be nervous because the interactions with the police officer make them nervous, or the man in the first example may be nervous because he is afraid that the police officer will not believe his explanation regarding why he is trying to unlock his bike with a screw-driver, similarly, the man in the second example may be nervous because he is afraid that the police officer will not believe his alibi and so on. Thus, their nervous behaviour makes both men appear suspicious (it may be an indicator of deception), but not necessarily guilt.

Furthermore, the fact that only signs of emotions, cognitive load and overcontrol exist implies that behavioural cues to deception may only become visible if at least one of these aspects is present in a deceptive situation. That is if a liar doesn't experience any fear, guilt or excitement and when the lie is not difficult to fabricate, behavioural cues to deception will not occur. A recent study conducted by DePaulo, Kashy, Kirkendol, Wyer and Epstein (1996) showed that most lies in everyday life fall in this category. They also found that these lies usually remain undetected.

Experimental studies of behavioural cues to deception

In the study of actual indicators of deception, participants are usually instructed to give either true or deceptive reports on certain issues. Their nonverbal behaviours are then analysed with particular coding systems and the average frequencies of occurrence of these behaviours during true and deceptive messages are compared. For instance DePaulo, a distinguished and leading researcher in this field, asked participants to describe in an honest way people they liked and people they disliked and also to describe the same people dishonestly, that is to pretend to like the people they really disliked and to pretend to dislike the people they really liked (DePaulo and Rosenthal, 1979; DePaulo, Lassiter and Stone, 1982). Ekman, another distinguished and leading researcher in this field, showed his participants (student nurses) a pleasant film showing colourful ocean scenes and asked them to describe their feelings frankly to an interviewer who could not see which film they were watching. Then he showed them a gruesome medical training film (including severe burns and an amputation) and asked them to conceal their feelings so that the interviewer would think that they were seeing another pleasant film, for instance about pretty flowers (Ekman and Friesen, 1974; Ekman, Friesen and Scherer, 1976). In order to raise the stakes in these experiments, subjects are usually offered some money if they successfully get away with their lies.

There have been numerous experiments conducted so far. A summary of the experiments being reviewed is given in Table 2.1. Box 2.1 provides an overview and descriptions of the behaviours to be discussed.

The first part of Table 2.1 (vocal characteristics) reveals one clear actual indicator of deception: liars have a higher pitched voice than truth tellers. As mentioned before, this is believed to be caused by stress.

With regard to speech disturbances (both ah and non-ah) and speech rate the findings of Höfer, Köhnken, Hanewinkel and Bruhn (1993), Vrij (1995) and Vrij and Winkel (1991a) differ from the findings of all of the others. Höfer and Vrij found a *decrease* in speech disturbances and a *faster* speech rate during deception whereas the other studies have found the opposite pattern, namely an *increase* in speech disturbances and a *slower* speech rate during deception. It is reasonable to suggest that this has to do with the type of lie used in these studies. In the studies of 'the others' participants in the deception condition have to *fabricate* an answer (as in the DePaulo and Ekman-like research approach, as described above). Höfer's and Vrij's paradigms are slightly different. Vrij asked participants in the deception condition to deny the possession of a set of headphones they actually possessed. Hence, participants only had to *conceal* some information, which is cognitively probably easier than fabricating an answer. In Höfer's study, participants had to recall a film they had just seen. In the deception condition they were requested to include details in their account which in fact did not occur in the film. However, Höfer *et al. instructed and coached* them in what they should say. Hence, these participants did not have to invent an answer either and were therefore probably facing an easier task than participants in studies who have to fabricate an answer. In summary, it seems (although it is speculative because it has never been tested) that cognitively more difficult lies, lies in which people have to

TABLE 2.1 *Objective indicators of deception*

| | Vocal characteristics | | | | |
	ah	non-ah	pitch of voice	speech rate	latency period
Bond et al. (1985)	–	–			
Bond et al. (1990)	–				
Buller et al. (1987)			–	–	
Buller et al. (1994a)	>	–			<
Cody et al. (1983)					<
Cody et al. (1984)	>	>			
DePaulo et al. (1982)	–	>		–	
DePaulo et al. (1989)	–	–			
DeTurck et al. (1985)	>				>
Ebesu et al. (1994)	–			<	
Ekman (1988)			>		<
Ekman et al. (1976)			>		
Ekman et al. (1991b)			>		
Fiedler et al. (1993)	>		–	<	
Hocking et al. (1980)	–	>		–	–
Höfer et al. (1993)	–	<		–	<
Kalma et al. (in press)					<
Knapp et al. (1974)	–	–			
Kraut, exp 1 (1978)	–	–			>
Kraut, exp 2 (1978)	–	–			<
Kraut, et al. (1980)		–			–
Mehrabian (1972)		>		–	
O'Hair et al. (1981)					<
Riggio et al. (1983)	–				
Stiff et al. (1986)	–				–
Stiff et al. (1994)					>
Streeter et al. (1977)			>		
Vrij (1995)	<	–	>	–	
Vrij et al. (1991a)	<	–	–	>	

| | Non-vocal characteristics | | | | | | | |
	gaze	smile	self manip.	arm/ hand	leg/ foot	trunk	head	shifting position
Bond et al. (1985)	>	–	–	>			–	–
Bond et al. (1990)	–	–	–	–			–	
Buller et al. (1987)	<	–	<	–	–	–	–	–
Buller et al. (1989)	<	–		–			–	
Buller et al. (1994a)		–					–	
Buller et al. (1994b)							<	
Cody et al. (1983)	–	–	–	<	<			>
Davis et al. (1995)				<				
DePaulo et al. (1989)	–			–			–	

(Continued)

TABLE 2.1 *(Continued)*

DeTurck *et al.* (1985)	–		>	>	–		
Ebesu *et al.* (1994)			–	–			>
Ekman (1988)		>	<	<	<		
Ekman *et al.* (1972)			>	<			
Ekman *et al.* (1976)				<			
Ekman *et al.* (1988)		>					
Ekman *et al.* (1991b)				<			
Fiedler *et al.* (1993)		>	–			<	
Hocking *et al.* (1980)	<	–	–	–	<	–	–
Höfer *et al.* (1993)	–	–	–	<	<	–	–
Kalma *et al.* (in press)	<	–		<	>		
Knapp *et al.* (1974)	<	–	>	–	–	–	
Kraut, exp 1 (1978)		–	–			–	–
Kraut *et al.* (1980)	–	–	–	–		–	–
McClintock *et al.* (1975)	–	–	>	–		>	>
Mehrabian (1972)				–	<	–	
O'Hair *et al.* (1981)	–	<	>	–	–	>	–
Riggio *et al.* (1983)	>	–	–	–	–	–	–
Stiff *et al.* (1986)		–	–	–	–		–
Vrij (1995)	–	–	–	<	<	–	–	–
Vrij *et al.* (1991a)	–	–	<	<		–	–	–
Vrij *et al.* (1996a)			–	<	–	–	
Vrij *et al.* (1996d)			–	<	<	–	–
Vrij *et al.* (1997a)				<			
Zuckerman *et al.* (1979)		<					

The signs refer to the actual behaviour–deception relationship (> = increase during deception, < = decrease during deception, – = no relationship with deception, blank = relationship was not investigated).

fabricate an answer, result in an increase in speech disturbances and a slower speech rate, a pattern predicted by the cognitive approach, whereas cognitively less difficult lies (concealing information or being coached concerning what to say) result in a decrease in speech disturbances and a faster speech rate, a pattern predicted by the control approach. The findings concerning latency period are not consistent. Hence, there does not seem to exist a clear relationship between latency period and deception.

The second part of Table 2.1 (nonvocal characteristics) shows a very confusing pattern. A detailed look reveals two actual indicators of deception, suggesting that liars tend to move their hands, arms, feet and legs less than truth tellers. With regard to hand and arm movements, particularly Vrij's (1995) research shows a decrease in subtle, non-functional hand and finger movements. These findings could be explained by both the cognitive approach and the control approach. All other nonvocal characteristics do not seem to be reliable indicators of deception. The fact that the facial characteristics mentioned in the scheme (gaze aversion and smiling) are unrelated to deception does not imply that the face cannot be used to detect deception. Ekman (1985) showed that it is possible to detect deception by using facial clues. His work reveals that brief expressions of emotions, which do not fit in the context, give people's lies away. For instance assume that both men in the opening examples are lying. In that case, they might be frightened about getting caught and might therefore show a brief microexpression of fear in their interactions with the police officers. Ekman found that these emotional microexpressions are very short (1/25 of a second, can easily be missed by an observer who happens to blink at the moment when they are expressed). They are short because the person tries to conceal them (which might be a cue for deception); they occur because they are very difficult to suppress. The fact that they are short, makes them very difficult to detect by untrained observers. However, detecting these microexpressions can be easily learned (Ekman, 1985).

Field studies of behavioural cues to deception

Not a single field study examining nonverbal behaviours of suspects in real police interviews has been published so far. The study that most resembles such a field study has been published recently by Davis and Hadiks (1995). They observed and scored Iraq's President Saddam Hussein's behaviour during his interview with Peter Arnett (CNN) during and about the Gulf War. The interview was broadcast on CNN. Afterwards, it was clear that Hussein lied at least once, namely when he fabricated an answer about Iraqi planes landing in Iran. Davis and Hadiks pointed out that during this statement Hussein refrained from making hand and arm movements. This finding corresponds with the findings of laboratory studies, that liars tend to move their hands and arms less during deception. Of course, it is too premature to draw conclusions on the basis of one study, in which only one individual from a particular culture is examined. More field studies are needed in this area.

Why are only a few indicators associated with deception?

There are at least two reasons why deception research reveals only a few indicators of deception. In the first place, the experimental designs in deception research which have been used so far are perhaps not suitable to reveal more indicators of deception, that is perhaps the tasks requested from the deceiver are too easy and the stakes (consequences for being caught) too low to reveal more indicators. The second explanation is that there does not exist one typical pattern of deceptive behaviour. Different people show different behaviours, that is some people give their lies away via voice-related cues, others via speech-related cues, a third group via movements and so on. The objective indicators findings thus only suggest that a relatively large number of people give their lies away via their pitch of voice and via their hand movements. Moreover, behaviours will differ per deceptive situation. The next paragraph deals with this second explanation.

Which factors influence deceptive behaviour?

As outlined above, there does not exist one typical pattern of deceptive behaviour. Different people show different behaviours and behaviours will differ per deceptive situation. At least five factors influence deceptive behaviour, namely cognitive complexity, stakes, motivation, planning and individual characteristics.

Cognitive complexity

As mentioned previously, behaviours during cognitively difficult lies will probably differ from behaviours during cognitively easy lies, differences between speech disturbances and speech rate are an illustration of this. Consider the following situation: A man who lives alone left his house at 1 a.m., he committed a crime and went back home at 2 a.m. The police suspect him of committing the crime and interview him. It is easy for the man to lie when there is no evidence at all that he committed the crime. An answer like 'I went to bed at 12 p.m. and woke up at 7 a.m.' seems realistic. The situation is much more complicated though when the police confront him with a witness who actually saw him after 1 a.m. at the scene of crime. The man then suddenly has to come up with an explanation regarding what he was doing at the scene of crime in the middle of the night. It is likely that in the latter case his account will be accompanied with more speech disturbances and will be spoken with a slower speech rate than his account in the first case.

Stakes

There may be differences in nonverbal behaviour between lies in which the stakes are high (a suspect who is accused of murder) compared to lies in which the stakes are rather low (a participant who has to lie in an experimental study). Unfortunately, there are no research data on this. It may be that liars in high stakes situations are more nervous than liars in low stakes situations and therefore display more nervous behaviours, such as making different sort of movements. However, it is not clear whether this is actually the case, for several reasons.

■ Experimental studies do differ in the stakes which are involved. Ekman's experiments are probably the studies with the highest stakes. He enhanced the stakes by using student nurses and identifying the study as a study of communication skills relevant to nursing and telling them that success in this study was a likely predictor of success as a nurse. The Ekman studies generally showed a decrease in (hand) movements during deception (see Table 2.1).

■ One may argue that the stakes were high for Saddam Hussein in his CNN interview. Similarly, the results showed not an increase but a decrease in movements during deception.

■ In a recent study, Vrij, Semin and Bull (1996d) examined correlations between being nervous and making hand movements in honest and deceptive interviews. These correlations were not significant, that is there was no relationship between the anxiety experienced by the participants and the number of hand movements they made.

■ In police interviews the police officer may react suspiciously to the suspect's answers. Stiff and Miller (1986) showed that people who realize that they are under suspicion, try even harder to make a credible impression (e.g. trying to avoid showing nervous behaviours).

Motivation

People who are highly motivated to get away with their lies may behave differently from people who care less about the outcome. In their meta-analysis, Zuckerman and Driver (1985) compared studies in which the motivation was high with those in which the motivation was lower. Motivation was considered high if participants were promised some monetary rewards for doing well on the deception task or if the deception was described as a test of some skill. The analysis revealed that highly motivated liars made fewer head movements and fewer shifts in position, spoke slower, spoke with a higher pitched voice and made more speech disturbances than less motivated liars. The explanation of these differences is speculative. The vocal differences (speech rate, pitch of voice and speech disturbances) might be caused by higher arousal in motivated liars, the nonvocal differences (head movements and shifting positions) might be caused by the fact that highly motivated liars try harder to control their behaviour and consequently move less and display more behavioural rigidity. DePaulo and Kirkendol (1989) refer to this as 'the motivational impairment effect'.

Planning

People who get the opportunity to plan their lie may behave differently from people who have to lie spontaneously. In their meta-analysis, Zuckerman and Driver (1985) also made a comparison between studies with low and high planning. Level of planning was considered high if the deceptive communication was rehearsed with the participants or if the participants needed only to say yes (or no) in response to all questions. Level of planning was considered low if participants did not know in advance the content of the questions and were not given time to prepare their answers. The meta-analysis revealed three differences: compared with deception under a low level of planning, the highly planned deceptions were associated with fewer arm and hand movements, shorter response latencies and faster speech rate. The shorter response latency and faster speech rate may be the result of the fact that planned lies are cognitively easier than spontaneous lies. The three differences may also be caused by an overcontrol of behaviour: the fact that planned lies are cognitively easier than spontaneous lies may give the liar better opportunities to try to control his or her behaviour, which may result in an even stronger overcontrol of behaviour.

Individual characteristics

Finally, it may be the case that personality characteristics can explain behaviours displayed during deception. Unfortunately, individual characteristics are rarely taken into account in deception studies and individual differences are seldomly reported. To date, there appear to be only two studies reporting frequency distributions in relation to individual differences in deception. Both studies deal with hand movements (Ekman, O'Sullivan, Friesen and Scherer, 1991b; Vrij, Akehurst and Winkel, 1997b).[1] These two studies revealed that a substantial number of subjects (about 25 per cent) did not show any difference at all in hand movements between truth telling and deception and that of those subjects who showed differences in hand movements between truth telling and deception, 65 per cent showed a decrease and 35 per cent showed an increase in hand movements during deception. These data suggest that, although most people decrease their hand movements during deception, a substantial number of people exhibit an increase in hand movements during deception or display no behavioural differences at all between truth telling and deception. In a recent study, Vrij, Akehurst and Morris (1997a) examined which individual differences may account for these different deception strategies. They found that particularly participants who were high in public self-consciousness and who were skilled in controlling their movements (both skills were measured with a questionnaire) refrained from making more hand movements during deception (only six per cent of these participants increased their hand movements during deception), whereas 75 per cent of their counterparts (participants who were low in public self-consciousness and not so skilled in controlling their movements) made more hand movements during deception than while telling the truth. They explained these findings by arguing that two aspects are important in deception strategies, namely (1) being aware of how to make a credible impression and (2) possessing the skills necessary to make a credible impression. Individuals high in public self-consciousness know how to make a reliable impression (public self-consciousness refers to people's ability to become aware of another's perspective and the willingness to act from that perspective). Individuals who possess the skills to control their behaviour will be successful in acting from that perspective and less threatened by the possibility of appearing awkward in public.

Is it possible to generalize these findings to police interviews?

There are reasons to believe that laboratory studies give good insight into suspects' behaviour during police interviews. There are many differences between these studies and real-life police interviews, probably particularly in motivation and stakes. However, as mentioned before, motivation and stakes will not radically influence the nonverbal behavioural pattern displayed by people, especially not as far as nonvocal behaviours are concerned. However, we have to be cautious. Studies dealing with situations in which the stakes are *extremely* high (comparable perhaps to the stakes for suspects who are accused of serious crimes) and in which the cognitive load is *extremely* high have not been carried out yet and behaviour in these circumstances may differ from behaviour displayed in situations with lower stakes (see 'Directions for future research' paragraph).

Predicting a particular suspect's behaviour during a police interview remains a difficult task. As mentioned before, it is certainly not the case that deception is associated with a specific, well-defined pattern of nonverbal behaviours. Many factors influence the nonverbal behaviour displayed during deception (cognitive complexity, stakes, individual characteristics and so on). Ideally, all these factors should be taken into account in order to make an adequate prediction.

Subjective (perceived) indicators of deception

Subjective indicators of deception are those cues used by observers to assess the truthfulness of communicators. In the examples at the opening of this chapter, an interesting question would be, what would lead the police officers to judge the men guilty? In the typical paradigm, observers are given videotapes or audiotapes and asked to judge whether each of a number of people is lying or telling the truth. These judgements are then correlated with the actual cues that were or were not present in each clip (for example Hemsley and Doob, 1978; Kraut, 1978; Kraut and Poe, 1980; Vrij and Winkel, 1992c, 1994). Another procedure determining perceived indicators of deception is to ask subjects directly what they think that they (or others in general) do differently when lying compared to when telling the truth (for example Gordon, Baxter, Rozelle and Druckman (1987); Vrij and Bull, 1992a; Vrij and Semin, 1996c; Zuckerman, Koestner and Driver, 1981b).

Table 2.2 summarizes studies concerned with the subjective nonverbal indicators of deception. These studies have been conducted in different Western countries, including Germany, the USA, the Netherlands and Great Britain. Mostly, they used college students as observers, but in some studies the observers were police officers (West (1992) and all the Vrij studies, except Vrij and Bull (1992a)) or customs officers (Kraut and Poe, 1980). In spite of this variety in research locations and variety in observers, the findings are highly similar. Hence, it appears that there exist clear and unanimous beliefs among observers (both lay persons and law enforcement personnel) in different cultures about the relationship between nonverbal behaviour and deception. Table 2.2 gives an overview of these beliefs.

TABLE 2.2 *Subjective indicators of deception*

			Vocal characteristics		
	ah	non-ah	pitch of voice	speech rate	latency period
Akehurst *et al.* (1996)	>	>	>	<	>
Apple *et al.* (1979)			>	<	
Baskett *et al.* (1974)		>			>
Baskett *et al.* (1974)					<
Bond *et al.* (1985)	–	–			
Bond *et al.* (1990)	–				
DePaulo *et al.* (1982)	>	>		<	
DePaulo *et al.* (1989)	>	–		<	
Ekman (1988)			–		
Fiedler *et al.* (1993)	–		>		–
Gordon *et al.* (1987)	>	>		>	
Kraut, exp 1 (1978)	–	–			>
Kraut *et al.* (1980)		–			>
McCroskey *et al.* (1969)		>			
Nigro *et al.* (1989)	>	>			
Riggio *et al.* (1983)	–	–		<	
Stiff *et al.* (1986)	>				–
Streeter *et al.* (1977)			>		
Vrij *et al.* (1992a)	>	>	–	>	>
Vrij *et al.* (1992b)	>	>			
Vrij *et al.* (1994)	>	>			
Vrij *et al.* (1996c)	>	>	–	>	–
West (1992)					>
Westcott *et al.* (1991)	>	>			>
Woodall *et al.* (1983)				<	
Zuckerman *et al.* (1981b)	>	>	>	>	>
Total:	>	>	>	–	>

(Continued)

TABLE 2.2 *(Continued)*

	gaze	smile	self manip.	arm/ hand	leg/ foot	trunk	head	shifting position
			Non-vocal characteristics					
Akehurst *et al.* (1996)	<	>	>	>	>	>	>	>
Bond *et al.* (1985)	<	>	–	–			–	–
Bond *et al.* (1990)	<	–	>	<			<	
Bond *et al.* (1992)	<							
Bond *et al.* (1992)	>							
Brookes *et al.* (1986)	–							
Burgoon *et al.* (1985)	<							
Desforges *et al.* (1995)	<							
Desforges *et al.* (1995)	>							
DePaulo *et al.* (1989)	–		–				–	>
Ekman (1988)		–	–	–	–			
Fiedler *et al.* (1993)		–	–				–	
Gordon *et al.* (1987)	<	>	>	>	–	>		
Hemsley *et al.* (1978)	<							
Koppelaar *et al.* (1986)			>			>		
Kraut, exp 1 (1978)		>	<			>		>
Kraut *et al.* (1980)	<	–	–	–		>		>
O'Sullivan *et al.* (1988)				>	>			
Riggio *et al.* (1983)	–	<	>	–	–		<	–
Rozelle *et al.* (1978)	<			>		>		
Schneider *et al.* (1977)					–			
Stiff *et al.* (1986)		>	–	–	–			>
Vrij *et al.* (1991b)	<							
Vrij *et al.* (1992a)	<	–	>	>	>	–	>	>
Vrij *et al.* (1992b)	<	>	–	–			–	–
Vrij *et al.* (1992c)		>	>	>				
Vrij *et al.* (1996a)			>	>	>			
Vrij *et al.* (1996b)			>	>	>			
Vrij *et al.* (1996c)	<	>	>	>	>	–	–	>
West (1992)	<		>	>				>
Westcott *et al.* (1991)	>	>						
Zuckerman *et al.* (1981b)	<	>	>	–	>		>	>
Total:	<	>	>	>	>	>	–	>

The signs refer to people's beliefs about behavioural cues to deception (> = observers associate an increase in the behaviour with deception, < = observers associate a decrease in the behaviour with deception, – = observers do no associate the behaviour with deception, blank = relationship was not investigated).

Observers associate deception with many speech disturbances (both ah and non-ah), a high-pitched voice, a long latency period, gaze aversion, smiling and many movements (self-manipulations, movements of the hands/arms, feet/legs and trunk and shifting positions). Interestingly, all these behaviours are signs of nervousness. Hence, this suggests that the two men in the situations outlined in examples 1 and 2 are likely to convey an impression of guilt when they act nervously. Observers are looking for cues of nervousness, probably because they assume that liars are nervous and will act accordingly (Knapp *et al.*, 1974; Köhnken, 1989; Kraut and Poe, 1980; Riggio and Friedman, 1983).

Bond, Omar, Pitre, Lashley, Skaggs and Kirk (1992) give a different explanation for subjective indicators of deception. They claim that not nervous behaviours but nonverbal behaviours that violate normative expectations create suspiciousness. Hence, not only many movements but also a total rigidity would create suspiciousness according to this suggestion. Their ideas are supported by research findings. To determine how observers use nonverbal norm violations when judging messages, Baskett and Freedle (1974) varied response latency. Responses were judged to be deceptive if they came too slowly or too quickly. The only responses to be judged truthful were those that followed an intermediate delay. Bond *et al.* (1992) found that subjects who maintained eye contact and subjects who showed complete gaze aversion made a more suspicious impression than subjects who showed intermediate levels of gaze aversion. Desforges and Lee (1995) also found that both maintenance of eye contact and complete gaze aversion evoked suspicion. Bond *et al.*'s suggestion has important implications. It implies that people will not appear to be honest when they show the 'opposite' behavioural pattern to that depcited in Table 2.2. People will only appear honest when they show behaviour that corresponds with normative expectations. However, when Vrij and Semin (1996c) asked participants to indicate in a questionnaire whether liars compared to truth tellers show 'an increase in gaze behaviour' (towards the conversation partner), 'a decrease in gaze behaviour' or 'similar levels of gaze behaviour', most participants filled in 'decrease in gaze behaviour'. A possible explanation for why people expect gaze aversion (and not eye contact) is that they can explain gaze aversion more effectively. Gaze aversion can be related to nervousness, whereas eye contact can only be explained by overcontrol of behaviour. We believe that observers think more about nervousness than about overcontrol when they think of deception and deceptive behaviour.

A comparison between objective and subjective indicators of deception

Since people have their own beliefs about what indicates that a person is deceiving, it is necessary to investigate how accurate these beliefs are in reality. A comparison of the research findings concerning actual and perceived indicators of deception reveals that the answer to this question is negative. Research has identified only one characteristic that is both a believed and an actual indicator, namely a high-pitched voice. Observers further associate an increase in speech disturbances and a longer latency period with deception, which are actual indicators of some lies (cognitively difficult lies) but not for other lies (such as cognitively easy lies), as has been argued before. Moreover, observers associate more nonverbal behaviours with deception than in fact actually indicate deception. For example perceived indicators such as gaze aversion, trunk movements, self-touches and shifting positions are not actual indicators of deception. Finally, observers believe that deception is associated with an *increase* in hand/arm and foot/leg movements, while, in fact, actual deception is associated with a *decrease* in hand/arm movements (particularly non-functional subtle hand/finger movements) and foot/leg movements.

The fact that both lay persons and law enforcement personnel hold similar but mostly incorrect beliefs about the relationship between nonverbal behaviour and deception indicates that law enforcement personnel do not seem to learn from their daily work experience how to interpret nonverbal behaviour. It may be that daily-life experience in detecting lies results in better insight among law enforcement personnel only when they receive adequate outcome feedback, that is information regarding whether their true/lie judgements are either right or wrong. In daily life such outcome feedback is usually lacking (DePaulo and Pfeifer, 1986). For example, customs officers will almost never find out whether or not the travellers they decide not to search further are smuggling goods. Vrij and Semin (1996c) therefore hypothesized that prisoners would have more accurate beliefs about the deception–nonverbal behaviour relationship than college students or law enforcement personnel because prisoners are likely to have the most adequate feedback. In their words: 'Criminals live in a culture that is a much more deceptive one than the world that "normal" people live in. Associating with other criminals as well as generally unsavoury people in the underworld may expose any sample of prisoners to a great deal of posing, bluffing, threats, promises, "cons" and so forth, many of which may be false or dishonest. Being successful in and adapting to, such a world depends in part on the ability to tell when you are being lied to' (p. 67). They investigated, via a questionnaire, beliefs about nonverbal indicators of deception of various groups, including college students, uniformed police officers, police detectives and prisoners. The results supported the hypothesis: prisoners had more accurate beliefs than any of the other groups. The beliefs of the other groups did not differ significantly from each other.

Why do differences between actual and perceived indicators of deception exist?

The core differences between actual and perceived indicators of deception are simply that observers expect liars to be nervous and to act accordingly, whereas in fact deceivers usually do not display nervous behaviour, because they try to (and quite often successfully) suppress these signs of nervousness. Hence, the mistake observers make is that they wrongly expect signs of nervous behaviour during deception. There are at least two explanations regarding why observers expect nervous behaviours. Almost everybody can think of somebody who has acted nervously during deception. Apparently, observers do not realize that these cases are exceptional and that in most cases people are successful in suppressing their nervous behaviour. Moreover, as a recent study of Vrij, Semin and Bull (1996d) revealed, liars are not aware that they successfully suppress their nonverbal behaviour during deception. On the contrary, they think that they exhibit nervous behaviour during deception! Hence, while detecting lies in others they are looking for cues which they think (incorrectly) reveal their own lies.

Accuracy rates

Obviously, the ability to detect deception depends upon the circumstances. For instance when the stakes are low, the lie is cognitively easy and the observers are not suspicious, it will be rather easy for a liar to successfully get away with the lie. It is perhaps more difficult to lie when the stakes rise and the lie is cognitively getting more difficult. In the scientific studies concerning the detection of deception, observers are typically given videotapes or audiotapes and asked to judge whether each of a number of people is lying or telling the truth. In most studies the liars had to immediately fabricate an answer, which makes these lies cognitively rather complicated. Moreover, there were usually some negative consequences involved for those who were not successful in lying, hence, the stakes were moderately high (although, of course, never as high as in some real-life police interviews). The percentages of lie detection (or the accuracy rate), in most of these studies ranges from 45 to 60 per cent when 50 per cent accuracy is expected by chance alone (DePaulo *et al.*, 1985; Kraut, 1980; Zuckerman *et al.*, 1981a). Although not impressive, deception accuracy slightly, but significantly, exceeds chance in almost all published studies. If accuracy at detecting lies is computed separately from accuracy at detecting truth, results usually show a truthfulness bias, that is, truthful messages are identified with more accuracy than are deceptive ones (Köhnken, 1989).

Theoretically, accuracy in detecting deception should vary with the ability to control the channels of communication. Liars should be most successful in deceiving others when using facial expressions (because this is the easiest channel to control) and least successful when using body movements and tone of voice cues (because these channels are less controllable). The combined results of more than 30 studies support this expectation. Observers are able to detect deception slightly above the level of chance when only body cues or voice cues are available, but they do no better than chance in detecting deceit if they only have access to facial cues. Furthermore, observers performed worse when facial cues were available in combination with other channels than when they only had access to these other channels (DePaulo *et al.*, 1985). Hence, these data suggest that, when trying to detect lies, the best strategy may be not to pay attention to the face at all and to pay attention to body movements and vocal characteristics only! However, this strategy may be too rigid because, as Ekman (1985) suggested, facial microexpressions of emotions may also reveal lies. The problem, however, is that observers usually miss these microexpressions and only pay attention to smiles and gaze aversion, neither of which are reliable indicators of deception.

Most of these studies, however, suffer from two important limitations. First, it could be argued, perhaps, that the deception task is not very realistic in these studies. For instance the observers are not able to interact with the potential deceiver, so detection of deception is perhaps easier during real-life interviews in which interaction with the interviewee takes place. Research findings do not support this suggestion. In experiments conducted by Stiff, Kim and Ramesh (1992) and Kalbfleisch (1994), for instance, in which observers actually interviewed the potential deceiver, the detection rate was not higher than the accuracy rate in the 'classical studies'. Secondly, the observers are usually college students. However, several studies included accuracy rates of 'professional lie detectors' (DePaulo and Pfeifer, 1986; Ekman and O'Sullivan, 1991a; Köhnken, 1987; Vrij, 1994). DePaulo and Pfeifer asked their participants (258 federal law enforcement officers, both experienced (n = 114) and new recruits (n = 144)) to detect deception when listening to audiotapes of target persons who were answering questions about their attitudes and opinions in front of a panel. In Ekman and O'Sullivan's deception task, observers (including 34 members of the Secret Service, 60 federal polygraphers and 126 police officers) were asked to detect deception on the basis of videotapes of nurses who described how they felt about a film they were watching. Köhnken showed 80 police officers videotapes of people who recalled a film (about a theft and a fight) they had just seen. Vrij showed 91 police detectives videotapes of people who denied the possession of a set of headphones. The accuracy scores of these 'professional lie catchers' are given in Table 2.3.

TABLE 2.3 *Accuracy scores of professional lie catchers*

	Accuracy rates		
	truth	lie	total
DePaulo and Pfeifer (federal law enforcement personnel, experienced)	64%[a]	42%[a]	52%
DePaulo and Pfeifer (federal law enforcement personnel, new recruits)			53%
Ekman and O'Sullivan (Secret Service)			64%
Ekman and O'Sullivan (Federal polygraphers)			56%
Ekman and O'Sullivan (police officers)			56%
Köhnken (police officers)	58%	31%	45%
Vrij (police detectives)	51%	46%	49%

[a] accuracy rates for experienced officers and new recruits together.

The results show, first, a truthfulness bias, that is truthful messages were identified with more accuracy then deceptive ones. Second, Table 2.3 shows that the professional lie catchers' accuracy rates fall in the 45–60 per cent range, which was previously found in studies with college students as observers. Hence, we may conclude that professional lie catchers were no better in detecting deception than were college students. The two studies conducted by DePaulo and Pfeifer and by Ekman and O'Sullivan actually support this conclusion. In both studies college students were included as observers as well. DePaulo and Pfeifer found that law enforcement personnel (both new recruits and experienced officers) were no better in detecting deception than college students, Ekman and O'Sullivan found that only members of the Secret Service were better in detecting lies than college students. It is interesting to see that even in Ekman and O'Sullivan's study the accuracy rates were rather low. These observers were exposed to videoclips of people who were facing a difficult task: (1) they had to say that they were amused while they were watching burns and amputations and (2) the stakes were high because they were led to believe that being successful in the deception task was associated with being successful in their career. The results thus show that even in such a difficult situation many people can successfully get away with their lies.

There are four possible explanations why the ability to detect deception is usually low.

- As Vrij (1994) argued, differences between liars and truth tellers are usually very small, perhaps too small to be detected.

- It might be the case that observers use the wrong cues to detect deception, that is they are usually looking for cues of nervous behaviour whereas liars often do not show such behaviour.

- As mentioned before, if people show nervous behaviour (for instance during police interviews) it does not necessarily mean that they are lying. A truthful suspect who is worried that he will not be believed by the police officer may, because of that fear, show the same nervous behaviour that a liar may manifest who is afraid of being caught. This is the so-called Othello effect (Ekman, 1985).

- Observers possibly fail to take account of individual differences in behaviour, as shown by Vrij (1993). He found, for instance that socially anxious people made an unreliable impression on police detectives, due to the fact that they exhibit nervous behaviour during police interviews. The problem, however, is that nervous behaviour during police interviews is typical behaviour of socially anxious people. For them, nervous behaviour is not a sign of lying, it is just the way they behave in these situations and has been labelled the Brokaw hazard (Ekman, 1985) or idiosyncrasy error (Ekman and Frank, 1993). The last three reasons suggest that detecting lies may be possible, but that accuracy rates are usually low because most observers make unnecessary mistakes. This idea is supported by Ekman and O'Sullivan's (1991a) study, which revealed that some observers, namely Secret Service agents, are rather accurate lie detectors. What makes them so accurate? We will refer to this question in the next paragraph.

Training

Bull (1989) noticed that a number of police recruitment advertisements and police training books seem to imply that the detection of deception from behavioural cues is a simple affair and that training with regard to these cues can enhance the detection of deception. Bull reviewed the published literature on the effects of training and found no evidence of a training effect. He concluded that 'until a number of publications in refereed journals appear demonstrating that training enhances the detection of deception, it appears that some police recruitment advertisements and police training books are deceiving their readers' (p. 83). Recent studies (DeTurck and Miller, 1990; Fiedler and Walka, 1993; Vrij, 1994) showed some, but only very limited effects, of training. Although training people in detecting deception is certainly not an easy task, it is perhaps too premature to conclude that it is not possible. As mentioned before, Ekman and O'Sullivan (1991a) found that Secret Service agents are better at detecting deception than others. They found for instance that 53 per cent of these agents achieved an accuracy rate of at least 70 per cent and 29 per cent an accuracy rate of 80 per cent or more. Hence, many of them seemed able to detect deception rather accurately. When some people are able, why then should others not be able to learn to detect deception as well? It is important to know which cues good lie catchers use when detecting deception. Ekman and O'Sullivan's (1991a) preliminary results showed that good lie detectors use different cues when observing different people (for instance they mention speech-related cues when detecting a lie in one person, voice-related cues for a second person and body movement-related cues for a third person), whereas inaccurate lie detectors seem to use a 'rule of thumb' strategy using the same cues in order to detect lies in different people. As mentioned before, this strategy is doomed to fail because different people show different behaviours.

Confidence

Despite people's low ability to detect lies, they are usually very confident in their ability to detect lies (Kalbfleisch, 1992; Köhnken, 1990, Vrij, 1993). Köhnken (1996) pointed out that people, when they are asked to estimate their ability to detect deceptions, usually remember only the gross and awkward lies which were easily detected and neglect the fact that most skillful, clever lies were rarely noticed by them. Moreover, the correlation between the accuracy of credibility judgements and the confidence about these is usually not statistically significant (DePaulo and Pfeifer, 1986; Ekman and O'Sullivan, 1991a; Vrij, 1994). Hence, inaccurate lie detectors are as confident as accurate lie detectors.

Finally, DePaulo and Pfeifer (1986) found that, although police officers were not better in detecting deception than were college students, they were more confident in their judgements than college students. Hence, daily experience in detecting lies seems to enhance confidence but not accuracy.

Consequences of police officers' incorrect beliefs about indicators of deception: cross-racial nonverbal communication errors

Police officers' incorrect beliefs about indicators of deception have negative consequences for some groups, such as black citizens during police interviews with white police officers, as Vrij and colleagues pointed out (Vrij and Winkel, 1990, 1991a, 1992c, 1994; Vrij, Winkel and Koppelaar, 1988, 1991b). Previous studies revealed several differences in nonverbal behaviour between black and white people: black people, for instance display more gaze aversion (Fugita, Wesley and Hillery, 1974; Ickes, 1984) and make more movements (Garratt, Baxter and Rozelle, 1981; Smith, 1983) than white people do. Vrij and Winkel (1990, 1991a) and Vrij et al. (1988) investigated nonverbal behavioural patterns of Dutch (white) and Surinam (black) citizens during simulated police interviews. The outcomes revealed many behavioural differences between Dutch and Surinam citizens in these interviews. Surinam people made more speech disturbances, exhibited more gaze aversion, smiled more often and made more self-manipulations and hand, arm and trunk movements. These findings combined with the findings concerning subjective indicators of deception show a big overlap which give rise to possible cross-racial nonverbal communication errors during cross-cultural police interviews. That is, nonverbal behavioural patterns that are typical for black people may be interpreted by white observers as being betrayed attempts to hide the truth (this is another example of the Brokaw hazard). Several experiments (Vrij and Winkel, 1992c, 1994; Vrij et al., 1991b) revealed that such cross-racial nonverbal communication errors might well occur. Vrij and Winkel (1992c), for instance exposed white police officers to a filmed interview with an actor showing 'black' movements or 'white' movements, using normative data derived from

Vrij and Winkel (1991a)). The outcomes revealed that the actor made a more suspicious impression in the black nonverbal behaviour condition (72 per cent found him suspicious) than in the white nonverbal condition (41 per cent found him suspicious).

CONCLUSION

Observers very often have incorrect beliefs about cues to deception and are hardly ever able to detect deception on the basis of nonverbal behaviour displayed by deceivers. This lack of ability to detect deception is perhaps not surprising bearing in mind that nonverbal behaviour displayed during deception depends on the characteristics of the individual, type of lie and the circumstances under which the lie takes place. The findings, however, also give some hope for those who want to detect lies. Specialized lie catchers, agents of the Secret Service, are rather accurate in detecting lies by observing nonverbal behaviour. This implies that nonverbal lie detection is an art, a skill that perhaps can be learned. More research is needed to find out which cues they use and how difficult it is to train people to use these cues. For the time being, it may be useful to train professional lie detectors (police officers for instance) to get rid of their incorrect, stereotyped beliefs about cues to deception, because they lead to undesired effects, such as cross-racial nonverbal communication errors.

Guidelines for the detection of deception

Some conclusions can be drawn from research for those who have to detect lies. These are as follows:

- Lies may only be detectable via nonverbal cues if the liar experiences fear, guilt, or excitement, or when the lie is difficult to fabricate.

- It is important to pay attention to mismatches between speech content and nonverbal behaviour and to try to explain these mismatches. Keep the possibility in mind that the person is lying, but consider this as only one of the possibilities for this mismatch.

- Attention should be directed at deviations from a person's 'normal' or usual patterns of behaviour, when these are known. The explanation for such deviations should be established. Each deviation may indicate that the person is lying, but do not disregard other explanations for these deviations.

- The judgement of untruthfulness should only be made when all the other explanations are negated.

- A person suspected of deception should be encouraged to talk. This is necessary to negate the alternative options regarding somebody's behaviour. Moreover, the more the liars talk, the more likely it is that they (finally) will give their lies away via verbal and/or nonverbal cues (as they continuously have to pay attention to both speech content and nonverbal behaviour).

- There are stereotyped ideas about cues to deception (such as gaze aversion, fidgeting and so on), which research has shown to be unreliable indicators of deception. The actual indicators are listed in Table 2.1. These can be a guide, but keep in mind that not everyone will exhibit these cues during deception and the presence of these cues *may* indicate deception but do not in every case.

Directions for future research

As mentioned before, deceptive behaviour may differ per situation and per person. For instance when the stakes are low, liars will experience less emotional arousal than when the stakes are high. It might be the case that liars will be successful in suppressing nervous behaviours (the result of stress) when the stakes are low but will not be able to suppress various nervous behaviours successfully when the stakes are high. Hence, high-stakes lies may result in more nervous behaviours than low-stakes lies. Similarly, liars will need less cognitive effort when the lie is easy than when the lie is difficult. It might therefore be the case that liars will be successful in suppressing behaviours associated with cognitive load when the lies are easy to fabricate but will not be able to suppress these behaviours successfully when the lies are difficult. Hence, difficult lies might result in more behaviours associated with cognitive load than easy lies. One might also expect that individual differences will influence deceptive nonverbal behaviour. For instance labile people will be more sensitive to high stakes than more stable people and will therefore perhaps show more nervous behaviours in high-stake lies than stable people. We are currently planning research to address these issues.

Moreover, although the accuracy rates in detecting deception are usually low, research has revealed considerable individual differences in people's ability to detect lies. Why are some people good at detecting lies and others poor? Which cues do good lie detectors use? Can poor lie detectors benefit from good lie detectors, i.e. can their ability to detect lies be improved when they obtain insight into how good lie detectors detect lies? It is up to us to find this out.

NOTE

1. In a recent study, Kashy and DePaulo (1996) reported individual differences in the frequency of lying in daily life situations.

REFERENCES

Akehurst, L. Köhnken, G., Vrij, A. and Bull, R. (1996). Lay persons' and police officers' beliefs regarding deceptive behaviour. *Applied Cognitive Psychology*, **10**, 461–471.

Apple, W., Streeter, L.A. and Krauss, R.M. (1979). Effects of pitch and speech rate on personal attributions. *Journal of Personality and Social Psychology*, **37**, 715–727.

Baskett, G.D. and Freedle, R.O. (1974). Aspects of language pragmatics and the social perception of lying. *Journal of Psycholinguistic Research*, **3**, 117–131.

Bond, C.F., Kahler, K.N. and Paolicelli, L.M. (1985). The miscommunication of deception: an adaptive perspective. *Journal of Experimental Social Psychology*, **21**, 331–345.

Bond, C.F., Omar, A., Pitre, U., Lashley, B.R., Skaggs, L.M. and Kirk, C.T. (1992). Fishy-looking liars: deception judgment from expectancy violation. *Journal of Personality and Social Psychology*, **63**, 969–977.

Bond, C.F., Omar, A., Mahmoud, A. and Bonser, R.N. (1990). Lie detection across cultures. *Journal of Nonverbal Behaviour*, **14**, 189–205.

Brooks, C.I., Church, M.A. and Fraser, L. (1986). Effects of duration of eye contact on judgments of personality characteristics. *Journal of Social Psychology*, **126**, 71–78.

Bull, R. (1989). Can training enhance the detection of deception? In J.C. Yuille (ed.), *Credibility Assessment* (pp. 83–97). Dordrecht, The Netherlands: Kluwer.

Buller, D.B. and Aune, R.K. (1987). Nonverbal cues to deception among intimates, friends and strangers. *Journal of Nonverbal Behavior*, **11**, 269–290.

Buller, D.B., Burgoon, J.K., Busling, A.L. and Roiger, J.F. (1994a). Interpersonal deception VIII. Further analysis of nonverbal and verbal correlates of equivocation from the Bauelas *et al.* (1990) research. *Journal of Language and Social Psychology*, **13**, 396–417.

Buller, D.B., Burgoon, J.K., White, C.H. and Ebesu, A.S. (1994b). Interpersonal deception VII. Behavioural profiles of falsification, equivocation and concealment. *Journal of Language and Social Psychology*, **13**, 366–395.

Buller, D.B., Comstock, J., Aune, R.K. and Strzyzewski, K.D. (1989). The effect of probing on deceivers and truthtellers. *Journal of Nonverbal Behavior*, **13**, 155–170.

Burgoon, J.K., Kelly, D.L., Newton, D.A. and Keely-Dyreson, M.P. (1989). The nature of arousal and nonverbal indices. *Human Communication Research*, **16**, 217–255.

Burgoon, J.K., Manusov, V., Mineo, P. and Hale, J.L. (1985). Effects of gaze on hiring, credibility, attraction and relational message interpretation. *Journal of Nonverbal Behavior*, **9**, 133–147.

Cody, M.J., Marston, P.J. and Foster, M. (1984). Deception: paralinguistic and verbal leakage. In R.N. Bostrom and B.H. Westley (ed.), *Communication Yearbook 8* (pp. 464–490). Beverly Hills, CA: Sage.

Cody, M.J. and O'Hair, H.D. (1983). Nonverbal communication and deception: differences in deception cues due to gender and communicator dominance. *Communication Monographs*, **50**, 175–193.

Davis, M. and Hadiks, D. (1995). Demeanor and credibility. *Semiotica*, **106**, 5–54.

DePaulo, B.M. (1988). Nonverbal aspects of deception. *Journal of Nonverbal Behavior*, **12**, 153–162.

DePaulo, B.M. (1992). Nonverbal behaviour and self–presentation. *Psychological Bulletin*, **111**, 203–243.

DePaulo, B.M., Kashy, D.A., Kirkendol, S.E., Wyer, M.M. and Epstein, J.A. (1996). Lying in everyday life. *Journal of Personality and Social Psychology*, **70**, 979–995.

DePaulo, B.M. and Kirkendol, S.E. (1989). The motivational impairment effect in the communication of deception. In J.C. Yuille (ed.), *Credibility Assessment* (pp. 51–70). Dordrecht: Kluwer.

DePaulo, B.M., Lassiter, G.D. and Stone, J.I. (1982). Attentional determinants of success at detection deception and truth. *Personality and Social Psychology Bulletin*, **8**, 273–279.

DePaulo, B.M. and Pfeifer, R.L. (1986). On-the-job experience and skill at detecting deception. *Journal of Applied Social Psychology*, **16**, 249–267.

DePaulo, B.M. and Rosenthal, R. (1979). Telling lies. *Journal of Personality and Social Psychology*, **37**, 1713–1722.

DePaulo, B.M., Rosenthal, R., Rosenkrantz and Green, C.R. (1982). Actual and perceived cues to deception: a closer look at speech. *Basic and Applied Social Psychology*, **3**, 291–312.

DePaulo, B.M., Stone, J.L. and Lassiter, G.D. (1985). Deceiving and detecting deceit. In B.R. Schenkler (ed.), *The Self and Social Life* (pp. 323–370). New York: McGraw-Hill.

DePaulo, P.J. and DePaulo, B.M. (1989). Can deception by salespersons and customers be detected through nonverbal behavioural cues? *Journal of Applied Social Psychology*, **19**, 1552–1577.

Desforges, D.M. and Lee, T.C. (1995). Detecting deception is not as easy as it looks. *Teaching of Psychology*, **22**, 128–130.

DeTurck, M.A. and Miller, G.R. (1985). Deception and arousal: isolating the behavioural correlates of deception. *Human Communication Research*, **12**, 181–201.

DeTurck, M.A. and Miller, C.R. (1990). Training observers to detect deception: Effects of self-monitoring and rehearsal. *Human Communication Research*, **16**, 603–620.

Ebesu, A.S. and Miller, M.D. (1994). Verbal and nonverbal behaviours as a function of deception type. *Journal of Language and Social Psychology*, **13**, 418–442.

Ekman, P. (1981). Mistakes when deceiving. *Annals of the New York Academy of Sciences*, **364**, 269–278.

Ekman, P. (1985). *Telling Lies*. New York: W.W. Norton.

Ekman, P. (1988). Lying and nonverbal behaviour: theoretical issues and new findings. *Journal of Nonverbal Behavior*, **12**, 163–176.

Ekman, P. (1989). Why lies fail and what behaviours betray a lie. In J.C. Yuille (ed.), *Credibility Assessment* (pp. 71–82). Dordrecht, The Netherlands: Kluwer.

Ekman, P. and Frank, M.G. (1993). Lies that fail. In M. Lewis and C. Saarni (eds), *Lying and Deception in Everyday Life* (pp. 184–201). New York: Guildford Press.

Ekman, P. and Friesen, W.V. (1972). Hand movements. *Journal of Communication*, **22**, 353–374.

Ekman, P. and Friesen, W.V. (1974). Detecting deception from the body or face. *Journal of Personality and Social Psychology*, **29**, 288–298.

Ekman, P., Friesen, W.V. and Scherer, K.R. (1976). Body movement and voice pitch in deceptive interaction. *Semiotica*, **16**, 23–27.

Ekman, P., Friesen, W.V. and O'Sullivan, M. (1988). Smiles when lying. *Journal of Personality and Social Psychology*, **54**, 414–420.

Ekman, P. and O'Sullivan, M. (1991a). Who can catch a liar? *American Psychologist*, **46**, 913–920.

Ekman, P., O'Sullivan, M., Friesen, W.V. and Scherer, K.R. (1991b). Face, voice and body in detecting deceit. *Journal of Nonverbal Behavior*, **15**, 125–135.

Fiedler, K. and Walka, I. (1993). Training lie detectors to use nonverbal cues instead of global heuristics. *Human Communication Research*, **20**, 199–223.

Fugita, S.S., Wexley, K.N. and Hillery, J.M. (1974). Black-white differences in nonverbal behaviour in an interview setting. *Journal of Applied Social Psychology*, **4**, 343–351.

Garratt, G.A., Baxter, J.C. and Rozelle, R.M. (1981). Training university police in black-American nonverbal behaviour. *Journal of Social Psychology*, **113**, 217–229.

Goldman-Eisler, F. (1968). *Psycholinguistics: Experiments in Spontaneous Speech*. New York: Doubleday.

Gordon, R.A., Baxter, J.C., Rozelle, R.M. and Druckman, D. (1987). Expectations of honest, evasive and deceptive nonverbal behaviour. *Journal of Social Psychology*, **127**, 231–233.

Hemsley, G.D. and Doob, A.N. (1978). The effect of looking behaviour on perceptions of a communicator's credibility. *Journal of Applied Social Psychology*, 8, 136–144.

Hocking, J.E. and Leathers, D.G. (1980). Nonverbal indicators of deception: a new theoretical perspective. *Communication Monographs*, 47, 119–131.

Höfer, E., Köhnken, G., Hanewinkel, R. and Bruhn, C. (1993). Diagnostik und attribution von glaubwürdigkeit. *Kiel: final report to the Deutsche Forschungsgemeinschaft*, KO 882/4-2.

Ickes, W. (1984). Compositions in black and white: determinants of interactions in interracial dyads. *Journal of Personality and Social Psychology*, 47, 330–341.

Kalbfleisch, P.J. (1992). Deceit, distrust and the social milieu: application of deception research in a troubled world. *Journal of Applied Communication Research*, 20, 308–334.

Kalbfleisch, P.J. (1994). The language of detecting deceit. *Journal of Language and Social Psychology*, 13, 469–496.

Kalma, A., Witte, M., Zaalberg, R. (in press). Authenticity: operationalization, manipulation and behavioural components: An exploration. *Medium Psychologie*.

Kashy, D.A. and DePaulo, B.M. (1996). Who lies? *Journal of Personality and Social Psychology*, 70, 1037–1051.

Knapp, M.L., Hart, R.P. and Dennis, H.S. (1974). An exploration of deception as a communication construct. *Human Communication Research*, 1, 15–29.

Köhnken, G. (1987). Training police officers to detect deceptive eyewitness statements. Does it work? *Social Behaviour*, 2, 1–17.

Köhnken, G. (1989). Behavioral correlates of statement credibility: theories, paradigms and results. In H. Wegener, F. Lösel and J. Haisch (eds), *Criminal Behavior and the Justice System: Psychological Perspectives* (pp. 271–289). New York: Springer-Verlag.

Köhnken, G. (1990). *Glaubwürdigkeit: Untersuchungen zu einem psychologischen konstrukt*. München: Psychologie Verlags Union.

Köhnken, G. (1996). Social psychology and the law. In G.R. Semin and K. Fiedler (eds), *Applied Social Psychology* (pp. 257–282). London, England: Sage.

Koppelaar, L., Winkel, F.W. and Steen, J.C. van der (1986). Psychologische kanttekeningen bij art 27 Sv.: een experiment rond etnische origine, ritmisch gedrag en verdacht zijn. *Delikt en Delinkwent*, 16, 25–38.

Kraut, R.E. (1978). Verbal and nonverbal cues in the perception of lying. *Journal of Personality and Social Psychology*, 36, 380–391.

Kraut, R.E. (1980). Humans as lie detectors: some second thoughts. *Journal of Communication*, 30, 209–216.

Kraut, R.E. and Poe, D. (1980). On the line: the deception judgments of customs inspectors and laymen. *Journal of Personality and Social Psychology*, 36, 380– 391.

McClintock, C.C. and Hunt, R.G. (1975). Nonverbal indicators of affect and deception in an interview setting. *Journal of Applied Social Psychology*, 5, 54–67.

McCroskey, J.C. and Mehrley, S. (1969). The effects of disorganization and nonfluency on attitude change and source credibility. *Speech Monographs*, 36, 13–21.

Mehrabian, A. (1972). *Nonverbal Communication*. Chicago, IL: Aldine-Atherton.

Nigro, G.N., Buckley, M.A., Hill, D.E. and Nelson, J. (1989). When juries 'hear' children testify: the effects of eyewitness age and speech style on jurors' perceptions of testimony. In S.J. Ceci, D.E. Ross and M.P. Toglia (eds), *Perspectives on Children's Testimony* (pp. 57–70). New York: Springer-Verlag.

O'Hair, H.D., Cody, M.J. and McLaughlin, M.L. (1981). Prepared lies, spontaneous lies, machiavellianism and nonverbal communication. *Human Communication Research*, 7, 325–339.

O'Sullivan, M., Ekman, P. and Friesen, W.V. (1988). The effect of comparisons on detecting deceit. *Journal of Nonverbal Behavior*, 12, 203–216.

Riggio, R.E. and Friedman, H.S. (1983). Individual differences and cues to deception. *Journal of Personality and Social Psychology*, 45, 899–915.

Rozelle, R.M. and Baxter, J.C. (1978). The interpretation of nonverbal behaviour in a role-defined interaction sequence: the police–citizen encounter. *Environmental Psychology and Nonverbal Behavior*, 2, 167–181.

Schneider, S.M. and Kintz, B.L. (1977). The effect of lying upon foot and leg movement. *Bulletin of the Psychonomic Society*, 10, 451–453.

Smith, A. (1983). Nonverbal communication among black female dyads: an assessment of intimacy, gender and race. *Journal of Social Issues*, 39, 55–67.

Stiff, J.B., Corman, S., Krizek, B. and Snider, E. (1994). Individual differences and changes in nonverbal behaviour. *Communication Research*, 21, 555–581.

Stiff, J.B., Kim, H.J. and Ramesh, C.N. (1992). Truth biases and aroused suspicion in relational deception. *Communication Research*, 19, 326–345.

Stiff, J.B. and Miller, G.R. (1986). 'Come to think of it...': interrogative probes, deceptive communication and deception detection. *Human Communication Research*, 12, 339–357.

Streeter, L.A., Krauss, R.M., Geller, V., Olson, C. and Apple, W. (1977). Pitch changes during attempted deception. *Journal of Personality and Social Psychology*, 24, 12–21.

Vrij, A. (1993). Credibility judgments of detectives: the impact of nonverbal behaviour, social skills and physical characteristics on impression formation. *Journal of Social Psychology*, 133, 601–611.

Vrij, A. (1994). The impact of information and setting on detection of deception by police detectives. *Journal of Nonverbal Behavior*, 18, 117–137.

Vrij, A. (1995). Behavioural correlates of deception in a simulated police interview. *Journal of Psychology: Interdisciplinary and Applied*, 129, 15–29.

Vrij, A. and Akehurst, L. (1996a). Hand movements during deception: some recent insights. Manuscript submitted for publication.

Vrij, A., Akehurst, L., Van Dalen, D., Van Wijngaarden, J.J. and Foppes, J.H. (1996b). Nonverbaal gedrag en misleiding. *Tijdschrift voor de Politie*, 58, 11–14.

Vrij, A., Akehurst, L. and Morris, P.M. (1997a). Individual differences in hand movements during deception. *Journal of Nonverbal Behavior*, in press.

Vrij, A., Akehurst, L. and Winkel, F.W. (1997b). Police officers' incorrect beliefs about nonverbal indicators of deception and its consequences. In J.F. Nijboer and J.M. Reijntjes (eds), *Proceedings of the First World Conference on New Trends in Criminal Investigation and Evidence* (pp. 221–239). Lelystad: Koninklijke Vermande.

Vrij, A. and Bull, R. (1992a). Subjective indicators of truthful and deceptive statements. Unpublished datafile. University of Portsmouth, Psychology Department.

Vrij, A., Foppes, J.H., Volger, D.M. and Winkel, F.W. (1992b). Moeilijk te bepalen wie de waarheid spreekt: nonverbaal gedrag belangrijkste indicator. *Algemeen Politie Blad*, **141**, 13–15.

Vrij, A. and Semin, G.R. (1996c). Lie experts' beliefs about nonverbal indicators of deception. *Journal of Nonverbal Behavior*, **20**, 65–80.

Vrij, A., Semin, G.R. and Bull, R. (1996d). Insight in behaviour displayed during deception. *Human Communication Research*, **22**, 544–562.

Vrij, A. and Winkel, F.W. (1990). Culturele verschillen in spreekstijl van Surinamers en Nederlanders: de relatie tussen 'zakelijkheid' en 'misleiding' bij een politieverhoor. *Recht der Werkelijkheid*, **11**, 3–15.

Vrij, A. and Winkel, F.W. (1991a). Cultural patterns in Dutch and Surinam nonverbal behaviour: an analysis of simulated police/citizen encounters. *Journal of Nonverbal Behavior*, **15**, 169–184.

Vrij, A. and Winkel, F.W. (1992c). Crosscultural police–citizen interactions: the influence of race, beliefs and nonverbal communication on impression formation. *Journal of Applied Social Psychology*, **22**, 1546–1559.

Vrij, A. and Winkel, F.W. (1994). Perceptual distortions in cross-cultural interrogations: the impact of skin color, accent, speech style and spoken fluency on impression formation. *Journal of Cross-Cultural Psychology*, **25**, 284–296.

Vrij, A., Winkel, F.W. and Koppelaar, L. (1988). Culturele verschillen in nonverbaal gedrag: de persoonlijke ruimte van Nederlanders en Surinamers. *Migrantenstudies*, **4**, 40–49.

Vrij, A., Winkel, F.W. and Koppelaar, L. (1991b). Interactie tussen politiefunctionarissen allochtone burgers: twee studies naar de frequentie en het effect van aan-en wegkijken op de impressieformatie. *Nederlands Tijdschrift voor de Psychologie*, **46**, 8–20.

West, I. (1992, March). Decision making in the detection of deception. Paper presented at the British Psychology Society, Division of Criminological and Legal Psychology. Harrogate, England.

Westcott, H.L., Davies, G.M. and Clifford, B.R. (1991). Adults' perceptions of children's videotaped truthful and deceptive statements. *Children and Society*, **5**, 123–135.

Woodall, W.G. and Burgoon, J.K. (1983). Talking fast and changing attitudes: a critique and clarification. *Journal of Nonverbal Behavior*, **8**, 126–143.

Zuckerman, M., DeFrank, R.S., Hall, J.A., Larrance, D.T. and Rosenthal, R. (1979). Facial and vocal cues of deception and honesty. *Journal of Experimental Social Pychology*, **15**, 378–396.

Zuckerman, M., DePaulo, B.M. and Rosenthal, R. (1981a). Verbal and nonverbal communication of deception. In L. Berkowitz (ed.), *Advances in Experimental Social Psychology, volume 14* (1–57). New York: Academic Press.

Zuckerman, M. and Driver, R.E. (1985). Telling lies: verbal and nonverbal correlates of deception. In A.W. Siegman and S. Feldstein (eds), *Multichannel Integrations of Nonverbal Behaviors* (pp. 129–147). Hillsdale, NJ: Lawrence Erlbaum.

Zuckerman, M., Koestner, R. and Driver, R. (1981b). Beliefs about cues associated with deception. *Journal of Nonverbal Behavior*, **6**, 105–114.

CHAPTER 3

FACIAL APPEARANCE AND CRIMINALITY

Ray Bull and Stephen McAlpine

INTRODUCTION

In 1984 Udry and Eckland (p. 47) made the following claims:

> Everyone knows that it is better to be beautiful than to be ugly. There may be some people who would prefer to be bad than good. Some might even prefer to be poor than rich. But we take it on faith that no one prefers to be ugly. The reason for this must be that people expect good things to come to the beautiful. Folklore tells us that beautiful girls marry handsome princes and live happily ever after. Heroes are handsome and villains are ugly.

The aim of this chapter is to consider some of the available literature on the question of whether there exists a relationship between facial appearance and criminality. This will include (i) a review of research on the extent to which people assume there to be such a relationship, (ii) an examination of studies on the impact upon prisoners' recidivism rates of surgery designed to improve their facial appearance, and (iii) an overview of the work on the effects on 'mock' jurors of defendant and victim facial attractiveness, as well as a description of the very few studies which exist of the effects of facial appearance in real-life court proceedings. When reading this chapter consideration should be given not only to the methodological rigour of the studies but also to their ecological validity.

Goldstein, Chance and Gilbert (1984) claimed that:

> the degree to which a particular individual's face invites facial stereotyping may influence the outcomes of any legal process in which they become involved (p. 552).

This chapter presents an overview of research relevant to this point.

MATCHING FACES TO CRIMES

Psychological research has shown that members of the general public do associate certain crimes with various types of facial appearance. In the USA in 1939 Thornton chose from the Nebraska State Penitentiary files the records of 20 criminals without looking at the file photograph of each criminal. These photographs were shown one at a time to a group of adults who were required to write down which one of four crimes each photographed person had been found guilty of. The adults' decisions were correct more so than could be expected by chance. In Germany Kozeny (1962) divided several hundred photographs of convicted criminals into 16 crime categories depending on the type of crime committed. For each of these 16 categories a composite photograph was made from those in the category. When asked to match one of the 16 crimes to each facial composite members of the public were found to be able to do this more so than would be expected by chance.

A study somewhat similar to those of Kozeny and of Thornton was conducted in London by Bull and Green (1980), with the exception that their photographs were not of criminals (but of the researchers' friends). The photographs all had the same background and the males photographed (aged between 27 and 33 years) had a similar, rather bland, facial expression. Participants (i.e. whom research psychologists used to refer to as 'subjects') were required to say which of the 11 listed crimes the 10 males had committed, more than one face being allowed for each crime. The data demonstrated that for company fraud, gross indecency, illegal possession of drugs, mugging, robbery with violence, soliciting, and taking and driving away, one of the faces was chosen significantly more often than the others, and it was a different face for each of these seven crimes. For the crimes of arson, burglary, rape and theft no one particular face was chosen more so than would be expected by chance.

In another US study, Goldstein *et al.* (1984) found participants to agree in their choices of which faces (in an album of actors' faces) looked like an armed robber, a mass murderer, a rapist, a clergyman or a medical doctor. When the chosen 'criminal' or 'non-criminal' faces were shown to other participants they rated the criminals' faces less positively on the dimensions of calm–excited, cautious–brash, clean–dirty, friendly–unfriendly, good–bad, kind–cruel, refined–vulgar, and sane–insane.

Attractiveness

In 1988 Saladin, Saper and Breen examined the relationship between criminal facial stereotypes and attractiveness. Participants were asked to say how likely were each of eight male stimulus photographs (previously rated for attractiveness) to commit each of two crimes: murder and armed robbery. Attractive faces were deemed less likely to carry out either act than were unattractive faces.

Yarmey and Kruschenske (1995) reported a study which found that undergraduates indicated that women likely to be battered (i.e. those suffering from domestic violence) would be of low facial attractiveness, as would women likely to kill their abuser. Yarmey and Kruschenske noted that cognitive schemata produce expectations about individuals who fit the schema and organize information input and output. (For more on forming impressions and stereotypes, see Kunda and Thagard (1996).) In their study one group of students rated each of 60 facial photographs of women for attractiveness, with facial expression similar across all photographs. The photographs which were rated as the most and least attractive were then shown to other students who were asked either to select the two 'who best represented a battered woman and the two who least represented a battered woman' (p. 343), or to select the ones most and least likely to kill their abuser, although non-selection of any photographs was allowed. From this study Yarmey and Kruschenke concluded that 'students were able to compare their perceptions of women's faces with a conceptual memory schema that represented their personal prototypical battered woman face' (p. 347). They suggested that if the results of this study are generalizable to the courtroom then jurors and judges may stereotype women on the basis of their facial attractiveness which 'could have far-reaching effects on due process and impartiality of decisions in the justice system.... Battered women do not deserve to be victimized twice – once by their abusive partner and a second time by triers of fact who may be influenced by facial stereotypes' (p. 349). Whether jurors, judges or others relevant within the criminal justice system are actually influenced by such factors has barely been researched (see below).

In 1993 Yarmey noted that the fourth amendment to the constitution of the USA (which is concerned with unreasonable search and seizure) could be interpreted as protecting citizens from being subjected to police harassment on the basis of imprecise stereotypes of what criminals look like. (This was an issue for the Supreme Court in the 1989 case of United States *v*. Sokolow.) In his study videorecordings were made of similarly dressed men reading the same text. These recordings were played to participants (students) some of whom saw and heard the men, some only saw them (the sound being turned off), and others only heard them. These people were then asked to select, if possible, the man who best represented a mass murderer, then a sexual assault felon, an armed robber, a clergyman, a medical doctor, and an engineer (only one man per category). Yarmey found that the participants showed high consensual agreement concerning which men they independently chose for each of these six categories, and that their confidence in their judgements was high. (He noted that his 1993 study did not specifically relate attractiveness to criminality.)

Macrae and Shepherd (1989a) controlled for the possible effects of physical attractiveness in their study of criminal stereotypes. They noted that 'the general public... possess stereotypical conceptions of the likely appearance of criminals', and that 'the selection of a particular individual from an identity parade may be influenced by the degree to which he or she resembles the commonly held stereotype for the incident in question' (p. 189). They pointed out that most prior studies of facial criminal stereotypes had involved faces which probably varied in attractiveness, and that such attractiveness may have mediated the criminality judgements. In their own study male faces rated similar in attractiveness were used and students (again!) were asked to select those faces most and least likely to commit assault or theft. The faces chosen as most and least likely to commit each offence were shown to other students who, having read an account of the criminal incident, were asked to judge the person as guilty or innocent. Guilt judgements were significantly influenced by whether the faces had been evaluated, by other people, as being likely to commit the offence.

Macrae and Shepherd concluded that their results support the contention that 'stereotypes function as schemata' (p. 190) and that with facial attractiveness being kept constant, these stereotypes are different for different crimes. They noted (1989b) that 'the psychological laboratory is far removed from the courtroom, and extrapolations and generalizations from experimental data will rightly be viewed skeptically by many legal practitioners' (p. 198). Nevertheless, they suggested that such biases may operate in the judicial process.

Police officers

In Bull and Green's (1980) study only a few of the participants were police officers, and their data did not differ from that of the general public. Recently Rowan Thorley and Ray Bull (Thorley, 1996) conducted a study somewhat similar to Bull and Green's to see if replication could be achieved. In this study a larger proportion of the participants were police officers (n = 46). These officers, and members of the public (n = 49), were shown 10 photographs taken against a similar plain background of young men each with a neutral facial expression. The participants were provided with a list of 10 offences and had to match a different face to each offence. Members of the public chose a particular, separate face more so than by chance for the eight offences of robbery/mugging, dealing in drugs, car theft, arson, murder, violence against the person, kidnapping, and handling stolen goods. For the two offences of burglary and criminal damage no one face was particularly chosen. The police officers matched the same faces to the same offences as did the general public for mugging/robbery, violence against the person, and kidnapping, but chose a different face for car theft. For the remaining six offences the police officers' choice of face did not fall on any one particular face but mostly on two or three faces, one of which was chosen by most members of the general public. Thus, this study found (as did Bull and Green, 1980) that members of the public concur when independently matching a male face to 8 of the 10 offences. However, the police officers' choices of which offence went with each face were rather more distributed across offences with strong agreement among them only for four of the 10 offences. Nevertheless, the police officers' data do reveal that at least for some offences they concur on the face most likely to be associated with a crime.

Research has also been conducted on the influence on police officers of a number of other appearance factors (e.g. skin colour) and of behavioural aspects (e.g. deference). For more on these topics see Vrij and Winkel (1992; 1994) and Bull and Horncastle (1989).

Children

A recent study by Elizabeth Price and Ray Bull (Price, 1996) examined whether children would concur when independently matching faces to crimes. In this study children aged eight, 12 and 16 years were asked to assign 10 crimes to photographs of 10 young men. They were allowed, if they wished, to assign more than one crime to each photograph, but each crime could be assigned only once. The procedure was then repeated using photographs of 10 young women. It was found that overall, regarding the male photographs for the crimes of murder, drug dealing and physical assault, the children's choice of face differed significantly from what would be expected by chance. This applied regarding the female photographs for the same three crimes of murder, drug dealing and physical assault, but also for burglary. For the male photographs age of child had little effect. However, for the female photographs the one most frequently chosen for a particular crime varied to a small but noticeable extent across age groups. Twelve adults independently indicated which of the 10 crimes used in the study were the five most serious. They concurred in choosing murder, arson, drug dealing, physical assault and kidnapping (rather than our other five crimes of theft, burglary, mugging, car theft and criminal damage). Thus children's significant agreement concerning which crimes go with which faces were for crimes considered serious by adults.

In this study other children from the three age groups were asked independently to say how attractive each face was. These children's resultant mean attractiveness rating were then correlated with the number of times a crime had been assigned to each face by the children in the main study. No relationship for male faces was found, but for the female faces there was a strong, significant negative relationship which emanated largely from the eight- and 12-year-old children in the main study. Thus, this second recent study again found that people, this time children, do associate some crimes with particular faces, and that for female faces these faces were the least attractive ones. (For more on children's stereotyping of faces and on the association between attractiveness and liking see Bull and Rumsey, 1988).

ARE APPEARANCE AND CRIME RELATED?

In 1982 Yarmey made the point that a main characteristic of stereotypes is the holder's belief in an assumed relationship between psychological attributes and category membership (e.g. criminals have a tough appearance). He argued that people 'attend to and encode such co-occurrences' and that 'these encodings are possible sources of distortion when memory is searched at a later time' (p. 207). Evidence to support this view comes from a variety of studies including one by Shepherd, Ellis, McMurran and Davies (1978). In this study women were asked to construct a 'photo-fit' of a man's face that they had just seen in a photograph. Half of the women were under the impression that the photograph was of a murderer and the other half that he was a lifeboatman. In fact all of them saw the same photograph. The 'photofits' made by these women were shown to other women (who were told nothing about a lifeboatman or murderer). These other participants rated the 'photofits' on a number of evaluative dimensions. The faces in 'photofits' constructed by women who believed the face was of a murderer were rated by these other women as significantly less attractive than were the faces in the 'photofits' of the (alleged) lifeboatman. Shepherd *et al.* concluded that differences in the 'photo-fit' constructors' impressions of the original face affected the 'photofits' they constructed from memory.

If less attractive faces are thought to be more likely to be associated with crime what would happen if these faces were made more attractive.

Facial surgery for criminals

In North America in the 1960s plastic surgery was performed on prison inmates in the hope of reducing their recidivism rates. One of the reasons for this was the belief that appearance and crime are related. For example the director of the Texas Department of Corrections was cited by Spira, Chizen, Gerow and Hardy (1966) as stating that facial deformities may contribute to criminality and that reduction of such deformities 'enhances the chance of an inmate making a satisfactory adjustment to society after release' (p. 370). In 1965 the *British Medical Journal* stated that: 'There is no need to justify the correction of cosmetic and other surgical disabilities in offenders' (p. 1449), and in 1948 Pick argued that juvenile delinquents would benefit from plastic surgery.

Recidivism rates

Of Texas offenders released from prison Spira *et al.* (1966) reported that usually 32 per cent returned to prison within a few years. However, only 17 per cent of those offenders who received plastic surgery while in prison did so. They noted that the within-prison plastic surgery facility was popular, with prisoners actually requesting treatment. They also noted that: 'Often a prison official will make the convict cognisant of his defect and will suggest the service ... available' (p. 364)! The prisoners who received such surgery exhibited 'a most appreciative attitude' (p. 364). Spira *et al.* pointed out that no definite conclusions could be drawn from their relatively uncontrolled comparison of the effect of plastic surgery on recidivism rates. Indeed, the possible positive effect upon inmates of society doing something for them (i.e. improving their physical appearance) may partly have been the reason for the lowered recidivism rate, rather than society's direct reaction to the prisoners' improved appearance. From Spira *et al.*'s study it is not possible to be sure why the recidivism rate was lower in the surgery group.

A similar study was reported by Kurtzberg, Safar and Cavior (1968) involving prison inmates (chronic petty offenders) in New York. Over one and a half thousand inmates volunteered for plastic surgery and of these several dozen (apparently chosen at random) received it prior to being released from prison. Others requesting such surgery were not given it. In each of these two 'surgery' and 'no surgery' groups half received social and vocational services preparing them for release from prison and half did not. Thus, in total there were four groups of participants. During the 12-month post-treatment interval, of the inmates having been released from prison, the recidivism rates (save for those guilty of heroin offences) were: 33 per cent for the surgery and services group; 30 per cent, for the surgery and no services group; 89 per cent, for the no surgery and services group; and 56 per cent, for the no surgery and no services group. Thus surgery, but not the social and vocational services, was related to reduced recidivism. (For those guilty of heroin offences the overall surgery group recidivism rate was 59 per cent, and for the no-surgery group it was 64 per cent.) Kurtzberg *et al.* concluded that their findings indicated that plastic surgery (much of which was facial) reduces recidivism and aids rehabilitation. They also noted that while the surgery is not cheap it costs less than keeping someone in prison for several months. However, as with the study by Spira *et al.* (1966), one has to ask to what extent the recidivism rate of the no-surgery participants was affected by their request for surgery being turned down. This criticism also applies to a Canadian study reported by Lewison in 1974 involving several hundred inmates on short sentences who had received in-prison plastic surgery for facial disfigurement in the previous 20 years. Those whose requests for such surgery were granted had lower recidivism rates than those whose requests were turned down (again except for drug offenders).

Frequency of facial abnormality

In 1967 Masters and Greaves attempted to discern the frequency of facial abnormality in convicted criminals. They used the police files from several large cities in the USA, and chose the crimes of homicide, rape, prostitution, sex deviation and suicide 'since there could be little doubt concerning the personal or social maladjustment of the individual' (p. 204) in such cases. (Now, however, within contemporary society, some people may not agree with this.) Eleven thousand (no less!) criminal faces were examined and 60 per cent of these were judged (their paper does not say how) to have surgically correctable facial defects compared to 20 per cent from 'a control group composed of the general population' (p. 210) (details of whom are not given). This difference of 40 per cent seems striking. However, one should ask whether this study may have had some major methodological weaknesses (for example the photographs of the criminals were almost certainly police 'mug shots' whereas those of the comparison group were not). Masters and Greaves' paper was published in the 1960s in a plastic surgery journal rather than in a scientific journal. Nowadays many surgical/medical journals set higher standards for the reporting of investigative methodology.

A critical appraisal of plastic surgery programmes in prisons was published in a criminal justice journal in 1990. In this review Thompson noted that research has consistently shown that attractive people are perceived more positively within society than are unattractive people, and that disfigured people tend to evoke negative perceptions by others (see Bull and Rumsey (1988) for an overview). For the disfigured individual, these reactions may become internalized, and feelings of rejection result. One cause of deviance may be individuals' inability to establish themselves within society's conventional groups. This social rejection may lead to status frustration, a process in which (i) the development of a positive self-image is curbed, (ii) employment opportunities decline, (iii) there is an inability to form stable relationships, and (iv) good grades at school are unattainable. Consequently, Thompson suggested social acceptance is sought elsewhere, within a deviant group in which there is a collective disdain towards society's rules, expressed in terms of violations of those rules. Plastic (or corrective) surgery was thought to be a solution to this problem for incarcerated inmates, the belief being that if an offender's outward appearance is improved, that person becomes more desirable and employable. Internally, this new feeling of self-worth may subsequently enhance self-esteem. Requests for plastic surgery within institutions were voluntary, and not everyone who requested treatment received it. Good behaviour on the part of the inmate was often a prerequisite to acceptance for surgery. Some inmates regarded corrective surgery as the answer to their problems, that by improving outwardly there will be a corresponding internal (or psychological) improvement also. When surgery failed to remedy an inmate's problems reactions ranging from aggression to withdrawal may have followed (Thompson, 1990).

Weak methodologies

Thompson (1990) further pointed out that despite the continuing use of such practices, very little research has been carried out on this topic and of those which have, the findings are inconclusive, and methodological problems abound: (i) follow-up periods vary from several months to several years making comparisons between studies difficult; (ii) participants, because surgery is not indiscriminately granted, are not really randomly assigned to experimental and control groups; and (iii) recidivism rates in some studies are compared to a baseline recidivism rate for a larger population such as that for the entire prison. Also, different studies use different measures to gauge recidivism (e.g. rearrest, reconviction and return-to-prison rates). Hence it is extremely difficult to explain differences between control and experimental groups solely in terms of corrective surgery. Age, type and number of prior offences, and length of sentence are all factors which could influence outcomes.

Of the nine studies reviewed by Thompson, the majority failed to rule out alternative explanations of the results. Therefore, more effective research in this area is required before conclusions regarding the efficacy of plastic surgery in reducing offending can be determined. Nevertheless, as already discussed in this chapter, there is accumulating research evidence that people do associate certain types of facial appearance with crime. Let us now turn to research on the question of whether facial appearance may have an influence in the courtroom.

DOES FACIAL APPEARANCE HAVE AN EFFECT IN THE COURTROOM?

Defendant appearance

The earliest published study of the possible effects of facial appearance on judgements of guilt was by Efran (1974). In this study students received a folder containing a facts summary sheet concerning alleged cheating in an examination and were asked to rate the guilt of the accused and the degree of punishment. The facial attractiveness of the accused person (in a photograph) was varied, ratings of facial attractiveness having been gained from other participants. Attractiveness was found to be related significantly to ratings of guilt and punishment, but only for the male raters (for whom all the accused were females). The female raters (for whom all the accused were males) were not affected by facial attractiveness. In fact the female raters did not rate the accused (male) attractive faces as highly for attractiveness as did other females who had rated the faces but who were not involved in the main study. Efran seemed at a loss to explain the lack of an attractiveness effect upon his female raters in the main study other than to suggest that they may not have looked at the faces. However, one possible explanation of why these participants did not rate the 'attractive' (male) faces as highly as did the other female raters is that only the participants in the main study read that the person whose face they saw had been accused of cheating. It may be that the association with cheating made the faces less attractive for these participants. Thus, while this chapter's main focus is on the question of whether facial appearance influences legal/criminality decisions, it is a feasible proposition that 'bad' information about a person (e.g. committed a crime) may influence evaluations of their facial appearance. This reversal of the 'what is beautiful is good' notion (i.e. 'what is ugly is bad' or 'what is bad is ugly') has rarely been researched (but see the 1978 study on 'photofits' by Shepherd, Ellis, McMurran and Davies mentioned above).

Since Efran's study a number of others have examined the extent to which 'mock' jurors' judgements are influenced by the facial appearance of a so-called 'defendant' or 'victim'. Those published prior to 1986 were reviewed by Bull and Rumsey (1988) who pointed out that the vast majority of these studies were ecologically invalid and that many of them were methodologically weak. Since then a small number of better studies have been published.

A study by Darby and Jeffers (1988) examined the effect of defendant physical attractiveness and of 'mock' jurors' self-perceived levels of attractiveness. In accord with Shaver's (1970) finding that less blame was attributed for an accident to those similar to 'jurors' in terms of attitudes, values and feelings, it was hypothesized that the more similar defendant and juror were in terms of attractiveness the more likely the defendant was to be found innocent or, to receive a lighter sentence. Shaver contended that such decisions are the result of defensive attributions made by the individual in which they act in the same way they would hope others would towards them, should the situation ever be reversed.

Participants in Darby and Jeffers' study were given a written account of one of six crimes, each accompanied by a photograph of either a highly attractive, a moderately attractive or an unattractive young woman. Each of the six cases differed in their degree of ambiguity regarding the guilt or innocence of the defendant. Overall, attractive defendants received fewer guilty verdicts, and lesser sentences (if found guilty). Attractive defendants were also rated as more likeable, trustworthy, and happy, and less responsible for the offence than were less attractive defendants. For participants rating themselves as attractive, the more attractive the defendant the less likely a conviction – an effect which also arose in the sentencing phase. For participants rating themselves as less attractive guilt was less affected by defendant attractiveness. When sentencing, these participants were most severe on moderately attractive defendants and least severe with very attractive defendants. Thus, there was some, limited support for Shaver's notion.

In 1991 Wuensch, Castellow and Moore attempted to replicate the oft-cited finding of Sigall and Ostrove (1975) that the effect of defendant attractiveness interacts with the nature of the crime (i.e. that if the attractiveness of the perpetrator could, in any way, have influenced his or her likelihood of success when committing the crime, then the tendency of leniency in favour of the attractive defendant is counteracted). Sigall and Ostrove found that whereas an attractive looking female burglar was sentenced by 'mock' jurors to significantly fewer years of imprisonment than an unattractive burglar, no significant effect of attractiveness was found for a female swindler. This was attributed to the fact that in the case of the swindler, her attractiveness may have been a significant factor in the success of the crime. Wuensch *et al.*, however, found no evidence that the leniency effect of attractiveness disappeared when the crime was attractiveness related.

Victim appearance

Some studies have examined the effects of the attractiveness of the victim, especially of alleged rape. Again many of these studies lack ecological validity. Ferguson, Duthie and Graf (1987) noted that a common misconception may exist within the general population regarding motives associated with rape. While most people believe such crimes to be exclusively sexually motivated, in many cases rape may be a show of (i) power or (ii) anger, the expression of which is through a sexual act (see Groth, 1981). As such, victim vulnerability rather than victim sexuality may be associated with their being raped, yet society, perversely continues to attribute some of the responsibility for rape to the victims: how provocatively the victims were dressed, their attractiveness, and whether they were known to the rapist have all been posited, and indeed shown empirically, as factors which at least displace some of the blame on to the victim. This 'myth' of rape being primarily sexually motivated is most evident when considering victim attractiveness, where some research has found attractive victims to be deemed less responsible for the rape simply because they are attractive, and therefore more desirable. Conversely, it is sometimes assumed that unattractive women, being less desirable, must, in some way, have provoked an attack (e.g. Thornton and Ryckman, 1983).

Attributions of responsibility

Ferguson *et al.* (1987) examined the effect of informing male undergraduates of the reasoning behind a rapist's actions on their attribution of responsibility for the rape to attractive and unattractive 'victims'. As found in previous studies, participants given no rape information attributed less blame to the rapist when the victim was unattractive. In the informed condition, however, blame was attributed regardless of the attractiveness of the victim. Ferguson *et al.* concluded that educating jurors concerning the motivations which may explain rape may reduce attractiveness bias. In neither condition, however, was full responsibility for the rape attributed to the rapist, a phenomenon which can be explained by just-world theory – the idea that by attributing at least some blame to the victim we subsequently reduce the possibility of our own victimization. They were victimized, but they did something to deserve it (which we wouldn't do). If no blame could be attributed to the victim the implication would be that rape can happen to anyone.

In their study Gerdes, Danmann and Heilig (1988) varied not only the attractiveness of the rape victim but also that of the defendant. They also varied whether the alleged perpetrator and victim were acquainted or not. Participants read one of eight versions of a 'newspaper article' in which the defendant was undoubtedly guilty of the rape. This lack of ambiguity allowed a test of Jacobson and Popovich's (1983) hypothesis that attractiveness effects should not be present in situations where the offence is indisputable (i.e. there was a rape, and the defendant was the assailant). The blame attributed to the unattractive victim was greater in the acquainted than unacquainted condition (i.e. such victims were deemed as having provoked an attack), while it was in the acquainted condition that attractive victims were viewed as most responsible for the rape (perhaps because attractive women are held responsible for their ability to arouse men). Victims were thought to be less responsible when raped by an unattractive assailant.

In 1988 Kanekar and Nazareth found no effect of victim attractiveness on the length of sentence given or the attribution of blame to the victim in a rape case. In their study attractiveness, physical hurt, and emotional distress were manipulated in a passage describing a rape. Longer imprisonment, particularly by female participants, was only recommended when the victim was physically hurt and emotionally disturbed, and attractive which suggests that punishment largely reflected participants' perceived seriousness of the rape.

Physically attractive people have often been shown (see Bull and Rumsey, 1988 for a review) to be evaluated more positively than less attractive people and in studies of mock jurors' judgements attractive defendants (even those whom participants were informed were definitely guilty) are commonly treated more leniently. McKelvie and Coley (1993) sought to test whether this effect existed independently of crime severity. Participants read one of two crime descriptions: an armed robbery, or an armed robbery plus murder, both of which stated that the person was guilty of the crime. Participants were also assigned to one of three cueing conditions: a low cue, where a picture of the offender (attractive or unattractive) was attached to the case description; a moderate cue, which also included a verbal description of the offender, drawing attention to his attractiveness; and a high cue, which also included another picture of the offender this one attached to the actual judgement sheet.

No effect of offender attractiveness on length of sentence was found for either crime. Length of sentence however, did vary as a result of crime seriousness. However, the less attractive offenders were more likely to receive recommendations for psychiatric care, suggesting the existence of a negative relationship between attractiveness and attribution of mental illness. (For more on this see Bull and Rumsey, 1988.)

Burke, Ames, Etherington and Pietsch (1990) attempted to evaluate the effect of physical attractiveness in a case of domestic violence. Participants read a hypothetical domestic violence scenario in which pictures of the husband and wife were presented. In the scenario the husband claims his wife fell onto a table, the wife claims the husband punched her in the eye. There was no support for the contention that physical attractiveness affected decision making, whether it be for the victim or the defendant. Burke *et al.* questioned the validity of using undergraduates as representatives of the general population, a criticism of almost all of the research on the topic.

Group decision making

In 1990 MacCoun pointed out that research purporting to examine the possible effects of defendant or victim appearance on jurors had merely studied individuals' decisions, whereas juries deliberate in groups upon their verdict. He noted that some juror deliberation studies (not on appearance) had found individuals' biases to be attenuated by the deliberation process (e.g. Kaplan and Miller, 1978) whereas other studies (e.g. Bray and Noble, 1978; Davis, Spitzer, Natao, and Stasser, 1978) had not found this. MacCoun attempted to determine whether jury deliberation would attenuate or enhance the effects of the victim and defendant attractiveness. Participants listened to an audiotaped trial simulation of a car theft, with victim and defendant attractiveness, in the form of photographs presented with the tape, being varied. Following the 'trial' participants completed a pre-deliberation questionnaire, then deliberated in groups of two, three, or four people and, following the 'jury' decision, they completed a further questionnaire. 'Juries' were found more likely to acquit the physically attractive rather than the unattractive defendant, and during deliberation, participants' evaluations of the attractive defendant became more lenient, while for unattractive defendants these ratings did not change. Thus, the deliberation process seemed to exacerbate rather than alleviate the problem.

Meta-analysis

This chapter's brief overview of some of the major publications examining the effects of facial appearance on mock jurors has revealed a lack of consistency in the findings. In their 1994 meta-analysis of previously published studies on this topic Mazzella and Feingold pointed out that: 'According to law, juridic decisions should be reached exclusively from admissible evidence presented during the course of a trial' (p. 1315). However, their meta-analysis of the 24 studies (involving 4804 participants) resulted in the outcome that 'mock jurors were less likely to find physically attractive defendants guilty than physically unattractive defendants although the effect size was small. Mock jurors also recommended less punishment for better looking defendants, but the mean effect size was trivial' (p. 1325). Thus the simulation studies they reviewed overall suggest that in real-life trials jurors in deciding guilt/innocence could be affected to some extent by defendant attractiveness. The 'trivial' effect size regarding punishment need not be generalized to real-life criminal trials since in these it is usually the judge not the jury who decides upon this. Mazzella and Feingold also found in their meta-analysis that: 'The physical attractiveness of the victim had no effects on judgements of mock jurors' (p. 1325).

In connection with generalizing from mock juror research to real-life trials Mazzella and Feingold made the important point that such research 'has often been criticized for being simplistic and lacking ecological validity. A common criticism has been that experimental manipulations are unduly potent because of the brevity of the scenarios, inflating effects of extralegal characteristics' (p. 1336). They made the crucial point that 'the generalizability issue must not be ignored, and the results obtained in this meta-analysis should not be assumed to apply to actual jury outcomes' (p. 1336).

This being the case, why have researchers used mock jurors rather than real jurors? One reason for this is that in some countries studying real-life jurors is legally impossible. Another reason is that psychologists, for various reasons, often take the easy way and study available students' reactions in easily accessible situations (e.g. the classroom). Only a few researchers have examined real-life court settings.

Real-life court proceedings

Stewart (1980, 1985) has reported upon criminal trials attended by members of his observational team who rated the physical attractiveness of defendants. He found that the attractiveness ratings (for which there was significant inter-rater agreement) correlated significantly not with subsequent judgements of guilt/innocence, but with the sentences received. This appears to be contrary to the outcomes of Mazzella and Feingold's meta-analysis and therefore underlines their point about generalizing from simple-minded simulations to the real world. Stewart noted that the less attractive defendants were being tried for more serious crimes, and when crime seriousness was partialled out of the relationship between appearance and sentence severity the relationship between these two was weaker. However, it was still significant. We need to ask (i) why were the less attractive defendants being tried for more serious crimes? We don't know, but the psychological research reviewed earlier in this chapter could be used to begin to try to answer this question. We also need to ask (ii) why the judges in the real-life trials reported upon by Stewart seemed influenced by defendant attractiveness. Perhaps judges are only human!

Zebrowitz and McDonald (1991) have also reported upon real-life court outcomes. They studied 506 proceedings in small claims civil courts. They pointed out that:

> A fundamental right guaranteed by the Fourteenth Amendment to the US Constitution is that of a fair trial. This constitutional right rests on the principle that there is a presumption of innocence in favour of the accused and that guilt must be proven beyond a reasonable doubt.... Because the influence of extralegal factors on judicial decisions poses a significant threat to this fundamental right, it is important to identify those factors that may bias a fact-finder's evaluation of evidence produced at a trial. One source of bias that has received considerable attention is the physical appearance of the litigants (pp. 603–604).

Zebrowitz and McDonald studied proceedings in the small claims civil courts for several reasons including (i) that decisions are made by an individual judge (thus group decision making did not occur), (ii) that in all cases each plaintiff is seeking financial damages, and therefore all outcomes will be on a common scale, (iii) such cases usually involve little evidence other than the testimony of the plaintiff and defendant (whereas in many criminal trials other sources of evidence are common), thus 'the appearance of the defendant and plaintiff should be a more significant variable than in a criminal trial' (p. 606), and (iv) such proceedings involve intentional acts as well as negligent acts which permit examination of the relationship between facial appearance and judgements of responsibility. They found that the court judgements favoured the more attractive plaintiffs, but this effect was only marginally significant when legal variables were controlled for (e.g. extent of legal support, whether responsibility was admitted or denied), and inversed for the most attractive plaintiffs. The attractiveness of the defendants was found to have no effect.

Zebrowitz and McDonald devote several hundred words of their discussion to attempts to explain why, unlike in published simulation studies, defendant attractiveness had no effect. Perhaps we, and they, should accept that in their study it had no effect precisely because it was irrelevant! However, they did find that as defendants increased in 'baby-facedness' (defined as the extent to which a person's facial features resemble those of a prototypical baby) they were more likely to win cases involving intentional actions, but less likely to win cases involving negligent actions.

These real-life court studies of Stewart and of Zebrowitz and McDonald do not concur on the effects of defendant attractiveness. The former found somewhat of an effect, the latter did not. The types of court cases in each study were different. Perhaps that explains the inconsistency, but if it does psychologists cannot generally claim that defendant attractiveness affects court outcomes. Indeed, one wonders (see Bull and Rumsey, 1988) how many studies finding null effects of appearance have been rejected for publication.

Other real-life settings

There exists a small amount of research on appearance in other 'law' settings. Let us now examine these. In 1973 Cavior and Howard suggested that facial unattractiveness may cause young people to be rejected by society and that this social rejection leads to delinquency. In their study photographs of male juvenile delinquents and non-delinquents were rated (blind) by students. They found that the delinquents' faces received lower attractiveness scores.

Cavior, Hayes and Cavior (1974) attempted to examine whether the faces of convicted young female offenders (aged 19 years) had any influence within prison. They found that facial attractiveness correlated with (i) frequency of reports of undesirable behaviour within prison using violent aggression (a negative relationship), and (ii) frequency of permitted trips into town (a positive relationship). Cavior *et al.* adopted a behavioural explanation (common in the early 1970s) of their findings and concluded that 'the differing environmental consequences for attractive versus unattractive individuals may shape divergent behavioural repertoires. The relationship between aggression-based behaviour and physical attractiveness is perhaps one such example. If attractive individuals are reacted to more positively they may find less reason for recourse to violent means to achieve their goals' (p. 330).

Agnew (1984) also claimed to have found a relationship between physical attractiveness and juvenile delinquency. He noted that efforts could be made to reduce discrimination against unattractive individuals by making people aware of their stereotypes and the influences these might have. In his study male adolescents' self-reported data on delinquency was found to be related to ratings of appearance. However, his raters may not have been blind to the adolescents' delinquency.

CONCLUSION

We now need to ask to what extent the studies reviewed above support the notion that facial appearance is related to criminality/wrong doing. The first main section in this chapter examined research on the extent to which people assume there to be a relationship between facial appearance and criminality. This research collectively seems strongly to suggest that such stereotypes do exist and are shared consensually. However, few studies have examined the accuracy or validity of these stereotypes.

Studies of the apparent effects of facial surgery upon prisoners' recidivism rates were then reviewed. These studies could be taken to suggest that facial appearance and criminality are related. However, the quality of their methodology and the presence of confounding variables need to be considered.

Research on the effects upon 'mock' jurors of defendant and victim facial attractiveness was then described. Many of these studies controlled/kept constant the very sources of information thought relevant in court cases (e.g. the nature of the evidence) and solely as a consequence may have found some effect of an extralegal factor such as facial appearance. Also, this type of study seems to lack many other qualities present in the real-life setting (e.g. consequences for the defendant of jury decisions). Furthermore, many of the studies used students as participants who may not be representative of the population of real-life jurors. Nevertheless, the two studies reported of real-life court decision making do claim to find some effect of facial appearance, though the two studies do not concur on the nature of this effect.

Overall, readers will have to decide whether Udry and Eckland (1984) (see the opening paragraph of this chapter) were correct in stating that: 'Everyone knows that ... Heroes are handsome and villains are ugly' (p. 47).

REFERENCES

Agnew, R. (1984). Appearance and delinquency. *Criminology: An Interdisciplinary Journal*, **22**, 421–440.

Bray, R. and Noble, A. (1978). Authoritarianism and decisions of mock juries: evidence of jury bias and group polarization. *Journal of Personality and Social Psychology*, **36**, 1424–1430.

British Medical Journal (1965). Physical disability and crime, **1**, 1448–1449.

Bull, R. and Green, J. (1980). The relationship between physical appearance and criminality. *Medicine, Science and the Law*, **20**, 79–83.

Bull, R. and Horncastle, P. (1989). An evaluation of human awareness training. In R. Morgan and D. Smith (eds), *Coming to Terms with Policing*. London: Tavistock.

Bull, R. and Rumsey, N. (1988). *The Social Psychology of Facial Appearance*. New York: Springer-Verlag.

Burke, D., Ames, M., Etherington, R. and Pietsch, J. (1990). Effects of victim's and defendant's physical attractiveness on the perception of responsibility in an ambiguous domestic violence case. *Journal of Family Violence*, **5**, 199–207.

Cavior, H., Hayes, S. and Cavior, N. (1974). Physical attractiveness of female offenders. *Criminal Justice and Behavior*, **1**, 321–331.

Cavior, N. and Howard, L. (1973). Facial attractiveness and juvenile delinquency. *Journal of Abnormal Child Psychology*, **1**, 202–213.

Darby, B. and Jeffers, D. (1988). The effects of defendant and juror attractiveness on simulated courtroom trial decisions. *Social Behaviour and Personality*, **16**, 39–50.

Davis, J., Spitzer, C., Natao, D. and Stasser, G. (1978). Bias in social decisions by individuals and groups: an example from mock juries. In H. Brandstatter, J. Davis and H. Schuler (eds), *Dynamics of Group Decisions*. Beverly Hills, CA: Sage.

Efran, M. (1974). The effect of physical appearance on the judgement of guilt, interpersonal attraction and severity of recommended punishment in a simulated jury task. *Journal of Research in Personality*, 8, 45–54.

Ferguson, P., Duthie, D. and Graf, R. (1987). Attribution of responsibility to rapist and victim: the influence of victim's attractiveness and rape-related information. *Journal of Interpersonal Violence*, 2, 243–250.

Gerdes, E., Danmann, E. and Heilig, K. (1988). Perceptions of rape victims and assailants: effects of physical attractiveness, acquaintance and subject gender. *Sex Roles*, 19, 141–153.

Goldstein, A., Chance, J. and Gilbert, B. (1984). Facial stereotypes of good guys and bad guys: a replication and extension. *Bulletin of the Psychonomic Society*, 22, 549–552.

Groth, A. (1981). Rape: the sexual expression of aggression. In P. Brain and D. Benton (eds), *Multidisciplinary Approaches to Aggression Research*. Elsevier: North-Holland Biomedical Press.

Jacobson, M. and Popovich, P. (1983). Victim attractiveness and perceptions of responsibility in an ambiguous rape case. *Psychology of Women Quarterly*, 8, 134–139.

Kanekar, S. and Nazareth, A. (1988). Attributed rape victim's fault as a function of her attractiveness, physical hurt and emotional disturbance. *Social Behaviour*, 3, 37–40.

Kaplan, M. and Miller, L. (1978). Reducing the effects of juror bias. *Journal of Personality and Social Psychology*, 36, 1443–1455.

Kozeny, E. (1962). Experimental investigation of physiognomy utilizing a photographic-statistical method. *Archiv fur die Gesamte Psychologie*, 114, 55–71.

Kunda, Z. and Thagard, P. (1996). Forming impressions from stereotypes, traits and behaviors: a parallel-constraint-satisfaction theory. *Psychological Review*, 103, 284–308.

Kurtzberg, R., Safar, H. and Cavior, N. (1968). Surgical and social rehabilitation of adult offenders. *Proceedings of the 76th Annual Convention of the American Psychological Association*, 3, 649–650.

Lewison, E. (1974). Twenty years of prison surgery: an evaluation. *Canadian Journal of Otolaryngology*, 3, 42–50.

MacCoun, R. (1990). The emergence of extralegal bias during jury deliberation. *Criminal Justice and Behavior*, 17, 303–314.

Macrae, C.N. and Shepherd, J. (1989a). Do criminal stereotypes mediate juridic judgements? *British Journal of Social Psychology*, 28, 189–191.

Macrae, C.N. and Shepherd, J. (1989b). The good, the bad and the ugly: facial stereotyping and juridic judgements. *Police Journal*, 2, 194–199.

Masters, F. and Greaves, D. (1967). The Quasimodo complex. *British Journal of Plastic Surgery*, 20, 204–210.

Mazella, R. and Feingold, A. (1994). The effects of physical attractiveness, race, socioeconomic status and gender of defendants and victims on judgements of mock jurors: a meta–analysis. *Journal of Applied Social Psychology*, 24, 1315–1344.

McKelvie, S. and Coley, J. (1993). Effects of crime seriousness and offender facial attractiveness on recommended treatment. *Social Behavior and Personality*, 21, 265–277.

Pick, J. (1948). Ten years of plastic surgery in a penal institution: preliminary report. *Journal of the International College of Surgeons*, **11**, 315–319.

Price, E. (1996). Stereotyping of criminality by children of different ages: Are facially attractive people perceived as less criminal? Unpublished BSc Psychology final year research project report. Department of Psychology, University of Portsmouth.

Saladin, M., Saper, Z. and Breen, L. (1988). Perceived attractiveness and attributions of criminality: what is beautiful is not criminal. *Canadian Journal of Criminology*, **30**, 251–259.

Shaver, K. (1970). Defensive attribution: effects of severity and relevance on the responsibility assigned for an accident. *Journal of Personality and Social Psychology*, **14**, 101–113.

Shepherd, J., Ellis, H., McMurran, M. and Davies, G. (1978). Effect of character attribution on photofit construction of a face. *European Journal of Social Psychology*, **8**, 263–268.

Sigall, H. and Ostrove, N. (1975). Beautiful but dangerous: effects of offender attractiveness and nature of crime on juridic judgement. *Journal of Personality and Social Psychology*, **31**, 410–414.

Spira, M., Chizen, J., Gerow, F. and Hardy, S. (1966). Plastic surgery in the Texas prison system. *British Journal of Plastic Surgery*, **19**, 364–371.

Stewart, J. (1980). Defendant's attractiveness as a factor in the outcome of criminal trials: an observational study. *Journal of Applied Social Psychology*, **10**, 348–361.

Stewart, J. (1985). Appearance and punishment: the attraction–leniency effect in the courtroom. *Journal of Social Psychology*, **125**, 373–378.

Thompson, K. (1990). Refacing inmates: a critical appraisal of plastic surgery programs in prisons. *Criminal Justice and Behavior*, **17**, 448–466.

Thorley, R. (1996). Criminality with respect to facial appearance. Unpublished BSc Psychology final year research project report. Department of Psychology, University of Portsmouth.

Thornton, B. and Ryckman, R. (1983). The influence of a rape victim's physical attractiveness on observers' attributions of responsibility. *Human Relations*, **36**, 549–562.

Thornton, G. (1939). The ability to judge crimes from photographs of criminals. *Journal of Abnormal and Social Psychology*, **34**, 378–383.

Udry, R. and Eckland, B. (1984). Benefits of being attractive: differential payoffs for men and women. *Psychological Reports*, **54**, 47–56.

United States *v*. Sokolow 109 S. Ct. 1581, (1989).

Vrij, A. and Winkel, F.W. (1992). Crosscultural police–citizen interactions: the influence of race, beliefs and nonverbal communication on impression formation. *Journal of Applied Social Psychology*, **22**, 1546–1559.

Vrij, A. and Winkel, F.W. (1994). Perceptual distortions in cross-cultural interrogations. *Journal of Cross-Cultural Psychology*, **25**, 284–295.

Wuensch, K., Castellow, W. and Moore, C. (1991). Effects of defendant attractiveness and type of crime on juridic judgement. *Social Behaviour and Personality*, **6**, 713–724.

Yarmey, A.D. (1982). Eyewitness identification and stereotypes of criminals. In A. Trankell (ed.), *Reconstructing the Past: The Role of Psychologists in Criminal Trials*. Stockholm: Norstedt.

Yarmey, A.D. (1993). Stereotypes and recognition memory for faces and voices of good guys and bad guys. *Applied Cognitive Psychology*, 7, 419–431.

Yarmey, A.D. and Kruschenske, S. (1995). Facial stereotypes of battered women and battered women who kill. *Journal of Applied Social Psychology*, 25, 338–352.

Zebrowitz, L. and McDonald, S. (1991). The impact of litigants' baby-facedness and attractiveness on adjudications in small claims courts. *Law and Human Behavior*, 15, 603–623.

4

PHYSIOLOGICAL PARAMETERS AND CREDIBILITY: THE POLYGRAPH

Aldert Vrij

INTRODUCTION

Apart from looking at speech content and nonverbal behaviour, there is, in principle, a third way of detecting lies, namely by examining the physiological reactions of deceivers. Throughout history it has been assumed that lying is accompanied by physiological activity within the liar's body. For example the Chinese forced suspected liars to chew rice powder and then to spit it out. If the resultant powder was dry then the person was judged to have been lying (Kleinmuntz and Szucko, 1984). The modern way of detecting physiological activity in liars is by using a polygraph. The polygraph (a composition of two Greek words, namely 'poly' = many, and 'grapho' = to write) is an accurate, scientific measurement device which can display, via ink writing pens onto charts or via a computer's visual display unit, a direct and valid representation of various sorts of bodily activity (Bull, 1988). The most commonly measured activities are palmar sweating, blood pressure and respiration (Ben-Shakhar and Furedy, 1990). Changes in these activities are signs of emotional arousal. The polygraph records these changes accurately, it detects smaller changes than can otherwise be observed, and records activities which are rarely visible (such as heart rate). It does this by amplifying signals picked up from sensors that are attached to different parts of the body. In the typical use of the polygraph four sensors are attached to the subject. Pneumatic tubes are stretched around the person's chest and stomach in order to measure changes in the depth and rate of breathing. A blood pressure cuff placed around the biceps measures changes in blood pressure, and metal electrodes attached to the fingers measure palmar sweating (Ekman, 1985). Recently it has been argued that measures of brain electrical activity (event-related brain potentials) can be used as well (Bashore and Rapp, 1993; Farwell and Donchin, 1991; Johnson and Rosenfeld, 1991; Rosenfeld, 1995; Rosenfeld, Angell, Johnson, and Qian, 1991).

The use of the polygraph is widespread in the USA. In the 1980s, it was believed that over one million tests were given each year (Ekman, 1985). This figure included tests as part of job selection, state security selection, and criminal investigation. Tests were used in applied settings by police personnel or specially trained investigators. Tests were also used in scientific investigations and the outcomes are presented by scientific psychologists who act as expert witnesses in court. About 90 per cent of the tests were used for personnel purposes. The number of tests heavily declined since the introduction of the *Polygraph Protection Act* in 1988, which banned most tests for personnel selection purposes. Nowadays, it is believed that around 40 000 polygraph test are given each year in the USA for personnel purposes (Raskin and Kircher, 1987).

The use of the polygraph as a lie detector is controversial, the arguments about this are usually heated. The faith in the accuracy of the polygraph among practitioners is high. The following quote of Gordon Barland (1988), a leading practitioner in the field of polygraph testing, is indicative of such faith:

> Polygraph results...often play a major role in police investigations and in helping prosecutors decide whether to indict a suspect and what to charge him with. A number of books provide a wealth of case histories in which polygraphs helped clear the innocent and solve crimes (p. 92).

Other countries which are known to use polygraph tests to detect deception are for instance Israel, Japan, South Korea and Turkey (Barland, 1988). On the other hand, polygraph tests are not used in West European countries. In Great Britain, following a well-known spy case, the government announced its intention to undertake pilot studies of the use of the polygraph. A number of distinguished psychologists from Great Britain formed a Working Group. Their aim was to provide a view of the present status of polygraph interrogation and its uses. Their conclusion in the final British Psychological Society report, published in 1986, was devastating:

> The procedures involved are not standardized to the extent that they may be described as satisfactory in psychometric terms. Nor is there an easy means of checking on the practices and procedures employed by individual polygraphers.... Polygraph descriptions include misleading the subject as to the efficacy of the procedure and inducing states of anxiety in order to increase compliance. Some aspects might be contrary to current British Law. Polygraph evidence has been accepted in some foreign courts in certain circumstances, but we believe it to be unlikely that it would be admissible in a British court of law. Polygraphic interrogation is probably most useful in police investigations

but it is not clear what aspect is responsible for success in securing confessions, nor whether other methods are equally effective or superior (p. 92).

Most of the polygraph testing conducted by law enforcement agencies in the USA is investigative in nature (Honts and Perry, 1992). That is, it is used to verify witness statements, to clear suspects and to serve as springboards for interrogations. Sometimes the polygraph tests are used as evidence, but this is less common (although there is a trend toward acceptance of polygraph evidence in the USA (Honts and Perry, 1992)). According to Patrick and Iacono (1991), 24 US states provide for the admission of polygraph evidence in criminal cases. Moreover, the Court of Appeals of the Fifth Circuit in United States *v.* Posado (57 F.3d 428 (1995)) stated that 'a *per se* rule against the admissibility of the results of a polygraph examination was no longer permissible' making the use of polygraph tests as evidence in criminal cases probably even more widespread. In many courts in the USA polygraph evidence is currently still inadmissible, but not necessarily because it is felt that the test is inaccurate. Honts (1994a) pointed out that polygraph tests have been held inadmissible because it is felt that juries may be overwhelmed by the scientific nature of the evidence.

Despite its widespread use in several countries, there is little scientific evidence about the polygraph's accuracy. However, the existing scientific literature reveals that, as well as an argument about the reliability and validity of polygraph use between opponents and supporters, there are also disagreements within the polygraph community. The two leading and probably most distinguished scientific polygraph researchers, David Raskin and David Lykken, have engaged in prolonged controversy over the reliability and validity of various polygraph tests. They have come into conflict in the scientific literature, as expert witnesses in court and as possible opponents in legal processes. This chapter provides an overview of the existing scientific literature regarding polygraph tests and the arguments of both Lykken and Raskin will be presented.

The polygraph is not a lie detector (people sometimes call the polygraph a lie detector but this is misleading). The polygraph measures changes in emotional arousal, and it is assumed that these changes occur during deception. The premise is that telling lies causes some stress or anxiety (see Chapter 2), and this stress and anxiety is translated into emotional arousal which will be recorded on the polygraph. However, an emotional change typical for lying does not exist (Saxe, 1991). In general, it is not possible to differentiate between emotions through the use of physiological reactions. For instance, conceptually distinctive emotions such as anger, fear, shame or guilt all result in similar physical reactions, and thus, all these emotions will give a similar output on the polygraph charts. In other words, the polygraph can tell that some kind of reaction is taking place within the subject, it cannot, however, tell what reaction that is (Ney, 1988).

Several different polygraph tests exist. One of the first tests widely used was the relevant/irrelevant technique (RIT: Larson, 1932). In the RIT, responses to crime-relevant questions (e.g. 'Did you break into a black Mercedes last night?') are compared with responses to irrelevant questions about everyday matters (e.g. 'Is it Tuesday today?'). The rationale with the RIT is that larger responses to relevant (crime-related) questions (to which, of course the suspects replies 'no') than to irrelevant questions indicate deception regarding the crime. In light of what is mentioned above, it is obvious that this premise is incorrect. The physiological response might be caused by the fact that the person is lying, but it might be caused by something else altogether. For example, suppose a lady is attached to a polygraph in order to find out whether she stole money from the office in the company where she is employed. She is innocent, but she realizes that a large response on the polygraph might imply that she will lose her job. Hence, the relevant question: 'Did you steal the money?', has major consequences for the employee and might therefore arouse her. Therefore, it is possible that this relevant question will result in a larger response on the polygraph than an irrelevant question about, for instance, the colour of her shirt. But a positive score in this case is a result of fear, and not the result of deception! One more example: suppose that somebody is attached to a polygraph in order to find out whether he murdered his wife. An example of a relevant question in this case is: 'Did you murder your wife?', whereas an example of an irrelevant question is: 'Are you wearing a watch?'. It is likely that an innocent person will show a higher emotional reaction to the relevant question than to the irrelevant question, due to the fact that the relevant question reminds him about his late wife.

Nowadays, there is an agreement among polygraph researchers that the RIT is inappropriate in detecting deception (Honts, 1991; Lykken, 1981; Raskin, 1986; Saxe, 1994). The fact that the RIT is not able to distinguish between different emotions makes this test completely unsuitable for detecting deceit in criminal investigations, and will therefore not be further discussed in this chapter. In fact, at present RIT is not very often used in criminal investigations in the USA. However, Honts and Perry (1992) reported that the RIT still plays a role in law enforcement in the USA and that the test is taught as a basic technique to all federal polygraph examiner trainees.

The two polygraph tests most often used are the control question test (CQT) and the guilty knowledge test (GKT). The CQT was initially developed by Reid (1947) and further conceptualized within the framework of current concepts in psychology and psychophysiology by Raskin (1979, 1982, 1986). The GKT was developed and described in detail by Lykken (1959, 1960, 1981, 1991). Both techniques will be explained in this chapter.

THE POLYGRAPH: HOW DOES IT WORK?

The control question test

The control question test is the polygraph test most widely used in the USA in criminal investigations. The typical control question polygraph test consists of four phases (Furedy, 1991b). In phase 1, the questions (neutral, relevant and control questions) are formulated by the examiner and discussed with the examinee. Neutral questions are general questions and are not expected to create any arousal, such as: 'Do you live in the United States?', 'Is your name Rick?', and so on. They are used as fillers, and the physiological responses to these questions are disregarded when scoring of the polygraph charts takes place. Fillers can, for instance, be used to check whether the examinee pays attention to the questions asked by the examiner, as will be discussed in the 'countermeasures' paragraph. The relevant questions (the questions about the crime) are carefully formulated and reformulated until the examinee indicates that he or she finds them unambiguous and can clearly answer 'no' to them, for instance: 'Did you take that ring?' (in case of a theft of a ring). These questions are expected to create arousal in guilty suspects (because they are lying), but not in innocent suspects (because they are telling the truth). Control questions deal with acts that are similar to the issue under investigation. They are always general in nature, deliberately vague, cover long periods of time and are meant to embarrass the suspects (both guilty and innocent). This is facilitated by giving the suspect no other choice than to lie when answering the control questions on one hand, and making clear to the suspect that the polygraph will detect this lie on the other hand. The examiner formulates a question for which, in his or her view, the examinee's answer 'no' is deceptive. The exact formulation of the question depends, of course, upon the examinee's circumstances, but a control question in an examination regarding theft might be: 'Before the age of 18, did you ever take something that did not belong to you?' Under normal circumstances, some examinees might admit this wrongdoing. However, during a polygraph examination they will not because the examiner will let the examinee think that admitting such a wrongdoing would cause the examiner to conclude that the examinee is the type of person to commit the crime in question and is therefore considered guilty.[1] Therefore, the examinee has no other choice than to deny this wrongdoing and thus to be untruthful in answering the control question. Further, the examiner will let the subject think that deceptive answers to control questions will result in physiological reactions during the test, which will be detected by the polygraph, and which will lead the examiner to conclude that the subject was also deceptive with respect to the relevant issues concerning the crime in question. (In fact, as will be described later on, the examiner will interpret stronger physiological reactions to a control question compared to a relevant question as being *truthful* but he will not inform the subject about this!)

Control questions are designed to create, in the innocent suspect, more arousal than the relevant questions. The same control questions, however, are expected to elicit less arousal in guilty suspects than the relevant questions. Raskin (1982) gives the following explanation for why control questions compared to relevant questions will elicit more arousal in innocent subjects but will elicit less arousal in guilty subjects:

> The manner in which the control question is posed to the subject and the behaviour of the examiner are both designed to make the subject feel defensive and embarrass him into answering 'no'.... That procedure is designed to create the possibility that an innocent subject will experience greater concern with regard to the truthfulness of his answers to the control questions than to the relevant questions. However, a guilty subject would still be more concerned about his deceptive answers to the relevant questions because those questions represent the most immediate and serious threat to him. However, the innocent subject knows that he is answering truthfully to the relevant questions, and he becomes more concerned about deceptiveness or uncertain of his truthfulness with regard to his answers to the control questions (p. 325).

Raskin (1989b) provided a typical CQT question sequence which is shown in Table 4.1.

TABLE 4.1 *Control question sequence*

N1 Do you live in the United States? 'Yes'
C1 During the first 20 years of your life, did you ever take something that did not belong to you? 'No'
R1 Did you take that ring? 'No'
N2 Is your name Rick? 'Yes'
C2 Prior to 1987, did you ever do something dishonest or illegal? 'No'
R2 Did you take that ring from the desk? 'No'
N3 Were you born in the month November? 'Yes'
C3 Before age 21 did you ever lie to get out of trouble or to cause a problem for someone else? 'No'
R3 Did you participate in any way in the theft of that ring? 'No'

After designing the questions, the second phase, the stimulation procedure, starts. The stimulation test must convince the examinee that the technique is highly accurate and that the polygraph is able to detect every lie.[1] Bashore and Rapp (1993) provided the following example of a stimulation test:

> Typically, the subject is asked to pick a playing card from a deck of cards, to take note of it, and to return it to the deck. The polygrapher then calls out the names of several cards, and the subject is instructed to respond with 'no' to each name. As the subject does so, the examiner pretends to evaluate the polygraphic response. After the last response is made, the polygrapher correctly informs the subject of the card he or she selected and asserts that the machine revealed the choice. Unbeknown to the subject, the deck of cards contains only one type of card (p. 4).

Most polygraphers, however, don't engage in this deceit but use different cards and rely upon the polygraph charts to spot which card was taken (this card trick, by the way, is a guilty knowledge technique, see below). The examinee is then told that the charts will reveal what his pattern of reaction looks like when he is lying or when he is telling the truth and that there should be no problem on the actual test if the examinee is truthful to all of the questions. The stimulation test is meant to have different effects on innocent and guilty suspects. It will augment fear of detection in the guilty suspect ('there is no way to cheat this machine'), and it will increase confidence in innocent people ('the machine works indeed, as I am innocent, I will therefore be exonerated').

After the stimulation test, phase three, the test proper follows, compromising a set of questions as shown in Table 4.1. The same question sequence is presented at least three times.

After the actual test, phase four, the interpretation of the polygraph charts starts. There are two interpretation approaches, the global approach and the numerical scoring approach. In the global approach the examiner forms a global impression of the subject's physiological responses to the test. This information is then combined in some unspecified manner with evaluations of the case facts and the subject's behaviour during the test in order to reach an overall decision about the truthfulness of the subject. The numerical scoring approach (advocated by Raskin) attempts to minimize the influences of sources other than the polygraph charts in the decision making, and attempts to score the charts systematically. Comparisons are made between the reactions to the control and relevant questions (R1 compared to C1, R2 compared to C2 and R3 compared to C3). If the observed reaction is *stronger* to the relevant question than to the control question, a negative score is assigned. If the observed reaction is *weaker* to the relevant question than to the control question, a positive score is assigned. The magnitude of scores can vary from 0 (no difference), to 1 (a noticeable difference), to 2 (a strong difference), to 3 (a dramatic difference). There exist, however, no standardized rules about what a 'noticeable', 'strong' and 'dramatic' difference means. According to Raskin (1989b) most assigned scores are 0 or 1, scores of 2 are less common, and scores of 3 are unusual. The examiner assigns a score for each physiological parameter for each comparison. The scores are then summed to provide a total score for the test. It might be the case that the different physiological measures taken provide different outcomes, particularly because it is known that these different physiological measures do not intercorrelate terribly well. However, it is only the total oucome that counts. The outcome of the test is based on this total. If the total is –6 or lower, the outcome is deceptive; if the total is +6 or higher, the outcome is truthful (or nondeceptive), and scores between –5 and +5 indicate an inconclusive outcome.

Criticism concerning the control question test

The control question test evokes major criticisms among its opponents. The most important ones are mentioned below.

A crucial role for the examiner in preparing the test. For the polygraph exam to work, the examiner should formulate control questions that, on the one hand, in innocent subjects should elicit *stronger* emotional responses than the relevant questions. That is, the examiner should phrase control questions that would ensure the eliciting of stronger reactions in an innocent person than would the relevant questions relating to the crime of which they had been accused, otherwise the outcome will be inconclusive (if both types of questions elicit the same emotional response) or will result in a deceptive outcome (if the relevant questions elicit more arousal than the control questions). On the other hand, in guilty suspects, these control questions should elicit *weaker* emotional responses than the relevant questions. Obviously, it is not easy for the examiner to formulate questions that meet these criteria, and it is not easy for the examiner to find out in the pre-test phase (phase 1) whether the control and relevant questions the examiner is going to ask are appropriate to achieve this aim. Reid and Inbau (1977) stated that this check should be based upon the examinee's behavioural symptoms. This, however, is a very difficult and risky task. As we saw in Chapter 2, Ekman and O'Sullivan (1991) found that polygraph examiners are not particularly good at detecting lies on the basis of behavioural cues. Lykken (1981) referred to the examiner's task in phase 1 as 'a very sophisticated piece of psychological engineering'. However, the control questions are crucial for the success of the test. Hence, much depends on the skills of the examiner, which is probably the major criticism about the CQT (Furedy, 1991a). Raskin (1989b) acknowledges this problem:

> The traditional CQT is difficult to administer, and the level of psychological sensitivity, sophistication, and skill of the examiner are crucial to obtaining an accurate outcome. Unfortunately, many polygraph examiners lack adequate training in psychological methods and do not understand the basic concepts and requirements of a standardized psychological test. These problems are exacerbated when the examiner formulates and introduces the control questions to the subject, because it is very difficult to standardize the wording and discussion of the questions for all subjects. A great deal depends on how the subject perceives and responds to the control questions when they are introduced and discussed during the pretest interview (p. 8).

The important role of the examiner may also influence the test itself. The examinee is usually not a complete stranger to the examiner, the examiner usually knows important details regarding the examinee (including case file information). Moreover, the examiner will get an impression of the examinee in the pre-test interview in which the control and relevant questions are formulated. It is always possible that this impression of the examinee, based upon case file information and pre-test interview, affects the exact formulation of control questions, which, in turn, may influence the outcomes of the test.

The test is not standardized. The second point is related to the first point. Which control questions should be asked is highly dependent on the examinee (one control question might be effective for one examinee but highly ineffective in another examinee). This means that the test is not standardized. Proponents of the CQT test responded to this criticism by developing 'directed lie' questions for use with all examinees as an alternative for control questions. Typical directed lie questions would be: 'Have you ever told a lie?' or 'Have you ever done something that you now wish you had not done?' (Honts, Kircher, and Raskin, 1995). Directed lie questions are less examinee-specific than control questions. The same question being asked to different examinees makes the test more standardized.

The scoring of the polygraph charts is not quantified. Differences between the control and relevant questions are scored as (1) noticeable difference, (2) strong difference, and (3) dramatic difference. As we saw above, there are, however, no rules about what a noticeable, strong and dramatic difference is. The scores are assigned on the basis of qualitative, subjective considerations of the examiner and may therefore vary per examiner, or, even worse, may be affected by the examiner's impression of the examinee (see next point of criticism). As a result, different examiners may reach different conclusions (whether the examinee failed or passed the test or whether the outcome is inconclusive) after scoring the same polygraph chart. Again, this emphasizes the important but not standardized role of the examiner. This problem may be overcome by using a computer-based method for scoring polygraph data as developed and advocated by Kircher and Raskin (1988), which rules out the interpretation of the examiner.

The final decision making is subjective. In the global approach, the examiner forms a global impression of the subject's polygraph charts and combines this information in some unspecified manner with non-polygraphic sources of information (case file information, subject's demeanor) in order to reach an overall decision. This means that the decision-making process is subjective and not verifiable. Raskin acknowledged this problem and therefore introduced the numerical scoring approach. But even in the numerical scoring approach some contamination can take place. The examiner usually knows important details of the examinee (see the first criticism). It is possible that this impression will influence the scoring of the polygraph charts, particularly because this scoring is not standardized. In a recent study, Elaad, Ginton and Shakhar (1994) showed that contamination problems do indeed to some extent occur. In their experiment they manipulated prior expectations about the examinee of experienced polygraph examiners working in familiar contexts. The outcomes revealed that these manipulated prior expectations affected the examiners' decisions, but only when the polygraph charts did not include clear indications of guilt or innocence. When the charts included strong indications that clearly contradicted these expectations, judgements were not affected by these expectations. The contamination problem could be reduced by the scoring of the charts being done by independent evaluators who are blind to the examinee and the crime under investigation. Barland (1988) states that most federally administered polygraph tests in the USA are checked by quality control officers who review the charts without having seen the behaviour of the examinees. Unfortunately, interagreement rates in field studies between different examiners are usually not available, whereas interagreement rates between examiners in laboratory studies range from modest (0.61) to satisfactory (0.95) (Carroll, 1988).

Is the test unethical? Misleading the examinee plays a crucial role in the control question test. First, the examinee must be convinced that the test is infallible, this usually happens by means of the stimulation test. Secondly, the examinee must be convinced that the control questions are important to them, otherwise they would not elicit emotional responses. One may argue whether these deceptive procedures are ethically acceptable. As mentioned above, the British Working Group on the use of the polygraph wondered whether these deceptive procedures would be acceptable under current British law.

Do people always believe in these deceptive procedures? A test whose validity depends on deception is vulnerable in the sense that the deception must be successful to make the test effective. Thus, all examinees must believe that the test is infallible, and all must believe that the control questions are crucial. According to Elaad (1993) and Lykken (1988) it is unlikely that all examinees believe these matters. There are dozens of books and articles about the CQT, in which the test is described, including details about the stimulation test, the nature of control questions, and the fact that the test sometimes does make mistakes. Of course, those who are taking polygraph tests have access to this literature. Obviously, the polygraph test will be ineffective when examinees do not believe that the test is infallible. For instance, in such a case innocent suspects have valid reasons to be very nervous during the relevant questions, as an incorrect test outcome, always possible when the test is not infallible, will accuse them of committing a crime they never committed!

Why should innocent suspects always show a stronger emotional response to control questions than to relevant questions? The CQT assumes that innocent suspects score higher on control questions than on relevant questions. Ekman (1985) gives five reasons why some innocent suspects may do the reverse and will be more emotional in their response to the relevant than to the control questions.

- The innocent suspect may think that the police are fallible. The innocent suspect asked to take a polygraph test knows the police already have made a mistake, namely suspecting her or him of a crime she or he has never committed. Perhaps she or he has already tried to convince the police of her or his innocence, without any success. Although, on one hand, she or he could see the test as an opportunity to prove her or his innocence, on the other hand it is also possible that she or he could fear that those who made the mistake of suspecting her or him will make further mistakes. In other words, if police methods are fallible enough to make them falsely suspicious, their polygraph test may also be fallible.

- The innocent suspect may think that the police are unfair. People may dislike or distrust the police and will therefore expect and fear that the polygraph examiner will misjudge them.

- The innocent suspect may think that machines are fallible. People may distrust the polygraph, which may be caused by a distrust in technology in general, or caused by books, articles and TV programmes about the polygraph.

- The innocent suspect is a fearful person. Someone who is generally fearful might respond more to the relevant questions than to the control questions.

- The suspect, even though innocent, has an emotional reaction to the events involved in the crime. Ekman (1985) gives the hypothetical example of an innocent person who is suspected of murdering his coworker, and who was very upset when he found his coworker's bloody, mutilated body. When asked about the murder, the memory of that scene might reawaken his feelings which will be recorded on the polygraph charts.

Why should guilty suspects elicit an even stronger response to relevant questions than to control questions? If the efforts of the examiner during the pre-test interview are successful, then all examinees are concerned about the control questions. As Ben-Shakhar and Furedy (1990) pointed out, it is not clear why a guilty suspect should be less concerned with the control questions, given that this suspect is under the impression that a deception to those questions might be harmful to his or her case.

As mentioned above, the debate about the polygraph is heated. The following quote of Furedy and Heslegrave (1988), two opponents of the CQT, provides a nice illustration of this debate:

> It is also important to recognize the important role played by the attitudes of evaluators toward accepting errors, and weighing these errors depending upon the circumstances. Because the circumstances are known by the evaluator prior to the administration of the polygraph, and because the test is not standardized, it is likely that not only will the outcome be judged on the basis of examinee circumstances and examiner attitude, but

also the administration of the test will be shaped by these prejudices. Because the test is psychological in the sense of involving a complex interview-like interaction between examiner and examinee, any biases in designing and administering the test are likely to produce outcomes that are consistent with those biases. So different individuals accused of different crimes may be given quite different tests, even though all of those tests are called by a single name polygraph test (p. 224).

The guilty knowledge test

The guilty knowledge test (also referred to as the concealed information test) is less extensively used than the control question test. In the USA, for instance, it is apparently considered so unimportant by federal law enforcement that it is not even mentioned in the US federal basic polygraph examiner course (Honts and Perry, 1992). However, in some countries, namely Japan and Israel, the GKT is more frequently used than the CQT (Ben-Shakhar and Furedy, 1990). The guilty knowledge test does not attempt to determine whether somebody is lying but, rather, whether the examinee possesses 'guilty knowledge', that is, whether the examinee recognizes pieces of information unique to the crime. It is assumed that the recognition of these pieces of information will produce arousal (interestingly, a heightened emotional response displayed on a polygraph chart will thus be interpreted by CQT examiners as 'concernedness about lying' and by GKT examiners as 'guilty knowledge'). In a GKT test the examiner will ask questions to which *only the examiner and the examinee* knows the answers (i.e. only a person involved in a rape would probably know what colour underpants the victim was wearing). The questions are asked in a multiple choice format. It is assumed that a guilty suspect will recognize the correct answer and will then produce a physiological reaction which will be recorded by the polygraph. Innocent suspects, of course, will not recognize anything and will therefore give the same physiological response to each of the alternatives (i.e. colour of underpants). The first choice, referred to as a buffer, is always incorrect. It is included to control for the fact that a large emotional response is generally induced by the first stimulus in a sequence, irrespective of its significance (Bashore and Rapp, 1993). Lykken (1988, p. 121) gives the following example of a typical GKT: while escaping through an alley a bank robber drops and leaves behind his hat. A likely suspect is later apprehended and, while attached to the polygraph, he is interrogated as follows (examinees are instructed to respond 'no' to all question alternatives):

1. 'The robber in this case dropped something while escaping. If you are that robber, you will know what he dropped. Was it: a weapon? a face mask? a sack of money? his hat? his car keys?'
2. 'Where did he drop his hat? Was it: in the bank? on the bank steps? on the sidewalk? in the parking lot? in an alley?'
3. 'What colour was the hat? Was it: brown? red? black? green? blue?'
4. 'I'm going to show you five red hats or caps, one at a time. If one of them is your hat, you will recognize it. Which of these hats is yours? Is it: this one? this one? ...etc'.

Theoretically, an innocent suspect has about one chance in five of reacting most strongly to the correct alternative in any of these questions. He has, however, only about two chances

(1.6 exactly) in a thousand of reacting most strongly to the correct alternative in all four questions. Hence, the more questions asked, the less likely the chance will be that an innocent suspect will be falsely accused.

It is probably preferable that the examiner does not know which answers are the 'correct' answers because this knowledge may result in 'experimenter expectancy-effects' (Rosenthal and Rubin, 1978), that is, the reactions of the examiner while giving the correct alternative (excitement for instance) may influence behaviour and physiological reactions of the examinee.

It should be emphasized that some precaution must be taken while constructing the questions and choosing the alternatives. Particularly, it is necessary to check whether all alternatives of a given question are *a priori* equivalent in the amount of arousal they elicit. It is for instance possible that the alternative 'weapon' elicits more arousal in subjects (guilty and innocent) than the alternative 'keys' or that black underpants are more arousing than pink underpants. According to Lykken (1988), this problem can be minimized by pre-testing the set of alternatives on known innocent persons.

Criticism concerning the guilty knowledge test

Criticisms about the guilty knowledge test are usually related to two aspects, namely its applicability and the knowledge of suspects.

Applicability. Raskin (1988) considers the limited applicability of the GKT as the greatest problem of the test:

> The basic premise of the test requires protected information known only by the perpetrator and investigators, but such information does not exist for most cases. In the majority of cases the salient details of the crime are made available to the suspects by the investigators, the media and defence attorneys. That eliminates the possibility of using the test. Also, many types of cases cannot employ the concealed information test because the suspect admits being present but denies the specific alleged acts. The most common example is an alleged sexual assault in which the witness claims that force was used and the suspect admits the sexual acts but claims that they were consensual. Similar problems arise in cases where there are several suspects who were involved in the crime and all deny having been the principal actor (pp. 102–103).

Podlesney (1993, cited in Rosenfeld, 1995) reviewed 61 Federal Bureau of Investigation (FBI) criminal case files in which CQTs were used and concluded that GKT examinations could have been conducted appropriately in only about 13–18 per cent of the cases. Bashore and Rapp (1993) believe that the limited applicability of the test is the principal obstacle to broader use of this technique.

Knowledge of the suspect. Another problem is that the GKT will be effective only when the suspect is aware of the details mentioned in the questions. This is, of course, not always the case. The guilty suspect may not have perceived the details the examiner is talking about or may have forgotten them at the time of the test. For instance, it might be the case that when the examiner asks a question about the colour of the hat which has been found at the scene of crime, the guilty suspect simply has forgotten the colour of the hat! The longer the period between the crime and the polygraph test, the more likely it is that the suspect has forgotten certain details. The test only works when questions are asked about details which are known to the suspect. The examiner, however, can never be sure which details are still known to the guilty suspect at the time of the test.

The polygraph: does it work?

In 1986, CBS (a US television station) enlisted the help of four polygraph testing firms in New York to ascertain which of four employees had stolen a valuable camera. The polygraph experts were advised that the manager's suspicions focused in particular on one individual. This was a charade. There was no missing camera and the employees were aware of this and were merely asked to deny that they had stolen anything (i.e. to tell the truth). As an incentive they were told they would get 50 dollars for passing the polygraph test. The outcome was that each polygrapher positively and confidently identified a culprit; in each case the one individual who was suspected to be the culprit (Lykken, 1988). This example shows that mistakes are made by examiners of US polygraph firms. The example, however, was given by Lykken, the most distinguished opponent of the polygraph test, and may therefore be selected in order to discredit the test. How likely is it that polygraph tests provide an incorrect outcome? Laboratory and field studies concerning polygraph tests may give an answer to this question. An overview of these studies is provided below.

The advantage of field studies is that suspects do really care about the polygraph outcome, and therefore strong emotions are likely. Another advantage is that real suspects are studied instead of college students participating in university laboratories. The major disadvantage of field studies is the ambiguity about ground truth, that is, it is very difficult to establish the actual guilt or innocence of the subjects. Confessions are usually used as ground truth but are not 100 per cent reliable. On the one hand, people who do not confess, and people considered as innocent may be actually guilty, as cases may be dismissed for lack of sufficient evidence rather than innocence. On the other hand, people considered as guilty by virtue of a confession may actually be innocent, as some innocent people do confess (as will be explained in Chapter 6). An alternative way to establish the ground truth is by having a panel of experts review all the evidence and come to a final decision about guilt or innocence. Also in this case, however, it is never certain whether the experts were actually right or wrong.

In a typical laboratory polygraph experiment, participants are randomly assigned to an innocent or guilty condition. Those in the guilty condition commit a mock crime, such as the theft of an object. Those in the innocent condition are given a description of the crime but do not enact in it. All are told to deny the theft. They may be promised a reward when they can convince the examiner of their innocence, or they may be threatened with punishment if they cannot (Bradley and Janisse (1981) for instance, threatened their guilty and innocent subjects with a 'painful but not permanently damaging electric shock' if they failed the test). The subject is then given a polygraph test by an examiner who is blind with respect to guilt or innocence. The major advantage of such a laboratory study is that there is absolute certainty about the ground truth, that is, absolute certainty about who is actually guilty or innocent. There is, however, in laboratory studies almost inevitably a lack of realism. In real-life situations, for instance, the stakes are much higher than in laboratory studies. It is never possible to elicit in a laboratory study the strong emotions possibly felt by a person who is accused of murder and whose guilt or innocence will be established by means of a polygraph test. For these reasons, polygraph critics such as Kleinmuntz and Szucko (1982) and Lykken (1981, 1988) have argued that laboratory polygraph tests are not useful to estimate field accuracy. Others (Kircher, Horowitz, and Raskin, 1988; Raskin, 1989a) have suggested that laboratory studies might be useful as long as certain criteria are met, namely representative subject populations (not only college students), and realistic polygraph practices (including expert examiners and some motivation for the examinee to deceive the examiner).

A unique attempt to conduct a polygraph study in a realistic setting and maintaining certainty about the ground truth was made by Ginton, Daie, Elaad, and Ben-Shakhar (1982). The subjects in the study were 21 Israeli policemen, participating in a police course, who took a paper and pencil test that was presented as a requirement for the course. Subjects were asked to score their own tests, which provided an opportunity to cheat by revising their initial answers. The test answer sheets, however, were chemically treated so that cheating could be detected. It turned out that seven out of the 21 subjects cheated. Later, all were told that they were suspected of cheating, were offered a polygraph examination, and were told that their future careers in the police force might depend on the outcome of this examination. (The option, by the way, to allow the police officers to refuse to take the test was a realistic one.) In criminal investigations taking a polygraph test is an option and not an absolute requirement of a suspect (Ekman, 1985)). Although initially all 21 agreed to be polygraphed, one guilty officer did not show up for the actual examination, and two (one guilty and one innocent) refused to take the polygraph test. Three other guilty subjects confessed just before the polygraph interrogation[2] so the final sample included only two guilty subjects and 13 innocent ones. The CQT was used, and both guilty officers were accurately detected. Two of the 13 innocent ones were mistakenly judged to be lying. No conclusions can be drawn from this study, however, because so few people were examined. Generally, it will, of course, be difficult to replicate such a realistic high stakes experiment, due to ethical difficulties.

Several reviews have recently been published concerning laboratory tests examining the accuracy of control question polygraph tests. They are listed in Table 4.2.[3]

First, Table 4.2 reveals that laboratory control question tests are rather accurate in detecting guilty subjects: A majority of guilty suspects (between 68 and 80 per cent) are usually detected and relatively small numbers (between 7 and 10 per cent) are incorrectly classified as innocent. A less positive picture emerges regarding proving innocence of innocent subjects. Between 55 and 84 per cent of these are correctly classified as innocent. The overall accuracy percentages for three of the four reviews are only slightly higher that the 50 per cent accuracy rate which can be expected by chance. Moreover, rather high percentages of subjects (usually more than 10 per cent) are falsely accused of being guilty.[4]

TABLE 4.2 *Results of laboratory study reviews testing the accuracy of the control question polygraph test*

	Guilty condition			Innocent condition		
	guilty	innocent	inconclusive	guilty	innocent	inconclusive
Ekman (1985, $n = 13$)	68%	10%	22%	15%	55%	30%
Honts (1995, $n = 8$)	77%	10%	13%	8%	84%	8%
Kircher *et al.* (1988, $n = 14$)	74%	8%	18%	12%	66%	22%
Ben-Shakhar *et al.* (1990, $n = 9$)	80%	7%	13%	15%	63%	22%

Note: n = number of studies reviewed.

The false accusation of an innocent suspect is called a *false-positive error*. Hence, Table 4.2 shows that laboratory control question polygraph tests are vulnerable to false-positive errors. This is perhaps not surprising. A false-positive error occurs when a subject reveals more emotional arousal when answering the relevant questions than when answering the control questions. In the above section about the disadvantages of the control question polygraph tests, several reasons why this might be the case were discussed (for instance, despite the examiner's efforts the subject realizes the major consequences of the relevant question and therefore shows emotional arousal when answering this question). Finally, it should be noted that the percentages of inconclusive outcomes are rather high in these studies. An inconclusive outcome means that the subjects were aroused to the same level when answering the control and relevant questions. Again, several reasons have already been given as to why this might occur.

Table 4.3 gives the outcomes of three literature reviews concerning the guilty knowledge polygraph test. Table 4.3 shows that the test is very accurate regarding innocent subjects. A vast majority of innocent people (94–99 per cent) are correctly classified, and only a small percentage of innocent people (1–6 per cent) are falsely accused. The test, however, is less accurate when detecting guilt in guilty subjects. Relatively high percentages of guilty subjects (between 14 and 22 per cent) are classified as innocent. (The GKT does not have

TABLE 4.3 *Results of laboratory study reviews testing the accuracy of the guilty knowledge polygraph test*

	Guilty condition		Innocent condition	
	guilty	innocent	guilty	innocent
Ekman (1985, $n = 6$)	78%	22%	5%	95%
Honts (1995, $n = 5$)	86%	14%	1%	99%
Ben-Shakhar *et al.* (1990, $n = 10$)	84%	16%	6%	94%

Note: The GKT does not have an inconclusive category.
n = number of studies reviewed.

an inconclusive category.) The classification of a guilty subject as innocent is called a *false-negative error*. The guilty knowledge test thus appears to be vulnerable to false-negative errors. This is perhaps not surprising. When discussing the disadvantages of the guilty knowledge test several reasons as to why this might be the case were given (the suspect did not perceive the details or has forgotten the details which are covered by the questions asked in the polygraph test).

Table 4.4 shows the outcomes of two literature reviews concerning field studies using the control question polygraph test and the outcomes of three recent field studies which were not included in the literature review. Only recent studies were included which fulfilled the following four criteria: (1) the subjects were suspects in real-life criminal cases, (2) the evaluations were based on the physiological data alone, (3) the evaluations were conducted by persons trained and experienced in doing 'blind' chart evaluations, and (4) a criterion for who was innocent and who was guilty was developed independently from the polygraph test. Most studies (for instance all the recent field studies) used confessions as the criterion. (It was noted above that confessions never provide certainty about the actual guilt or innocence of suspects.)

TABLE 4.4 *Results of field studies testing the accuracy of the control question polygraph test*

	Guilty condition			Innocent condition		
	guilty	innocent	inconclusive	guilty	innocent	inconclusive
Reviews						
Ekman (1985, *n* = 10)	88%	10%	2%	20%	78%	2%
Ben-Shakhar *et al.* (1990, *n* = 9)	84%	13%	3%	23%	72%	5%
Individual recent studies which were not included in the previous reviews						
Honts (1994b)[a]	91%	5%	4%	9%	55%	36%
Honts *et al.* (1988)	92%	8%	0%	15%	62%	23%
Patrick *et al.* (1991)	92%	2%	6%	24%	30%	46%

[a] All these data are from the blind scoring of the cases.
Note: *n* = number of studies reviewed.

Table 4.4 shows that accuracy concerning classifying guilty suspects is rather high. Vast majorities of guilty suspects (between 84 and 92 per cent) were correctly classified as guilty, whereas relatively small numbers of guilty suspects (between 5 and 13 per cent) were incorrectly classified as innocent. As in the laboratory studies, the picture for innocent suspects is less optimistic. Moreover, they show a big variety. Between 30 and 78 per cent of the innocent suspects were correctly classified. Some of these percentages were not higher, or were even below, the level of chance which is 50 per cent. Rather high percentages of innocent suspects (between 9 to 24 per cent) were falsely accused. This means that these suspects demonstrated more emotional arousal when answering the relevant questions than when answering the control questions. These percentages of false-positive errors are higher in the field studies than in the laboratory studies, which is not surprising. Especially in field studies the stakes are high, and especially in field studies suspects may realize the major consequences of the relevant questions. The occurrence of relatively high percentages of false-positives and the rather accurate decisions made for guilty suspects in control question tests (obtained in both laboratory studies and field studies) implies that somebody who passes a control question test is rather likely to be telling the truth.

It is important to bear in mind that the accuracy rates of the recent individual studies were obtained from the blind scoring of the cases. The accuracy rates are usually much higher when the cases are assessed by the original examiner, as can be seen in Table 4.5. Especially the accuracy scores concerning the innocent suspects are much better, that is, more innocent suspects are classified as innocent and fewer *false-positive errors* (the false accusation of an innocent suspect) are made. Particularly Honts *et al.* (1988) achieved very high accuracy rates.

TABLE 4.5 *Results of field studies testing the accuracy of the control question polygraph test using original examiners*

	Guilty condition			Innocent condition		
	guilty	innocent	inconclusive	guilty	innocent	inconclusive
Honts (1994b)	71%	5%	24%	0%	82%	18%
Honts *et al.* (1988)	92%	8%	0%	0%	91%	9%
Patrick *et al.* (1991)	98%	0%	2%	8%	73%	19%

The main difference between blind evaluators (Table 4.4) and original examiners (Table 4.5) is presumably caused by the additional, extra-polygraphical, information the original examiners have. Apparently, this additional information makes them more accurate. Or, even stronger, this additional information is necessary, as the accuracy rates in Table 4.4 are not satisfactory. This means that there is much reliance on the judgement skills of original examiners, which may be problematic in the sense that not all examiners may be equally skilled. The problem, however, is how to find out which examiners are skilled?

Few field studies using the guilty knowledge polygraph test have been published to date. As mentioned above, the application of this test is limited, which might be one of the reasons why so few studies are reported. To our knowledge only two studies have been published so far (Elaad, 1990; Elaad, Ginton and Jungman, 1992). Elaad (1990) examined a sample of 98 guilty knowledge polygraph test charts from the pool of verified polygraph tests of the Israel Police Scientific Interrogation Unit. The sampling was random and the actual guilt and innocence of the examinees was established by confession. In total, cases of 48 guilty and 50 innocent examinees were examined. The results revealed that almost all innocent suspects (98 per cent) were correctly classified. However, similar to the laboratory studies, the classification of guilty suspects was less accurate: only 42 per cent of the guilty suspects were correctly classified. Elaad *et al.* (1992) examined GKT records of 40 innocent and 40 guilty suspects, for whom actual truth (guilt or innocence) was established by confession. Again, the charts were taken from the pool of verified polygraph tests of the Israel Police Scientific Interrogation Unit. The main difference between this study and the 1990 study was that respiration response length was taken into account as an extra bodily activity measure. The outcomes revealed that 94 per cent of the innocent suspects and 76 per cent of the guilty suspects were correctly classified. Although it is perhaps too premature to reach any conclusions on the basis of these two field studies, they indicate that the guilty knowledge test is vulnerable to false-negative errors (to classify guilty suspects as innocent). The occurrence of relatively high percentages of false-negatives and the rather accurate decisions made for innocent suspects in guilty knowledge tests (obtained in both laboratory studies and field studies) implies that somebody who fails a guilty knowledge test is rather likely to be guilty.

COUNTERMEASURES

One of the problems in detecting deception via polygraph testing is the possible effectiveness of countermeasures. Countermeasures are 'deliberate techniques that some subjects use to appear truthful when their physiological responses are being monitored during a polygraph examination' (Gudjonsson, 1988, p. 126). Naturally, if such techniques could be shown to be effective, this might have major implications for the polygraph technique, because it will make the technique less effective. A distinction can be made between physical and mental countermeasure techniques. Physical countermeasures include physical activities such as tongue biting and foot tensing (by pressing the toes against the floor). This can for instance be done when answering the control questions, resulting in a stronger physical response concerning these questions. Examples of mental countermeasure techniques are counting sheep or counting backward. The result of this technique will be that the examinee does not process the questions (control question test) or the alternatives (guilty knowledge test). As a result, a similar physical response to each question or each question alternative is likely, which will lead to an inconclusive test outcome.[5] Reid and Inbau (1977) argued that it is highly improbable that countermeasures can succeed because the properly trained examiner would notice that the examinee tries to fool him. Indeed, the use of countermeasures has been found to be ineffective against the CQT (Honts, Raskin, Kircher and Hodes, 1988). However, an important limitation of this study was that subjects had to use the countermeasures spontaneously. One may argue that different outcomes can be established when subjects get the opportunity to practise countermeasures (which is more realistic, one might for instance expect that spies will be trained by their masters to defeat the test). Several studies showed that training in countermeasures can be very effective in defeating polygraph tests (Elaad, 1987, cited in Ben-Shakhar and Furedy, 1990; Honts, Hodes and Raskin, 1985; Honts, Raskin and Kircher, 1994). In the study conducted by Honts *et al.* (1994), subjects were trained (for 30 minutes) in the use of either physical countermeasures (biting the tongue or pressing the toes against the floor) or a mental countermeasure (counting backward from seven) to be applied in a polygraph test using the control question test. The mental and physical countermeasures were equally effective: each enabled approximately 50 per cent of the subjects to defeat the polygraph test. Moreover, the examiner's (who was experienced in control question polygraph tests) decisions of countermeasure use were correct for only 12 per cent of the physical countermeasure users, whereas none of the mental countermeasure users produced behaviour or physiological responses that the examiner considered to be indicative of countermeasure use. These latter findings contradict Reid and Inbau's (1977) claim that experienced examiners will detect the use of countermeasures. Recent studies by Honts, Devitt, Winbush and Kircher (1996) and Ben-Shakhar and Dolev (1996) revealed that countermeasures were successful in defeating the GKT polygraph test as well. On the basis of subjects' achievements in faking the polygraph one might perhaps conclude that polygraph testing is only successful in naïve suspects.

CONCLUSION

Field studies examining the accuracy of polygraph tests show that these tests (both CQT and GKT tests) make substantial amounts of mistakes. The proponents of the CQT tests will probably argue that this conclusion is incorrect, and they will then refer to the accuracy scores obtained in their field studies. The problem, however, is that these outcomes were accurate only when the original examiner evaluated the charts (Table 4.5), and not when blind evaluators evaluated the charts (Table 4.4). This suggests that extra, non-polygraph information (known to the original examiner but not to the blind evaluator) is essential to make an accurate decision. The accuracy of the test *itself*, however, can only properly be determined by using evaluators who have access solely to the test results, and their accuracy rates appeared to be less accurate (Table 4.4).

How this extra information leads to more accuracy is never defined. The lack of rules in this decision-making process implies that much depends on the skills, experiences, and intuition of the individual examiner. It also implies that some examiners may be accurate, but not necessarily all examiners. The proponents of the CQT test do not deny that much depends on the skills of the administrator. However, how do you find out in criminal investigations whether the particular investigator is a good or a bad one? You can never find this out. In our view, a test should only be used when the outcomes are verifiable and are independent of the skills of the particular examiner. This means that a decision should be based upon the polygraph charts alone. The fact that the scoring of the charts is not completely quantified also requires that the charts should be scored by at least two evaluators, in order to reduce the subjectivity of the scoring method. Once again, tests who met these criteria appear to be rather inaccurate (Table 4.4).

Moreover, the accuracy rates in the field studies are perhaps inflated, due to inaccurate ground-truth decisions. Confessions were taken as ground truth but they might have been affected by the polygraph outcomes. It is believed that about 30 per cent of the suspects confess after they have failed a polygraph test (Van Koppen, Boelhouwer, Merckelbach and Verbaten, 1996). This does not necessarily mean that these suspects are actually guilty. Perhaps, innocent suspects may confess as well after they have failed the test. They might do so because they see little opportunity anymore to convince the jury or judges of their innocence and decide to confess in order to get a lesser sentence. This might explain differences in accuracy rates between different original examiners as well (Table 4.5). That is, confessions after failing a test may be more likely to occur when the original examiner is famous, well-known or makes a powerful impression, as especially in these cases convincing the jury of their innocence may be difficult for innocent suspects. Failing a polygraph test may also lead to coerced-internalized false confessions, that is, innocent suspects may confess after failing a polygraph test because the test outcome makes them believe that they have committed the crime. Kassin (1997) illustrates this with the following case of 18-year-old Peter Reilly who returned home one night to find that his mother had been murdered:

> Reilly immediately called the police who, while interrogating the boy with the aid of a polygraph, suspected him of matricide. The police told Reilly that he failed an infallible lie-detector test, thus indicating that he was guilty even though he had no memory of the incident. Transcripts of the interrogation sessions revealed that Reilly underwent a remarkable transformation from denial to confusion, self-doubt, conversion ('Well, it really looks like I did it'), and the signing of a full written confession. Two years later, independent evidence revealed that Reilly could not have committed the murder, that the confession that even he came to believe was false (p. 226).

On the other hand, it is unlikely that a guilty suspect who passed the test will ever confess during subsequent police interviews (if these interviews ever take place).

The control question test procedure is especially vulnerable to false-positive errors, that is, the false accusation of an innocent subject. The guilty knowledge test is especially vulnerable to false-negative errors, that is, classifying the guilty subjects as innocent. We believe that false-positive errors are the most serious type of errors, as false-positive errors imply that an innocent suspect can be accused and convicted of committing a crime he or she never committed. False-positive errors go counter to most western legal systems which are founded on the ideal that it is better to acquit 10 guilty people than to convict one person who is innocent.

Taking into account the accuracy rates of blind examiners in field studies, we believe that polygraph evidence in criminal cases is undesirable, because too many mistakes are made to justify polygraph evidence. However, we acknowledge that polygraph interrogation may give valuable insight concerning whether or not a suspect is lying. We therefore believe that polygraph interrogation may be a useful tool in police investigations, for instance, to eliminate potential suspects, to check the truthfulness of informants or to examine contradicting statements of witnesses and suspects.

Directions for future research

At present, ongoing research seems to concentrate mainly on introducing new physiological measures, such as the above mentioned event-related potentials and the effectiveness of countermeasures. This chapter made clear that much depends on the examiner, some examiners achieve better accuracy rates than others. It will therefore be interesting to examine in scientific experiments differences in accuracy rates and differences in conducting polygraph tests and analysing outcomes between examiners who have proven to be very accurate and other examiners. Moreover, it may be worth while to investigate whether submitting a suspect to both the CQT procedure and the GKT procedure will increase the accuracy rates. This idea seems fruitful because the strength of one test may compensate the weakness of the other test, that is, the CQT procedure may compensate the GKT procedure's vulnerability to incorrectly classify guilty suspects, whereas the GKT procedure may compensate the GKT procedure's vulnerability to incorrectly classify innocent suspects. In such a combined experiment, the effectiveness of countermeasures may be investigated as well, as research has shown that the use of countermeasures has a negative effect on the accuracy of both the CQT procedure and the GKT procedure.

NOTES

1. This phase does not always take place. Other procedures employed by polygraphers to persuade the examinee of the standing of their procedures include having a well-appointed office with various framed diplomas and other certificates present on the walls (Bull, 1988).
2. Ekman (1985) pointed out that these figures support what polygraph examiners claim, namely that the threat of taking a polygraph exam does produce confessions among guilty suspects. However, the findings also suggest that refusal to take the test is no certain guarantee of guilt.
3. Some recent experiments which were not included in the reviews examining the accuracy of the control question test (Forman and McCauley, 1986; Podlesny and Truslow, 1993) and the guilty knowledge test (Bradley and Rettinger, 1992) provided outcomes similar to the findings in the reviews.
4. Ten per cent is high because falsely accusing an innocent person is a serious error in the context of most western legal systems which are founded on the idea that it is better to acquit 10 guilty people than to convict one person who is innocent. Also, in a particular investigation, there may be more innocent persons tested than guilty ones. If 10 out of 11 people tested are innocent, one of them will be deemed guilty.
5. The introduction of fillers may counteract this technique, as examinees are supposed to answer 'yes' to fillers but 'no' to the other questions. This forces examinees to listen to and process the questions, as answering 'no' to a filler may reveal that they are not paying attention to the questions.

REFERENCES

Barland, G.H. (1988). The polygraph test in the USA and elsewhere. In A. Gale (ed.), *The Polygraph Test: Lies, Truth and Science* (pp. 73–96). London, England: Sage Publications.

Bashore, T.R. and Rapp, P.E. (1993). Are there alternatives to traditional polygraph procedures? *Psychological Bulletin*, **113**, 3–22.

Ben-Shakhar, G. and Dolev, K. (1996). Psychophysiological detection through the guilty knowledge technique: effects of mental countermeasures. *Journal of Applied Psychology*, **81**, 273–281.

Ben-Shakhar, G. and Furedy, J.J. (1990). *Theories and Applications in the Detection of Deception*. New York: Springer-Verlag.

Bradley, M.T. and Janisse, M.P. (1981). Accuracy demonstrations, threat and the detection of deception: cardiovascular electrodermal and pupillary measures. *Psychophysiology*, 18, 307–315.

Bradley, M.T. and Rettinger, J. (1992). Awareness of crime-relevant information and the guilty knowledge test. *Journal of Applied Psychology*, 77, 55–59.

British Psychological Society (1986). Report of the Working Group on the use on the polygraph in criminal investigation and personnel screening. *Bulletin of the British Psychological Society*, 39, 81–94.

Bull, R. (1988). What is the lie-detection test? In A. Gale (ed.), *The Polygraph Test: Lies, Truth and Science* (pp. 10–19). London, England: Sage Publications.

Carroll, D. (1988). How accurate is polygraph lie detection? In A. Gale (ed.), *The Polygraph Test: Lies, Truth and Science* (pp. 20–28). London, England: Sage Publications.

Ekman, P. (1985). *Telling Lies*. New York: W.W. Norton and Company.

Ekman, P. and O'Sullivan, M. (1991). Who can catch a liar? *American Psychologist*, 46, 913–920.

Elaad, E. (1990). Detection of guilty knowledge in real-life criminal investigations. *Journal of Applied Psychology*, 75, 521–529.

Elaad, E. (1993). Detection of deception: a transactional analysis perspective. *Journal of Psychology*, 127, 5–15.

Elaad, E., Ginton, A. and Jungman, N. (1992). Detection measures in real-life criminal guilty knowledge tests. *Journal of Applied Psychology*, 77, 757–767.

Elaad, E., Ginton, A. and Shakhar, G. (1994). The effects of prior expectations and outcome knowledge on polygraph examiners' decisions. *Journal of Behavioral Decision Making*, 7, 279–292.

Farwell, L.A. and Donchin, E. (1991). The truth will come out: interrogative polygraphy ('lie detection') with event-related brain potentials. *Psychophysiology*, 28, 531–547.

Forman, R.F. and McCauley, C. (1986). Validity of the positive control polygraph test using the field practical model. *Journal of Applied Psychology*, 71, 691–698.

Furedy, J.J. (1991a). Alice in Wonderland terminological usage in, and communicational concerns about, that peculiarly flight of technological fancy: the CQT polygraph. *Integrative Physiological and Behavioral Science*, 26, 241–247.

Furedy, J.J. (1991b). On the validity of the polygraph. *Integrative Physiological and Behavioral Science*, 26, 211–213.

Furedy, J.J. and Heslegrave, R.J. (1988). Validity of the lie detector: a psychophysiological perspective. *Criminal Justice and Behavior*, 15, 219–246.

Ginton, A., Daie, N., Elaad, E. and Ben-Shakhar, G. (1982). A method for evaluating the use of the polygraph in a real-life situation. *Journal of Applied Psychology*, 67, 131–137.

Gudjonsson, G.H. (1988). How to defeat the polygraph tests. In A. Gale (ed.), *The Polygraph Test: Lies, Truth and Science* (pp. 126–136). London, England: Sage Publications.

Honts, C.R. (1991). The emperor's new clothes: the application of the polygraph tests in the American workplace. *Forensic Reports*, 4, 91–116.

Honts, C.R. (1994a). Assessing children's credibility: scientific and legal issues in 1994. *North Dakota Law Review*, **70**, 879–903.

Honts, C.R. (1994b). Field validity study of the Canadian police college polygraph technique. TR-07-94. Ottawa, Canada: Canadian Police Research Centre.

Honts, C.R. (1995). The polygraph in 1995: progress in science and the law. *North Dakota Law Review*, **17**, 987–1020.

Honts, C.R., Devitt, M.K., Winbush, M. and Kircher, J.C. (1996). Mental and physical countermeasures reduce the accuracy of the concealed knowledge test. *Psychophysiology*, **33**, 84–92.

Honts, C.R., Hodes, R.L. and Raskin, D.C. (1985). Effects of physical countermeasures on the physiological detection of deception. *Journal of Applied Psychology*, **70**, 177–187.

Honts, C.R., Kircher, J.C. and Raskin, D.C. (1995). Polygrapher's dilemma or psychologist's chimaera: a reply to Furedy's logico-ethical considerations for psychophysiological practitioners and researchers. *International Journal of Psychophysiology*, **20**, 199–207.

Honts, C.R. and Perry, M.V. (1992). Polygraph admissibility: changes and challenges. *Law and Human Behavior*, **16**, 357–379.

Honts, C.R. and Raskin, D.C. (1988). A field study of the validity of the directed lie control question. *Journal of Police Science and Administration*, **16**, 56–61.

Honts, C.R., Raskin, D.C. and Kircher, J.C. (1994). Mental and physical countermeasures reduce the accuracy of polygraph tests. *Journal of Applied Psychology*, **79**, 252–259.

Honts, C.R., Raskin, D.C., Kircher, J.C. and Hodes, R.L. (1988). Effects of spontaneous countermeasures on the physiological detection of deception. *Journal of Police Science and Administration*, **16**, 91–94.

Johnson, M.M. and Rosenfeld, P.J. (1991). Oddball-evoked p300-based method of deception detection in the laboratory: II. Utilization of non-selective activation of relevant knowledge. *International Journal of Psychophysiology*, **12**, 289–306.

Kassin, S.M. (1997). The psychology of confession evidence. *American Psychologist*, **52**, 221–233.

Kircher, J.C., Horowitz, S.W. and Raskin, D.C. (1988). Meta-analysis of mock crime studies of the control question polygraph technique. *Law and Human Behavior*, **12**, 79–90.

Kircher, J.C. and Raskin, D.C. (1988). Human versus computerized evaluations of polygraph data in a laboratory setting. *Journal of Applied Psychology*, **73**, 291–302.

Kleinmuntz, B. and Szucko, J.J. (1982). On the fallibility of lie detection. *Law and Society Review*, **17**, 85–104.

Kleinmuntz, B. and Szucko, J.J. (1984). Lie detection in ancient and modern times: a call for contemporary scientific study. *American Psychologist*, **39**, 766–776.

Larson, J.A. (1932). *Lying and its Detection: A Study of Deception and Deception Tests*. Chicago, Il: University of Chicago Press.

Lykken, D.T. (1959). The GSR in the detection of guilt. *Journal of Applied Psychology*, **43**, 385–388.

Lykken, D.T. (1960). The validity of the guilty knowledge technique: the effects of faking. *Journal of Applied Psychology*, **44**, 258–262.

Lykken, D.T. (1981). *Tremor in the Blood: Uses and Abuses of the Lie Detector*. New York: McGraw-Hill.

Lykken, D.T. (1988). The case against polygraph testing. In A. Gale (ed.), *The Polygraph Test: Lies, Truth and Science* (pp. 111–125). London, England: Sage Publications.

Lykken, D.T. (1991). Why (some) Americans believe in the lie detector while others believe in the Guilty Knowledge Test. *Integrative Physiological and Behavioral Science*, **126**, 214–222.

Ney, T. (1988). Expressing your emotions and controlling feelings. In A. Gale (ed.), *The Polygraph Test: Lies, Truth and Science* (pp. 65–72). London, England: Sage Publications.

Patrick, C.J. and Iacono, W.G. (1991). Validity of the control question polygraph test: the problem of sampling bias. *Journal of Applied Psychology*, **76**, 229–238.

Podlesny, J.A. and Truslow, C.M. (1993). Validity of an expanded-issue (modified general question) polygraph technique in a simulated distributed crime-roles context. *Journal of Applied Psychology*, **76**, 788–797.

Raskin, D.C. (1979). Orienting and defensive reflexes in the detection of deception. In H.D. Kimmel, E.H. van Olst and J.F. Orlebeke (eds), *The Orienting Reflex in Humans* (pp. 587–605). Hillsdale, NJ: Lawrence Erlbaum Associates.

Raskin, D.C. (1982). The scientific basis of polygraph techniques and their uses in the judicial process. In A. Trankell (ed.), *Reconstructing the Past* (pp. 317–371). Stockholm, Sweden: Norsted and Soners.

Raskin, D.C. (1986). The polygraph in 1986: scientific, professional and legal issues surrounding acceptance of polygraph evidence. *Utah Law Review*, **29**, 29–74.

Raskin, D.C. (1988). Does science support polygraph testing? In A. Gale (ed.), *The Polygraph Test: Lies, Truth and Science* (pp. 96–110). London, England: Sage Publications.

Raskin, D.C. (1989a). Polygraph techniques for the detection of deception. In D.C. Raskin (ed.), *Psychological Methods in Criminal Investigation and Evidence* (pp. 247–296). New York: Springer-Verlag.

Raskin, D.C. (1989b). Recent laboratory and field research on polygraph techniques. In J.C. Yuille (ed.), *Credibility Assessment* (pp. 1–24). Dordrecht, The Netherlands: Kluwer Academic Publishers.

Raskin, D.C. and Kircher, J.C. (1987). The validity of Lykken's criticisms: facts or fantasy? *Jurimetric Journal*, Spring, 271–277.

Reid, J.E. (1947). A revised questioning technique in lie detection tests. *Journal of Criminal Law, Criminology and Police Science*, **37**, 542–547.

Reid, J.E. and Inbau, F.E. (1977). *Truth and Deception: The Polygraph (Lie Detector) Technique*. Baltimore, MA: Williams and Wilkins.

Rosenfeld, J.P. (1995). Alternative views of Bashore and Rapp's (1993) alternative to traditional polygraphy: a critique. *Psychological Bulletin*, **117**, 159–166.

Rosenfeld, P.J., Angell, A., Johnson, M.M. and Qian, J. (1991). An ERP-based, control-question lie detector analog: algorithms for discriminating effects within individuals' average waveforms. *Psychophysiology*, **28**, 319–335.

Rosenthal, R.R. and Rubin, D.B. (1978). Interpersonal expectancy effects: the first 345 studies. *Behavioral and Brain Sciences*, **3**, 377–415.

Saxe, L. (1991). Science and the GKT polygraph: a theoretical critique. *Integrative Physiological and Behavioral Science*, **26**, 223–231.

Saxe, L. (1994). Detection of deception: polygraph and integrity tests. *Current Directions in Psychological Science*, 3, 69–73.

Van Koppen, P.J., Boelhouwer, A.J.W., Merckelbach, H. and Verbaten, M.N. (1996). *Leugendetectie in actie: Het gebruik van de polygraaf in de praktijk*. Leiden, The Netherlands: Nederlands Studiecentrum Criminaliteit en Rechtshandhaving.

Accuracy

5

PSYCHOLOGICAL FACTORS IN EYEWITNESS TESTIMONY

Aldert Vrij

INTRODUCTION

Seeing is believing

Evidence in criminal trials is often based upon eyewitness testimonies: it has been estimated that around 77 000 people a year in the USA are charged with crimes solely on the basis of eyewitness evidence (Goldstein, Chance and Schneller, 1989). Loftus (1974, 1979) was one of the first researchers to examine the impact of eyewitness testimony on mock juries. She provided 150 subjects (college students) with descriptions of a hypothetical case in which a small grocery store was robbed, the owner of the store was murdered and the police apprehended a suspect. One group of students was provided with only circumstantial evidence (for instance money was found in the defendant's room, and traces of ammonia used to clean the floor of the store were found on the defendant's shoes). In this situation, 18 per cent voted for conviction. A second group of subjects received the same information but with the addition of a single eyewitness who claimed that he saw the defendant shoot the victim. In this situation a remarkably higher percentage of students, namely 72 per cent, judged the defendant to be guilty, indicating the persuasiveness of eyewitness testimony on jurors. A third group of students received the same information as the second group, however, in this case the defendant's solicitor discredited the witness' testimony by showing that the witness had a vision poorer than 20/400 and had not been wearing his glasses on the day of the robbery, thus he could not have identified the culprit. In spite of the defence solicitor's remarks, 68 per cent of the subjects still voted for conviction! A possible explanation for the persuasiveness of eyewitness testimony is that vivid eyewitness accounts have a strong impact on observers and are easy to remember (Nisbett and Ross, 1980) and they are therefore difficult to erase from jurors' minds (Myers, 1996). It is therefore perhaps not surprising that eyewitness identifications tend to be one of the most compelling types of evidence presented in police investigations and criminal trials (Stern and Dunning, 1994).

Despite its persuasiveness, eyewitness identifications are often inaccurate, as shown by Cutler and Penrod (1995) in their meta-analysis of studies examining identification accuracy in realistic field settings. In these studies, customers (confederates) engaged in unusual (but safe) transactions with employees. These employees were, a couple of hours later, asked to identify the customers from photoarrays. Of the 536 employees participating in these studies, 42 per cent made a correct identification, but 36 per cent made a false identification, that is an 'innocent' person was falsely identified. A recent field study (Yarmey, Yarmey and Yarmey, 1994) found similar results.

A compelling example of mistakes in eyewitness testimony is given by Crombag, Wagenaar and Van Koppen (1996). Their study was based upon a real-life event, namely the crash of a cargo El Al Boeing 747 into an 11-storey apartment building in Amsterdam (The Netherlands) on 4 October 1992. The Dutch television reported extensively on this national disaster, showing the fire brigade fighting the blaze and rescuing people from the collapsing building. The disaster was the main news item for several days and eventually everyone in the country knew, or thought they knew, in great detail what had happened. In all these news programmes, the TV could only show what had happened after the crash, pictures of the crash itself were never filmed and thus never broadcast. Nevertheless, 61 (66 per cent) of the 93 students who participated in the study, answered the question: 'Did you see the television film of the moment the plane hit the apartment building?' affirmatively. Many 'witnesses' remembered further details of this non-existing TV footage of the crashing plane. For instance, 41 students remembered that they had seen that the plane hit the building horizontally, 10 students remembered that the plane hit the building vertically, and 14 students indicated that they had seen, on television, that the plane was already burning when it crashed (See Chapter 7 for a discussion of why such distortions occur.)

One might argue that the issue of erroneous eyewitness testimony is irrelevant when observers are able to distinguish between accurate and inaccurate witnesses. If this were the case, all observers would have to do is rely on the accurate witnesses and reject the inaccurate witnesses. Some studies have revealed that observers are able to distinguish between accurate and inaccurate witnesses, but only to a limited extent. The accuracy rates (percentages of correct answers) in these studies are about 60 per cent, while a 50 per cent accuracy rate can be expected by chance alone (Dunning and Stern, 1994; Leippe, Manion and Romanczyk, 1992; Schooler, Gerhard and Loftus, 1986; Stern and Dunning, 1994). Some recent studies provide insight in differences in verbal and nonverbal behaviour between accurate and inaccurate witnesses. Accurate witnesses for instance seem to make a lineup choice more quickly than inaccurate witnesses (Sporer, 1993, 1994), provide more sensorial details (Schooler et al. (1986), see also Chapter 1) and make their choice without much deliberation (Dunning and Stern, 1994). Dunning and Stern found that accurate witnesses often report that 'the face just popped out' without being able to provide any reasons why they believe that this might be the correct choice.

Most researchers hold a pessimistic view about observers' ability to distinguish between accurate and inaccurate witnesses. For instance based upon their own research, Wells, Lindsay and Tousignant (1980, p. 446) speculated 'that human observers have absolutely no ability to discern eyewitnesses who have mistakenly identified an innocent person'. After a recent review of the literature, Cutler and Penrod (1995, p. 195) concluded that 'jurors apparently have difficulty reliably differentiating accurate from inaccurate eyewitnesses'. The pessimistic view about jurors' ability to spot inaccurate witnesses is supported by a study conducted by Lindsay, Wells and Rumpel (1981). Witnesses viewed a crime under three different viewing conditions, in the *poor* condition the criminal was visible for only 12 seconds and wore a hat that completely covered his hair. The *moderate* condition was similar to the poor condition except that the hat was worn higher on the criminal's head so that his hair was more visible. In the *good* condition, the criminal's head was uncovered and he was visible for 20 seconds. Perhaps not surprisingly, accurate identifications differed per condition with the lowest accuracy (33 per cent) in the poor viewing condition, the highest accuracy (74 per cent) in the good viewing condition and an intermediate accuracy (50 per cent) in the moderate viewing condition.

In the next stage of the experiment, observers, who were aware of the viewing conditions of the witnesses, were asked whether they believed the witnesses' judgements. First, it was found that observers believed inaccurate witnesses as often as accurate witnesses, hence, they could not differentiate between accurate and inaccurate witnesses. Secondly, there was a strong belief in the accuracy of witnesses: observer belief rates for witnesses in the poor, moderate and good viewing conditions, were 62 per cent, 66 per cent, and 74 per cent, respectively. The belief scores in the poor viewing condition are especially remarkable. The viewing conditions were so poor that two-thirds of the witnesses had actually misidentified an innocent person, nevertheless 62 per cent of the observers still believed the witnesses in this condition. Lindsay *et al.*'s study demonstrates at least three aspects of eyewitness testimony. First, as mentioned earlier, people are not very accurate at distinguishing between accurate and inaccurate witnesses. Secondly, some factors make eyewitness identifications more difficult, such as wearing a hat (disguise) in this experiment. Which factors influence eyewitness identifications? The next part of this chapter deals with this question. Thirdly, people do not take into account the fact that the viewing conditions would have an impact on eyewitness accuracy in identification tests. To inform jurors about which factors influence identification accuracy is a task for eyewitness experts. What knowledge do jurors have about factors influencing eyewitness identifications? What can experts tell jurors in court? Are jurors influenced by what experts say in court? These questions will be discussed in the concluding parts of this chapter.

ESTIMATOR VARIABLES AND SYSTEM VARIABLES IN EYEWITNESS IDENTIFICATION

There are many reasons why false identifications occur. On the one hand, a long delay between the encounter and the recognition test, or the fact that the witness was intoxicated when he or she witnessed the crime, may impair the witness' memory of the culprit. These and similar factors are called *estimator variables* (Wells, 1978). Estimator variables are factors over which the criminal justice system exerts little or no control. Wells called these factors estimator variables because, although these variables may be manipulable in research, they cannot be controlled in the actual criminal situation and their influence on identification accuracy can therefore at best only be *estimated post hoc*. On the other hand, the witness may have made a wrong identification because the police conducted a lineup which was biased in some way. This factor and similar factors are called *system variables* (Wells, 1978). System variables are factors that are directly under control of the criminal justice system which can handle them in such a way as to reduce the inaccuracies of witnesses (for instance by conducting a fair, unbiased lineup).

Another way of classifying the factors is by the stage of memory at which they influence identification accuracy. Memory for person recognition might be seen as a three-stage process involving *encoding*, *storage* and *retrieval* (Sporer, Köhnken and Malpass, 1996). Stage 1 (encoding) refers to a witness' perceptions at the time of the event in question. At stage 2 (storage) the witness stores the acquired information in memory to avoid forgetting, at stage 3 (retrieval) the witness retrieves the information from storage when it is required. Errors can occur at each of these three stages. Estimator variables focus primarily on the first two stages, whereas system variables focus primarily on stage three.

Estimator variables

In the past few years several excellent meta-analyses about the impact of estimator variables on eyewitness identification have been published (Cutler and Penrod, 1995; Narby, Cutler and Penrod, 1996; Shapiro and Penrod, 1986). Altogether, these analyses included almost 150 experiments with more than 17 000 subjects. This section relies on these meta-analyses.

Estimator variables can be classified into seven categories: stable witness characteristics, malleable witness characteristics, style of presentation, stable target characteristics, malleable target characteristics, environmental conditions, and post-event factors.

Stable witness characteristics

Witness characteristics such as *intelligence*, *gender* and *race*, are not particularly useful predictors of identification accuracy. They are only weakly, if at all, related to making false or correct identifications. However, *age* has an impact, with children and the elderly performing less accurately than other adults.

The impact of *personality traits* on identification accuracy has received little attention so far (Hosch, 1994). The results of the few studies are conflicting and no firm conclusion about the impact of personality traits on identification accuracy can be drawn.

Malleable witness characteristics

Now and then groups of employees (bank tellers for instance) receive some kind of *training in face recognition*. The effect of training depends on the kind of training given. Training programmes focusing on facial feature analyses (learn to describe eyes, eyebrows, noses and so on) have proved to be unsuccessful (Malpass, 1981; Woodhead, Baddeley and Simmonds, 1979), whereas elaboration techniques (making inferential judgements about faces, such as personality judgements) are more successful (Devine and Malpass, 1985).

The impact of *alcohol intoxication* has hardly been examined to date, but the results suggest that some level of intoxication will deteriorate encoding and storage (Cutler and Penrod, 1995).

Style of presentation

Eyewitnesses are usually interviewed more than once. It is possible that these different accounts reveal *inconsistencies* in recall for certain details. Lawyers may highlight these inconsistencies in order to discredit the eyewitness (Cutler and Penrod, 1995). Research conducted by Fisher and Cutler (1996) has revealed that lawyers may be wrong in doing this, as their research revealed that inconsistencies were not related to accuracy.

Witnesses may differ in the level of *confidence* about the accuracy of their decision, that is, they may be convinced that the suspect they identified was the culprit or they may be less certain about their own decision. Jurors rely heavily on witnesses' confidence to infer witness accuracy (for example Lindsay, 1994b; Luus and Wells, 1994), which is not surprising. A witness who says: 'I'm sure, that's the one who robbed the shop', makes a more convincing impression than a witness who says: 'I think he is the one who robbed the shop, but I might be wrong'. Interestingly, most research has shown that confidence is not a valid indicator of accuracy, that is, accurate witnesses are as confident as inaccurate witnesses! A recent review of the literature (Sporer, Penrod, Read and Cutler, 1995) has resulted in a somewhat different conclusion. Sporer *et al.* found that the confidence–accuracy relationship is stronger for choosers (witnesses who make an identification in a lineup) than for nonchoosers (witnesses who reject lineups, that is, who say that the culprit is not present in the lineup). The authors, however, emphasize in their discussion of the data, that even choosers' confidence is a far from perfect indicator of witness accuracy. In a recent study, Robinson and Johnson (1996) found that recall memory conditions (in which no alternative answers were provided) by the researchers resulted in a higher eyewitness confidence–accuracy correlation than recognition memory conditions (in which alternative answers were provided).

Stable target characteristics

Gender and *race* of the suspect have no effects on face recognition accuracy, whereas *facial distinctiveness* has an effect. Faces that are rated as highly attractive or highly unattractive are better recognized than nondistinctive faces.

Malleable target characteristics

Malleable target characteristics are important predictors of identification accuracy. Identifications are less accurate if the culprit wore a *disguise* (hat, mask, glasses and so on) during the crime or *changed his or her facial appearance* between the crime and the recognition test. In the latter case, changing hair style may be the most efficient, as research has indicated that people when they are invited to describe faces from their memory refer mostly to hairstyle (in 27 per cent of the cases), followed by eyes (14 per cent), nose (14 per cent) and face shape (13 per cent) (Ellis, 1984; Shepherd and Ellis, 1996).

Environmental conditions

Most experiments on estimator variables have examined the impact of environmental factors on identification accuracy. These studies have revealed that identification accuracy becomes poorer if the *target is less salient* (that is, the more people in the scene the less salient the perpetrator is, and therefore the more difficult it is to identify him or her), the *exposure duration* (the amount of time for viewing a perpetrator) *is short*, and a *weapon is present*.

A lot of research has been conducted concerning the so-called weapon focus effect (see Steblay (1992) for a review). Weapon focus effect refers to the visual attention that eyewitnesses give to a perpetrator's weapon during the course of a crime, thereby paying less attention to the facial characteristic of the perpetrator which, in turn, will impair the ability to recognize the perpetrator on a subsequent identification test. Two explanations for the weapon focus effect are given, namely arousal level and focus of attention. The arousal level effect is compellingly demonstrated by Maass and Köhnken (1989). Subjects were approached by an experimenter who was either holding a syringe or a pen and who threatened the subject with an injection. Later on, the subjects were asked to identify the experimenter in a target-absent lineup (that is, the experimenter was not present in the lineup) and to recall details about the experimenter's face and hand. Prior to the experiment, subjects had answered some questions about their fear of injections. The results revealed that twice as many subjects in the syringe present condition (64 per cent) than in the pen present condition (33 per cent) made a false identification in the lineup task. Moreover, subjects recalled hand cues more accurately and facial cues less accurately the more afraid they were of the syringe.

A study conducted by Loftus, Loftus and Messo (1987) gave support to the attention focus explanation. Their study showed that even in harmless situations (in situations in which no arousal is involved) a witness's eyes are drawn like a magnet to a weapon. Witnesses saw slides of a customer who approached a bank teller and pulled out either a handgun or a chequebook. The number and duration of eye fixations on the gun or cheque book were recorded. They found that witnesses made both more eye fixations and longer eye fixations on the gun than on the chequebook.

Crime seriousness (another estimator variable) is also related to identification accuracy. People are worse in identification tests when they perceive the crime to be less serious (Cutler and Penrod, 1995). Personal involvement (another type of crime seriousness) seems not to be related to identification accuracy, that is, victims are as accurate as bystander witnesses. However, not many studies have investigated the victim/bystander factor.

The impact of *stress* and *arousal* on identification accuracy is not clear due to ethical restrictions concerning the experimental manipulations of high levels of arousal. Deffenbacher (1983) and Christiaanson (1992) refer to the 'Yerkes–Dodson Law' in their reviews of the literature concerning the relationship between stress and encoding. The Yerkes–Dodson Law describes an inverted U-shaped relationship between stress and encoding. Low levels of arousal produce low attentiveness (and therefore lead to poor encoding), very high levels of arousal weaken perceptual and encoding skills (and therefore lead to poor encoding), whereas moderate levels of arousal heighten perceptual and attentiveness skills (and therefore lead to better encoding). Students may recognize this phenomenon when revising for an exam. Starting to revise too long before an exam is inappropriate, because there is no pressure yet and it is therefore difficult to concentrate. Someone who starts too late runs the risk of panic, which makes it very difficult to encode the information.

As mentioned before, gender of witness or gender of target have no effect on identification accuracy. The interaction between the two factors, however, leads to the *cross-gender bias identification* effect, that is, identifications of someone of the opposite gender are less accurate than identifications of someone of the same gender.

Similarly, a *cross-race bias identification* effect exists: identifications of someone of the same race are more accurate than identifications of someone of another race (see Anthony, Cooper and Mullen (1992) for a extensive review of the cross-racial effect). The effect appears to be stronger for whites than for blacks. For instance, Cross, Cross and Daly (1971) found a cross-race bias in white subjects but not in black subjects. Chance and Goldstein (1996) suggested that the effect is caused by differences in frequency and, particularly, quality of contact between members of different groups. For example, Lavrakas, Buri and Mayzner (1976) found that in explaining white subjects' other-race recognition performance, quality of contact was more important than frequency:

> Being white and actually having black friends was found to be more positively related to recognition of black faces than merely having grown up in an integrated neighbourhood or having gone to school with blacks (p. 480).[exr]

Post-event factors
Common sense makes us believe that memory declines over time. Research has revealed that this *time delay* effect indeed exists, although, interestingly, time delay has a much smaller impact on false identifications than on correct identifications.

Witnesses are sometimes asked by the police to search through mugshots to identify (i) an unknown suspect, (ii) a suspect they have seen in the media, or (iii) a suspect that participated in an earlier lineup. Research has shown that having seen the suspect previously (in the media, in mugshots, in an earlier lineup) affects identification accuracy in subsequently presented lineups. Several experiments (Brigham and Cairns, 1988; Gorenstein and Ellsworth, 1980) have shown that when witnesses view a lineup after having looked at mugshots, they are inclined to identify a person whose mugshot photograph they have previously seen (regardless of whether that person is the perpetrator). Gorenstein and Ellsworth, for example, staged an event during a lecture. Half of the subjects who witnessed the event were asked to identify the intruder from a set of mugshots (a picture of the intruder was not included in this set of mugshots). The other half of the subjects did not see the set of mugshots. A couple of days later, all subjects attempted to identify the intruder from a photoarray. In the photoarray were photos of the intruder and of somebody who was included in the mugshots, but who was not the intruder. Of the subjects who were previously exposed to the mugshots, 44 per cent identified the one who was included in the mugshots as the intruder and 22 per cent identified the real perpetrator as the intruder. Of those who did not participate in the mugshot phase, 39 per cent correctly identified the intruder. There are two possible reasons for this so-called *repeated identification* effect (Köhnken, Malpass and Wogalter, 1996). It occurs because the witness recognizes the photo but forgets the circumstances in which she or he originally saw it (so-called 'unconscious transference' effect, Loftus, 1976), or it occurs because once a witness comes to a decision and expresses it, he or she feels committed and may be less willing to change the decision later (so-called 'commitment' effect, Kiesler, 1971). This implies, in criminal settings, that a witness who is exposed to a particular suspect (via mugshots, media or an earlier lineup) should not be used as a witness in a subsequent lineup procedure. Wagenaar and Loftus (1991) recommend that, if one witness identifies a suspect from a mugshot array, other witnesses should attempt the lineup identification (of course, this is only possible when there were at least two witnesses). The repeated identification effect is usually discussed in the estimator variables section. One might argue that it is a system variable as well, because the criminal justice system can exert control over this factor. This also applies to the next factor, experiential context.

Changes in experiental context may make an identification difficult. When someone 'knows' a person from one context, say as an employee in a shop, it is sometimes difficult to recognize the same person in another context, namely away from the shop. Research has shown that context reinstatement (going back to the original context) improves identification accuracy. Context reinstatement may occur physically (returning to the scene of crime when performing the identification task) or, if that is not appropriate, mentally (imagining the scene of crime when performing the identification task). In fact, the cognitive interview technique (described in Chapter 8) is a mental reinstatement technique. (See Chapter 8 for a review of the effects of reinstatement techniques.)

After somebody witnesses a crime, this person will be interviewed by the police about what he or she has seen. Additional information about the event (true or not true) which arises from this interview will distort the witness' memory (so-called *post-event information* effect), as an experiment of Loftus and Palmer (1974) has revealed. Subjects saw a film of a traffic accident and then answered questions about the event, including the question: 'About how fast were the cars going when they *contacted* each other?' Other subjects received the same information, except the verb contacted was replaced by either *hit*, *bumped*, *collided* or *smashed*. Even though all subjects saw the same film, the wording of the question affected their answers. The speed estimates (in miles per hour) were 31, 34, 38, 39 and 41, respectively. One week later, subjects were asked whether they had seen broken glass at the incident site. Although the correct answer was 'no', 32 per cent of the subjects in the 'smashed' condition said they had. Hence, the wording of the question had influenced their memory of the incident. Loftus calls this reconstructive memory, and argues that the additional information actually becomes integrated in the memory of the original event. As a result, the original event can never be retrieved again. Others argue that misled witnesses remember the event details just as well as the witnesses who were not misled, but also remember the suggested detail and follow this suggestion, but leaving their original memory intact for retrieval under the right conditions (Bekerian and Bowers, 1983; McCloskey and Zaragoza, 1985). The debate as to whether or not the post-event information becomes actually integrated in the memory of the original event still continues. From an applied perspective, the important issue is that eyewitness reports can be biased by post-event information (all researchers agree on this issue). Suggestive questions asked by the police which could interfere with the witness' original memory of the event should therefore be avoided. Unfortunately, not only the police but also others (friends, acquaintances) will talk with the witness about the event. Their suggestive information may distort the witness' memory as well. If Loftus is right, this distortion can never be corrected, if Loftus is wrong, the damage done by this post-event information can be restored. The current climate provides more arguments against than in favour of Loftus' point of view (see D.S. Lindsay (1994) for an overview of this discussion).

System variables

As mentioned earlier, system variables are factors that are under the control of the criminal justice system (Wells, 1978). These factors usually describe characteristics of a recognition test, and are related to the retrieval stage (the third memory stage). Following Cutler and Penrod's (1995) categorization, five biases that may occur in recognition tests (lineup tests) will be described here, namely lineup instruction bias, foil bias, clothing bias, presentation bias, and investigator bias.

Lineup instruction bias

As soon as witnesses are requested to come to the police station for a lineup test, they are likely to think that the police have reasons to believe that they have apprehended the perpetrator (Malpass and Devine, 1984). Why else would they make the effort to organize a lineup test and to call the witness? It is very hard to believe that the police will think: 'Well, it's Friday afternoon, we haven't got that much to do, let's organize a fake lineup'. Do these implicit beliefs of witnesses influence their identifications in lineups? According to research, it appears that they do. Malpass and Devine (1981) conducted an experiment in which subjects were asked to identify the vandal who they had previously seen in their lecture room during a (staged) act of vandalism. Half of the subjects were presented with a vandal-present lineup (the vandal was actually present in the lineup), the others were presented with a vandal-absent lineup (the vandal was not present in the lineup). Half of the witnesses in each condition were given 'biased' instructions (p. 484): 'We believe that the person...is present in the lineup....Which of these is the person you saw'. The other half were given 'unbiased' instructions: 'The person...may be...in the lineup. It is also possible that he is not in the lineup'. Results showed that the type of instructions did not have a substantial impact in the target-present condition, 75 per cent made a correct identification after a biased instruction and 83 per cent after an unbiased instruction. The instruction, however, had a huge impact in the target-absent condition: 33 per cent identified an innocent person after an unbiased instruction but 78 per cent did so after a biased instruction! The reason is clear. People in the biased instruction condition (like witnesses in a police station) expect the perpetrator to be present in the lineup and tend to choose somebody, probably the one who resembles most the fuzzy picture of the offender in their memory. It is therefore important that, before the lineup starts, the police point out explicitly to the witness that the offender may or may not be in the lineup; that not making a choice is also important information to the police; and that answers such as: 'The culprit is not present' and 'I cannot remember anymore' will be seen as legitimate answers (Köhnken, Malpass and Wogalter, 1996). Obviously, this procedure still does not rule out the possibility that some witnesses still feel an obligation to choose, even when the culprit is not there. One way of identifying these 'obliged choosers' is by starting with a 'blank' lineup in which the culprit is not present. However, this method has some several disadvantages: it is expensive and eventually it will become common knowledge that the police usually start with a blank lineup (Wells, Seelau, Rydell and Luus, 1994).

Foil bias

A suspect in a lineup deserves a fair test, that is, a test in which the suspect does not stand out from the other, innocent people ('foils') in the lineup. Although this sounds obvious, biased lineups do occur. One of the most notorious examples was the black suspect in an all-white lineup used by police in Minneapolis (Ellison and Buckhout, 1981). The police justified this lineup by explaining that there were no other blacks in the building when the lineup was constructed and that there were few blacks in Minneapolis so the lineup was representative for the population!

Constructing a fair lineup is not an easy task. For instance, which foils do you need to select? People who look like the suspect, or people who fit with the description that the witness gave of the perpetrator? Experts disagree on this issue (see Brigham and Pfeifer (1994), Lindsay, Martin, and Webber (1994), and Wells, Seelau, Rydell and Luus (1994) for a discussion). Another question is, how many foils do you need to select? The more people in the lineup, the less likely it is that the suspect will be chosen by chance. That is, when only two people are present (the suspect and one foil) there will be a 50 per cent chance of a random identification of the suspect, whereas this chance will be lowered to 20 per cent when five people will be present in the lineup. Of course, recruiting many foils can be a difficult and expensive task. A lineup of at least six people (one suspect and five foils) is usually recommended by experts (Wells *et al.*, 1994). An effective way of testing the validity (fairness) of a lineup is by conducting the lineup with pseudo witnesses or mock witnesses (people who have not seen any of the lineup members before). In a totally fair lineup, each of the members of the lineup should be chosen as 'the culprit' at a level of chance, that is, in a six people lineup, each of the members should gather $1/6 = 16.7$ per cent of the mock witnesses' votes.

Clothing bias

An important question that has only recently been addressed is how the members of a lineup should be dressed to ensure a fair identification procedure. It is obvious that the suspect should not stand out from the foils by his or her clothing. It is therefore recommended that all members of the lineup wear similar clothes. But should they all wear clothes similar to those worn by the perpetrator at the scene of crime, or is it better to wear clothes which differ from those worn by the perpetrator at the scene of crime? Lindsay, Wallbridge, and Drenman (1987) and Yarmey, Yarmey, and Yarmey (1996) addressed these questions and concluded that it is better if the people in the lineup do not wear clothes which are similar to those worn by the perpetrator at the scene of crime. Wearing different clothes gives the police the opportunity to conduct a second test (apart from the lineup) in which the witness will be requested to identify the clothes worn by the perpetrator.

Presentation bias

It is a common procedure to present suspect and foils simultaneously. Lindsay and Wells (1985), however, showed that it is better to show the lineup members sequentially, that is, one at a time. Subjects in their experiment witnessed a theft and were asked to identify the culprit afterwards from six photographs (the photo of the thief was not present). Half of the subjects were presented with a simultaneous presentation, the others with a sequential presentation. Fifty-eight per cent of the subjects in the simultaneous condition made a wrong identification, whereas only 17 per cent of the subjects in the sequential condition made a wrong identification. The reason seems obvious. In the simultaneous condition, the witness knows from the beginning the size of the set from which the choice may be made and is looking for the person who most resembles the culprit. In a sequential presentation, the size of the set is unknown. It is important that the witness is not informed about the number of alternatives that will be presented in a sequential lineup, otherwise it would increase the pressure on someone who feels an obligation to choose when the lineup is coming to the end.

We have already discussed the single-suspect lineup, that is a lineup with one suspect and some foils (preferably at least five foils). Other types of lineup are all-suspects lineups (a lineup in which all members are suspects) and the showup (a lineup with just one member, namely the suspect). Although both the all-suspects lineup and the one-suspect lineup are used by the police, they lead, compared to lineup with one suspect and some foils, to more false identifications of a look-a-like innocent suspect (Yarmey *et al.*, 1996) and have severe limitations and should therefore be avoided. Both types of lineup are inappropriate because they do not give any opportunity to discriminate between accurate and inaccurate witnesses. A guessing witness who mistakenly identifies an innocent lineup member, will do no harm to this person, when this person is a foil. Foils are always known to be innocent, and the incorrect decision of the witness will therefore immediately be discovered. It is a different story, however, if the innocent person who is mistakenly identified by the witness is a suspect, because he or she will then be accused of having committed the crime! In an all-suspects lineup and in a showup each incorrect decision will automatically lead to such an accusation, because each member is a suspect. In a one-suspect lineup, it is likely that a guessing suspect will identify a foil (for instance, the chances are five out of six that a foil will be identified by a guessing witness in a one suspect plus five foils lineup).

Investigator bias

An investigator who knows which member of the lineup the suspect is, may, perhaps unintentionally, pass on this information to an eyewitness through his nonverbal behaviour. For instance, when the witness is observing the suspect, the investigator may at that moment become anxious about whether or not the witness will recognize the suspect.

This anxiety will change his or her behaviour which in turn will lead the witness to believe that this particular person is the suspect (see demand characteristics, Rosenthal (1976)). In order to avoid this bias, the lineup should be conducted by an investigator who is blind to the identity of the suspect (Köhnken *et al.*, 1996). Köhnken *et al.* also recommend that in a live lineup, the foils should not know who the suspect is. They mention a case of a very upsetting crime, in which the foils actually distanced themselves from the suspect, giving (perhaps unintentionally) the witness a subtle cue as to the suspect's identity.

In fact, one might say that well-conducted lineups have similarities with a good psychological experiment (Wells and Luus, 1990). For instance, they include a control group (a lineup with mock witnesses in order to test the fairness of the lineup); they have an experimenter who is blind to the hypotheses (an investigator who doesn't know who the suspect is), and the questions are phrased in such a way that they do not demand a particular answer (the procedure does not imply for certain that the culprit is in the lineup). Given the fact that we cannot assume that practitioners (such as police officers) are aware of the ins and outs of conducting good experiments, it is therefore a task for expert witnesses to inform investigators how to conduct lineups.

PSYCHOLOGISTS' CONTRIBUTION TO THE COURT

Are the above findings common sense?

Several factors which may influence the accuracy of eyewitness testimonies have been discussed throughout this chapter. What do, for instance, jurors and lawyers know about these factors? Research has indicated that factors which influence memory and identification decisions are not common sense. For instance, Cutler and colleagues (Cutler, Penrod and Dexter, 1990; Cutler, Penrod and Stuve, 1988) and R.C.L. Lindsay (1994b) found that mock jurors were not sensitive to the effects of disguise, weapon focus, retention interval, instruction bias, foil bias and other factors that influence identification accuracy. Moreover, these jurors were particularly influenced by how confident the witness was, a factor which, as we saw earlier, does not predict accuracy. A study of Rahaim and Brodsky (1982) with regard to the knowledge of lawyers revealed similar results. Brigham and Wolfskeil (1983) investigated the beliefs of prosecutors, defence lawyers and law enforcement personnel about the accuracy of eyewitness identifications. When asked to estimate the percentage of eyewitness identifications they had observed which were probably correct, they found that the vast majority of the prosecutors (84 percent) felt that '90 per cent or more' of the identifications are probably correct, while 63 per cent of the law officers and only 36 per cent of the defence lawyers endorsed this view.

What do expert witnesses say in court?

Given the fact that jurors and lawyers are generally not aware of the impact of several factors on eyewitness accuracy, it is one of the tasks for the expert to inform them about these issues (another task, as described earlier, is to inform practitioners how to conduct a proper lineup). The nature of system and estimator variables implies that expert witnesses have different roles with regard to these two types of factor. One task is to inform others (jurors for instance) about the *impact* of *system and estimator* variables on eyewitness accuracy. A second task is to inform others (practitioners for instance) how to *prevent* errors caused by *system* variables (by telling them how to conduct proper lineups). Prevention regarding estimator variables is, by definition, not possible because estimator variables are not under the control of the criminal justice system.

In order to find out what experts tell jurors in court, Kassin, Ellsworth and Smith (1989) conducted a survey among 63 experts on eyewitness testimony. Kassin *et al.* asked their opinions about 21 phenomena related to eyewitness testimony. A selection of these phenomena are provided in Table 5.1. Also provided are the percentages of experts who said that the phenomena are reliable enough to present in courtroom testimony. The phenomena are rank-ordered from the one with the most support to the one with the least support.

TABLE 5.1 *What eyewitness experts say in court (from Kassin et al., 1989)*

Rank order and support	Factor	Statement
1. (97%)	Wording of questions	An eyewitness' testimony about an event can be affected by how the questions put to that witness are worded.
2. (95%)	Lineup instructions	Police instructions can affect an eyewitness' willingness to make an identification and/or the likelihood that he or she will identify a particular person.
3. (87%)	Postevent information	Eyewitness testimony about an event often reflects not only what they actually saw but information obtained later on.
4. (87%)	Accuracy–confidence	An eyewitness' confidence is not a good predictor of his or her accuracy.
7. (85%)	Repeated identification	Eyewitnesses sometimes identify as a culprit someone they have seen in another situation or context.
8. (83%)	Showups	The use of a one-person showup instead of a full lineup increases the risk of misidentification.
10. (79%)	Cross-racial/White	White eyewitnesses are better at identifying other white people than they are at identifying black people.
11. (77%)	Lineup fairness	The more the members of a lineup resemble the suspect, the higher the likelihood that identification of the suspect is accurate.
13. (70%)	Stress	Very high levels of stress impair the accuracy of eyewitness testimony.
17. (57%)	Weapon focus	The presence of a weapon impairs an eyewitness' ability to accurately identify the perpetrator's face.
19. (48%)	Cross-racial/Black	Black eyewitnesses are better at identifying other black people than they are at identifying white people.
21. (11%)	Sex differences	Women are better than men at recognizing faces.

Table 5.1 shows that many statements were viewed by a substantial number of the experts as reliable enough to be presented in court. The one with the weakest support is sex differences in eyewitness accuracy (as we saw before, gender is only weakly, if at all, related to accuracy). Eleven per cent of the experts believed that gender differences are reliable enough to present in court.

One should bear in mind that the statements presented in Table 5.1 are based upon findings of psychological laboratory research in eyewitness testimony (conducted before 1989 but the study is currently being replicated by Memon, Kassin, Hosch and Tubbs). Apparently, many experts feel themselves confident enough to present these findings in court and to relate these laboratory findings to the real world of crime. Many experts emphasize that one should be cautious in doing this (Egeth, 1993; Loftus, 1993; Wagenaar, 1988; Yuille, 1993). See for instance Egeth and McCloskey (1984), Egeth (1993), Elliot (1993), Kassin, Ellsworth, and Smith (1994) and Wells (1993) for a vivid discussion about this issue. For instance, what do all these laboratory studies tell us about the eyewitness memory of Second World War concentration camp survivors when they were asked to identify 'Ivan the Terrible' many years later (Wagenaar, 1988)? The concerns about the possibility of generalizing laboratory eyewitness findings to the real world are especially important with regard to estimator variables (Egeth, 1993).

Can experts educate jurors?

Psychologists disagree over whether receiving information from experts helps the jury. McCloskey and Egeth (1983) and, more recently, R.C.L. Lindsay (1994b) and Ebbesen and Konecni (1997) claim that the jury is usually not better off with help from experts, whereas Cutler and Penrod (1995) and Penrod, Fulero and Cutler (1995) express a more positive view based upon their own experiments. It is too early to draw firm conclusions, but expert testimony has a beneficial impact in at least one way. It makes jurors scrutinize the evidence more carefully, which is beneficial since people tend to place too much faith in eyewitness testimony (Brehm and Kassin, 1996). A study of Visher (1987) based upon post-trial interviews with 331 real jurors showed that several factors other than eyewitness evidence had a stronger effect on jurors' decision making. The results indicated that jurors' decisions are dominated by evidential issues, particularly evidence concerning the use of force (including victim injuries) and physical evidence which ties the defendant to the scene of crime.

CONCLUSION

Psychological eyewitness research has revealed substantial insight into which factors may influence the accuracy of eyewitness accounts. However, as the latter part of the chapter revealed, there still appear to be at least two important flaws.

First, almost all research has been conducted inside the laboratory using mock witnesses, and almost none of the research has been conducted with witnesses of actual crime. As Yuille (1993) and Ebbesen and Konecni (1997) have argued, it might be too premature to generalize laboratory-based findings to real-life settings, therefore, studies involving real-life eyewitnesses should be encouraged.

Secondly, gaining insight in the accuracy of eyewitness identification decisions is only one part of the job, informing others (police officers, jurors) how to implement these findings in their activities and decisions is important as well. Little attention has been paid, so far, to what police and jurors actually gain from the information they receive from expert witnesses. Some researchers believe that expert witnesses are only a small help to jurors. More attention should be paid to this issue. Particularly relevant are two questions, namely (1) Are experts presently of actual help to jurors? and (2) How can they improve their success in helping jurors? Perhaps the suggestion made earlier to conduct research with 'real' eyewitnesses offers an answer to the latter question. Jurors will probably be more convinced by experts' information when they realize that their knowledge is based upon research with real witnesses instead of upon research in laboratories using mock witnesses.

REFERENCES

Anthony, T., Cooper, C. and Mullin, B. (1992). Cross-racial facial identification: a social cognitive integration. *Personality and Social Psychology Bulletin*, **18**, 296–301.

Bekerian, D.A. and Bowers, J.M. (1983). Eyewitness testimony: were we misled? *Journal of Experimental Psychology: Learning, Memory and Cognition*, **9**, 139–145.

Brehm, S.S. and Kassin, S.M. (1996). *Social Psychology* (Third edition). Boston, MA: Houghton Mifflin Company.

Brigham, J.C. and Cairns, D.L. (1988). The effect of mugshot inspections on eyewitness identification accuracy. *Journal of Applied Social Psychology*, **18**, 1394–1410.

Brigham, J.C. and Pfeifer, J.E. (1994). Evaluating the fairness of lineups. In D.F. Ross, J.D. Read and M.P. Toglia (eds), *Adult Eyewitness Testimony: Current Trends and Developments* (pp. 201–222). New York: Cambridge University Press.

Brigham, J.C. and Wolfskeil, M.P. (1983). Opinions of attorneys and law enforcement personnel on the accuracy of eyewitness identifications. *Law and Human Behavior*, **7**, 337–349.

Chance, J.E. and Goldstein, A.G. (1996). The other-race effect and eyewitness identification. In S.L. Sporer, R.S. Malpass and G. Köhnken (eds), *Psychological Issues in Eyewitness Identification* (pp. 153–176). Mahway, NJ: Lawrence Erlbaum Associates.

Christiaanson, S. (1992). Emotional stress and eyewitness memory: a critical review. *Psychological Bulletin*, **112**, 284–309.

Crombag, H.F.M., Wagenaar, W.A. and Van Koppen, P.J. (1996). Crashing memories and the problem of source monitoring. *Applied Cognitive Psychology*, **10**, 93–104.

Cross, J.F., Cross, J. and Daly, J. (1971). Sex, race, age, and beauty as factors in recognition of faces. *Perception and Psychophysics*, **10**, 393–396.

Cutler, B.L. and Penrod, S.D. (1995). *Mistaken Identification: The Eyewitness, Psychology, and the Law*. New York: Cambridge University Press.

Cutler, B.L., Penrod, S.D. and Dexter, H.R. (1990). Juror sensitivity to eyewitness identification evidence. *Law and Human Behavior*, **14**, 185–191.

Cutler, B.L., Penrod, S.D. and Stuve, T.E. (1988). Juror decision making in eyewitness identification cases. *Law and Human Behavior*, **12**, 41–55.

Deffenbacher, K.A. (1983). Eyewitness accuracy and confidence: can we infer anything about their relationship? *Law and Human Behavior*, **4**, 243–260.

Devine, P.G. and Malpass, R.S. (1985). Orienting strategies in differential face recognition. *Personality and Social Psychology Bulletin*, **11**, 33–40.

Dunning, D. and Stern, L.B. (1994). Distinguishing accurate from inaccurate eyewitness identifications via inquiries about decision processes. *Journal of Personality and Social Psychology*, **67**, 815–835.

Ebbesen, E.B. and Konecni, V.J. (1997). Eyewitness memory research: probative v. prejudical value. *Expert Evidence*, **5**, 2–42.

Egeth, H.E. (1993). What do we not know about eyewitness identification. *American Psychologist*, **48**, 577–580.

Egeth, H.E. and McCloskey, M. (1984). Expert testimony about eyewitness behavior: is it safe and effective? In G.L. Wells and E.F. Loftus (eds), *Eyewitness Testimony: Psychological Perspectives* (pp. 283–303). New York: Cambridge University Press.

Elliot, R. (1993). Expert testimony about eyewitness identification. *Law and Human Behavior*, **17**, 423–437.

Ellis, H.D. (1984). Practical aspects of face memory. In G.L. Wells and E.F. Loftus (eds), *Eyewitness Testimony: Psychological Perspectives* (pp. 12–37). Cambridge, England: Cambridge University Press.

Ellison, K.W. and Buckhout, R. (1981). *Psychology and Criminal Justice*. New York: Harper and Row.

Fischer, R.P. and Cutler, B.L. (1996). The relation between consistency and accuracy of eyewitness testimony. In G. Davies, S. Lloyd-Bostock, M. McMurran and C. Wilson (eds), *Psychology, Law, and Criminal Justice* (pp. 21–28). Berlin, Germany: Walter de Gruyter.

Goldstein, A.G., Chance, J.E. and Schneller, G.R. (1989). Frequency of eyewitness identification in criminal cases. *Bulletin of the Psychonomic Society*, **27**, 71–74.

Gorenstein, G.W. and Ellsworth, P. (1980). Effect of choosing an incorrect photograph on a later identification by an eyewitness. *Journal of Applied Psychology*, **65**, 616–622.

Hosch, H. (1994). Individual differences in personality and eyewitness identification. In D.F. Ross, J.D. Read and M.P. Toglia (eds), *Adult Eyewitness Testimony: Current Trends and Developments* (pp. 328–348). New York: Cambridge University Press.

Kassin, S.M., Ellsworth, P.C. and Smith, V.L. (1989). The 'general acceptance' of psychological research on eyewitness testimony. *American Psychologist*, **44**, 1089–1098.

Kassin, S.M., Ellsworth, P.C. and Smith, V.L. (1994). Deja vu all over again: Elliot's critique of eyewitness experts. *Law and Human Behavior*, **18**, 203–210.

Kiesler, C. (1971). *The Psychology of Commitment*. New York: Academic Press.

Köhnken, G., Malpass, R.S. and Wogalter, M.S. (1996). Forensic applications of lineup research. In S.L. Sporer, R.S. Malpass and G. Köhnken (eds), *Psychological Issues in Eyewitness Identification* (pp. 205–232). Mahway, NJ: Lawrence Erlbaum Associates.

Lavrakas, P.J., Buri, J.R. and Mayzner, M.S. (1976). A perspective on the recognition of other-race faces. *Perception and Psychophysics*, **20**, 475–481.

Leippe, M.R., Manion, A.P. and Romanczyk, A. (1992). Eyewitness persuasion: how and how well do fact finders judge the accuracy of adults' and children's memory reports? *Journal of Personality and Social Psychology*, **63**, 181–197.

Lindsay, D.S. (1994). Memory source monitoring and eyewitness testimony. In D.F. Ross,

J.D. Read and M.P. Toglia (eds), *Adult Eyewitness Testimony: Current Trends and Developments* (pp. 27–55). New York: Cambridge University Press.

Lindsay, R.C.L. (1994a). Biased lineups: where do they come from? In D.F. Ross, J.D. Read and M.P. Toglia (eds), *Adult Eyewitness Testimony: Current Trends and Developments* (pp. 182–200). New York: Cambridge University Press.

Lindsay, R.C.L. (1994b). Expectations of eyewitness performance: jurors' verdicts do not follow from their beliefs. In D.F. Ross, J.D. Read and M.P. Toglia (eds), *Adult Eyewitness Testimony: Current Trends and Developments* (pp. 362–384). New York: Cambridge University Press.

Lindsay, R.C.L., Martin, R. and Webber, L. (1994), Default values in eyewitness descriptions. *Law and Human Behavior*, **18**, 527–541.

Lindsay, R.C.L., Wallbridge, H. and Drenman, D. (1987). Do the clothes make the man? An exploration of the effect of lineup attire on eyewitness identification accuracy. *Canadian Journal of Behavioral Science*, **19**, 463–477.

Lindsay, R.C.L. and Wells, G.L. (1985). Improving eyewitness identifications from lineups: simultaneous versus sequential lineup presentations. *Journal of Applied Psychology*, **70**, 556–564.

Lindsay, R.C.L., Wells, G.L. and Rumpel, C.H. (1981). Can people detect eyewitness-identification accuracy within and across situations? *Journal of Applied Psychology*, **66**, 77–89.

Loftus, E.F. (1974). Reconstructive memory: the incredible witness. *Psychology Today*, **8**, 116–119.

Loftus, E.F. (1976). Unconscious transference in eyewitness identification. *Law and Psychology Review*, **2**, 93–98.

Loftus, E.F. (1979). *Eyewitness Testimony*. Cambridge, MA: Harvard University Press.

Loftus, E.F. (1993). Psychologists in the eyewitness world. *American Psychologist*, **48**, 550–552.

Loftus, E.F., Loftus, G.R. and Messo, J. (1987). Some facts about 'weapon focus'. *Law and Human Behavior*, **11**, 55–62.

Loftus, E.F. and Palmer, J.C. (1974). Reconstructions of automobile destruction: an example of the interaction between language and memory. *Journal of Verbal Learning and Verbal Behavior*, **13**, 585–589.

Luus, C.A.E. and Wells, G.L. (1994). Eyewitness identification performance. In D.F. Ross, J.D. Read and M.P. Toglia (eds), *Adult Eyewitness Testimony: Current Trends and Developments* (pp. 348–361). New York: Cambridge University Press.

Maass, A. and Köhnken, G. (1989). Eyewitness identification: simulating the 'weapon effect'. *Law and Human Behavior*, **13**, 397–408.

Malpass, R.S. (1981). Training in face recognition. In G.H. Davies, H.D. Ellis and J. Shepherd (eds), *Perceiving and Remembering Faces* (pp. 271–285). London, England: Academic Press.

Malpass, R.S. (1996). Enhancing eyewitness memory. In S.L. Sporer, R.S. Malpass and G. Köhnken (eds), *Psychological Issues in Eyewitness Identification* (pp. 177–204). Mahway, NJ: Lawrence Erlbaum Associates.

Malpass, R.S. and Devine, P.G. (1981). Eyewitness identification: lineup instructions and the absence of the offender. *Journal of Applied Psychology*, **66**, 482–489.

Malpass, R.S. and Devine, P.G. (1984). Research on suggestion in lineups and photospreads. In G.L. Wells and E.F. Loftus (eds), *Eyewitness Testimony: Psychological Perspectives* (pp. 64–91). New York: Cambridge University Press.

McCloskey, M. and Egeth, H. (1983). Eyewitness identification: what can a psychologist tell a jury? *American Psychologist*, 38, 550–563.

McCloskey, M. and Zaragoza, M. (1985). Misleading post-event information and memory for events: arguments and evidence against memory impairment hypotheses. *Journal of Experimental Psychology*, **114**, 3–18.

Myers, D.G. (1996). *Social Psychology* (Fifth edition). New York: McGraw-Hill.

Narby, D.J., Cutler, B.L. and Penrod, S.D. (1996). The effects of witness, target, and situational factors on eyewitness identifications. In S.L. Sporer, R.S. Malpass and G. Köhnken (eds), *Psychological Issues in Eyewitness Identification* (pp. 23–52). Mahway, NJ: Lawrence Erlbaum Associates.

Nisbett, R.E. and Ross, L. (1980). *Human Inference: Strategies and Shortcomings of Social Judgment*. Englewood Cliffs, NJ: Prentice-Hall.

Penrod, S.D., Fulero, S.M. and Cutler, B.L. (1995). Expert psychological testimony in the United States: a new playing field? *European Journal of Psychological Assessment*, **11**, 65–72.

Rahaim, G.L. and Brodsky, S.L. (1982). Empirical evidence versus common sense: juror and lawyer knowledge of eyewitness accuracy. *Law and Psychology Review*, 7, 1–15.

Robinson, M.D. and Johnson, J.T. (1996). Recall memory, recognition memory, and the eyewitness confidence–accuracy correlation. *Journal of Applied Psychology*, **81**, 587–594.

Rosenthal, R. (1976). *Experimenter Effects in Behavioral Research*. New York: Irvington Press.

Schooler, J.W., Gerhard, D. and Loftus, E.F. (1986). Qualities of the unreal. *Journal of Experimental Psychology: Learning, Memory and Cognition*, **12**, 171–181.

Shapiro, P.N. and Penrod, S. (1986). Meta-analysis of facial identification studies. *Psychological Bulletin*, **100**, 139–156.

Shepherd, J.W. and Ellis, H.D. (1996). Face recall: methods and problems. In S.L. Sporer, R.S. Malpass and G. Köhnken (eds), *Psychological Issues in Eyewitness Identification* (pp. 87–116). Mahway, NJ: Lawrence Erlbaum Associates.

Sporer, S.L. (1993). Eyewitness identification accuracy, confidence, and decision times in simultaneous and sequential lineups. *Journal of Applied Psychology*, 78, 22–33.

Sporer, S.L. (1994). Decision times and eyewitness identification accuracy in simultaneous and sequential lineups. In D.F. Ross, J.D. Read and M.P. Toglia (eds), *Adult Eyewitness Testimony: Current Trends and Developments* (pp. 300–328). New York: Cambridge University Press.

Sporer, S.L., Köhnken, G. and Malpass, R.S. (1996). Introduction: 2000 years of mistaken identification. In S.L. Sporer, R.S. Malpass and G. Köhnken (eds), *Psychological Issues in Eyewitness Identification* (pp. 1–6). Mahway, NJ: Lawrence Erlbaum Associates.

Sporer, S.L., Penrod, S.D., Read, D. and Cutler, B.L. (1995). Choosing, confidence, and accuracy: a meta-analysis of the confidence–accuracy relation in eyewitness identification studies. *Psychological Bulletin*, **118**, 315–327.

Steblay, N.M. (1992). A meta-analytic review of the weapon focus effect. *Law and Human Behavior*, **16**, 413–424.

Stern, L.B. and Dunning, D. (1994). Distinguishing accurate from inaccurate eyewitness identifications: a reality monitoring approach. In D.F. Ross, J.D. Read and M.P. Toglia (eds), *Adult Eyewitness Testimony: Current Trends and Developments* (pp. 273–299). New York: Cambridge University Press.

Visher, C.A. (1987). Juror decision making: the importance of evidence. *Law and Human Behavior*, **11**, 1–17.

Wagenaar, W.A. (1988). *Identifying Ivan*. Cambridge, MA: Harvard University Press.

Wagenaar, W.A. and Loftus, E.F. (1991). Tien identificaties door ooggetuigen: Logische en procedurele problemen. In P.J. van Koppen and H.F.M. Crombag (eds), *Psychologie voor Juristen* (pp. 175–208). Arnhem, The Netherlands: Gouda Quint.

Wells, G.L. (1978). Applied eyewitness-testimony research: system variables and estimator variables. *Journal of Personality and Social Psychology*, **36**, 1546–1557.

Wells, G.L. (1993). What do we know about eyewitness identification? *American Psychologist*, **48**, 553–571.

Wells, G.L. and Luus, C.A.E. (1990). Police lineups as experiments: social methodology as a framework for properly conducted lineups. *Personality and Social Psychology Bulletin*, **16**, 106–117.

Wells, G.L., Lindsay, R.C.L. and Tousignant, J.P. (1980). Effects of expert psychological advice on human performance in judging the validity of eyewitness testimony. *Law and Human Behavior*, **4**, 275–285.

Wells, G.L., Seelau, E.P., Rydell, S.M. and Luus, C.A.E. (1994). Recommendations for properly conduced lineup identification tasks. In D.F. Ross, J.D. Read and M.P. Toglia (eds), *Adult Eyewitness Testimony: Current Trends and Developments* (pp. 223–244). New York: Cambridge University Press.

Woodhead, M.M., Baddeley, A.D. and Simmonds, D.C. (1979). On training people to recognize faces. *Ergonomics*, **22**, 333–343.

Yarmey, A.D., Yarmey, A.L. and Yarmey, M.J. (1994). Face and voice identifications in showups and lineups. *Applied Cognitive Psychology*, **8**, 453–464.

Yarmey, A.D., Yarmey, M.J. and Yarmey, A.L. (1996). Accuracy of eyewitness identifications in showups and lineups. *Law and Human Behavior*, **20**, 459–477.

Yuille, J.C. (1993). We must study forensic eyewitnesses to know about them. *American Psychologist*, **48**, 572–573.

6 INTERVIEWING SUSPECTS

Aldert Vrij

INTRODUCTION

The purpose of a police interview with a suspect should be to obtain further information about a crime which has been committed. Police officers use a variety of tactics and techniques in order to obtain this information. The first part of this chapter gives an overview of the literature about tactics and techniques used by the police. The implicit assumptions in most of the literature are that suspects are very likely to be guilty, not cooperative during police interviews and prefer to remain silent. As a result, the police officer must *force* the suspect to talk. This part of the literature is summarized in the section 'How to get the suspect to talk'. Only a few publications do not assume that suspects are almost certainly guilty, uncooperative and unwilling to talk. These publications outline techniques on how to *encourage* suspects to talk. This approach is summarized in the section 'How to let the suspect talk'.

After reading the literature one might get the impression that most suspects are uncooperative and unwilling to talk. To what extent is this true? Do suspects usually prefer to remain silent? And what makes them decide to talk? The second part of this chapter addresses these issues.

Research has shown that sometimes suspects do confess to crimes which they have not committed. The final part of this chapter deals with this topic of false confessions.

HOW TO GET THE SUSPECT TO TALK

Inbau, Reid and Buckley's nine-steps approach

Undoubtedly the most influential handbook about interrogation techniques was written by Inbau, Reid and Buckley (1986). They based their book on extensive interrogation experience and advocated a tough approach: that interrogation is meant to break the (guilty) suspect's resistance to tell the truth. They presented a 'nine-steps approach to effective interrogation', which was developed for *interrogating suspects whose guilt seems definite or reasonably certain.* These steps are:

- positive confrontation

- theme development

- handling denials

- overcoming objections

- retain subject's attention

- handling the suspect's mood

- creating an opportunity to confess

- oral confession

- converting an oral confession into a written one.

Step 1 consists of a direct presentation of real or fictional evidence and the suspect's involvement in the crime, e.g. 'Our investigation shows that you are the one who...'. After this accusation there is a brief pause, in which the suspect's behavioural cues are closely observed. The interrogator then repeats the accusation. Suspects who fail to make a denial after this second direct confrontation are considered to be deceptive. **Step 2** deals with theme development and differs for emotional and non-emotional suspects. In the case of emotional suspects the interrogator should try to build up a rapport with them, basically by offering them a moral excuse for having committed the offence. This could be done by telling them that anyone else in the same situation might have committed the same type of offence, minimizing the moral seriousness of the offence, suggesting a more morally acceptable motivation for the offence, condemning others, and so on. Suspects who seem to listen attentively to these suggestions are supposed to be guilty. Kassin and McNall (1991) called this approach the *minimization approach* and described it as a technique in which the police interrogator tries to lull the suspect into a false sense of security by offering sympathy. The following example, given by Inbau *et al.* (1986) illustrates this technique: 'Joe, no woman should be on the street alone at night looking as sexy as she did.... It's too much a temptation for any normal man. If she hadn't gone around dressed like that you wouldn't be in this room now' (p. 108).

Non-emotional suspects perceive an interrogation, according to Inbau *et al.*, as a 'contest of endurance', as 'pitting their willpower against the interrogator's persistence' (pp. 127–128). Effective techniques in this case are seeking an admission of lying about some incidental aspect of the crime (in that case the interrogator can say 'You lied to me once, and you will lie to me again'), trying to let suspects associate themselves with the scene of crime, pointing out that all the evidence leads to his or her guilt and that it is futile to resist telling the truth, and so on. Kassin and McNall (1991) called this the *maximization approach*, a technique in which the interrogator tries to scare and intimidate the suspect into confessing by exaggerating the seriousness of the offence and the magnitude of the charges and, if necessary, by making false claims about evidence (e.g. by staging an eyewitness identification or a rigged lie-detector test, by claiming to have fingerprints or other types of forensic evidence, or by citing admissions that were supposedly made by an accomplice (Kassin, 1997)). **Step 3** deals with handling denials of guilt. Basically, this step involves ending the suspect's repetition or elaboration of the denial (by using the techniques described in step 2), and is, according to Inbau *et al.*, a crucial step, because the more frequently guilty suspects repeat a lie, the harder it becomes for the interrogator to persuade suspects to tell the truth. Generally, innocent suspects, it is contended, will not allow their denials to be cut off, whereas guilty suspects are more likely to allow the interrogator to return to the conversation theme. Innocent suspects are said usually to stick with the denial but guilty suspects usually change their technique by providing a reason why the accusation is wrong, such as 'I couldn't have done that, I don't own a gun'. **Step 4** consists of overcoming these objections. An assumed efficient way of doing this is showing understanding and returning to the conversation theme: 'That may be true, but the important thing is...' (p. 158). Once suspects feel that the objections are ineffective, they are believed usually to become uncertain and begin to show signs of withdrawal. The interrogator should react to this by retaining the suspect's attention (**step 5**). This could be achieved by moving physically closer to the suspect, leaning towards him or her, touching gently, mentioning his or her first name, and maintaining eye contact. **Step 6** deals with handling the suspect's passive mood. When the suspect appears attentive the interrogator should focus the suspect's mind on possible reasons for committing the crime. The interrogator should exhibit signs of understanding and sympathy and should urge the suspect to tell the truth. Finally, the interrogator should attempt to create a remorseful mood, for instance by pointing out the negative consequences the crime has on the victim. **Step 7** is the usage of an alternative question. Suspects are given the opportunity to provide an explanation or excuse for the crime, which makes admissions much easier to achieve. An example is: 'Was this your own idea, or did someone talk you into it?'. Whichever alternative a suspect chooses, the net effect of an expressed choice is an admission. Following the selection of an alternative, **step 8** consists of the development of the initial admission into a detailed confession that discloses the circumstances, motives and details of the crime. Inbau *et al.* advise that the questions asked by the interrogator should be brief, clear and designed so that they can be answered in a few words. Furthermore, they should not contain harsh or emotionally charged terminology (p. 171). **Step 9** deals with converting an oral confession into a written one. This step is important because suspects sometimes deny that they ever made an oral confession.

Inbau *et al.*'s tactics and techniques for *interrogating suspects whose guilt or innocence is doubtful or uncertain* are less well developed. Basically, they consist of observing somebody's verbal and nonverbal responses in order to find out whether the suspect is telling the truth. Verbal responses claimed to be typical of the untruthful suspects include delayed, evasive or vague answers, unusually poor memory, injection of irrelevant matters into conversation, overpoliteness in answering questions and requests for repetition of the interrogator's questions. Assumed behavioural clues to deception include posture changes, self-manipulations, placing hand over mouth or eyes when speaking, and hiding hands (by sitting on them) or hiding feet (by pulling them under the chair).

A social-psychological explanation of the nine-steps approach

Theoretically, the effectiveness of Inbau *et al.*'s nine-steps model is easy to explain with social-psychological theories concerning attitude change (Ajzen and Madden, 1986). Attitudes are an individual's evaluations of particular persons, groups, things, actions or ideas and are important in predicting somebody's behaviour. Simply stated, somebody's attitude towards an attitude-object (for instance confessions) is based upon the perceived positive and negative aspects of that attitude-object. The more positive and/or the less negative aspects are perceived, the more positive the attitude will be; the more negative and/or the less positive aspects are perceived, the more negative the attitude will be. In sum, an attitude will become more positive when positive aspects are emphasized and negative aspects diminished. In police interview terms, a persuasive technique to make a suspect think more positively about confessions (and, as a result, make a person more willing to confess) is, first, eliminating negative consequences of admitting guilt. The major disadvantage of a confession compared to a denial is that a confession will lead to a conviction and a denial possibly not. An effective way of eliminating this negative aspect is by giving the suspect the impression that a denial will also lead to a conviction. This can be done by telling the suspect that there is already enough evidence for a conviction (step 1 of Inbau *et al.*'s approach). Subsequently, emphasize positive aspects of admitting guilt (minimization approach, step 2, step 6) and emphasize negative aspects of not making a confession (maximization approach, step 2) in order to create a more positive attitude towards a confession. The more positive the attitude towards a confession, the more likely it will be that the suspect will finally admit his or her guilt. Of course, by means of such a technique, the willingness to confess will become greater in both guilty and innocent suspects (see also the false confessions section).

Nine concerns with the nine-steps model

Despite its popularity among practitioners in some countries, numerous problems arise with Inbau *et al.*'s nine-steps approach, which are summarized in the following points.

▪ Trickery and deceit (providing fictional evidence, creating a false sense of security, exaggerating the seriousness of the offence and so on) is unlawful in several countries, which implies that the evidence obtained via trickery and deceit cannot be allowed. Moreover, defendants who involuntary confess on the basis of minimization techniques run the risk of being found guilty by a jury because jurors do not disregard confessions elicited by minimization methods. In Kassin and McNall's (1991) experiment, subjects read interrogation transcripts in which an interrogator used minimization methods to elicit a confession. Subjects judged the confession as involuntary but nevertheless proceeded to vote guilty, probably because the interview was noncoercive, a situation, it is believed, in which few truly innocent suspects are likely to confess.

▪ The nine-steps approach of psychologically manipulating people via trickery and deceit may lead to false confessions. The problem of tricks and deceit is that it not only makes guilty suspects more willing to confess but also the innocent ones. There exists no one trick that only makes guilty suspects more willing to talk. As a result, the more successful a trick is in eliciting confessions from guilty suspects, the more likely it is that this trick will result in false confessions as well. Inbau *et al.* acknowledge the problem of false confessions and give the following solution: 'A guideline that an interrogator may use in any case situation where he may be in doubt as to the permissibility of any particular type of trickery and deceit, is to ask himself the following question: "Is what I am about to do, or say, apt to make an innocent person confess?". If the answer is "no", the interrogator should go ahead and do or say what was contemplated. On the other hand, if the answer is "yes", the interrogator should refrain from doing or saying what he had in mind' (p. 217). The problem, not addressed by Inbau *et al.*, of course, is that the police interviewer can never know for sure whether she or he made a correct judgement. The issue of false confessions will be discussed later on in this chapter.

- Trickery and deceit may be considered unethical. Inbau *et al.* themselves do not deny this, but they believe that it is justified when dealing with criminals. They refer to a case of a man who confessed to murdering his sister-in-law and say: 'It involved the taking of a human life by one who abided by no code of fair play toward his fellow human beings. The killer would not have been moved one bit toward a confession by being subjected to a reading or lecture regarding the morality of his conduct. It would have been futile merely to give him a pencil and paper and trust that his conscience would impel him to confess. Something more was required – something that was in its essence an "unethical" practice on the part of the interrogator; but, under the circumstances involved in this case, how else would the murderer's guilt have been established?' (p. xvii). Williamson (1994) pointed out that unethical behaviour may undermine public confidence and social trust in the police (and other agencies).

- Pressing suspects to confess may, on occasion, result in the opposite effects to those intended by the police, that is, suspects who would normally confess may not confess at all when they feel they are being rushed or unfairly treated by the police ('boomerang effect': Gudjonsson, 1994a).

- When suspects feel that they have been induced to confess by unfair means they retain strong feelings of resentment towards the police, even many years afterwards (Gudjonsson, 1992).

- Moston and Stephenson (1992) illustrated that bluffing is a poor interview technique: 'Suppose an interviewer lies and tells a burglar that his fingerprints have been found at the scene of crime. If that burglar had been wearing gloves then he would know this statement is a lie and he will probably view anything the interviewer says from that moment on with either contempt, or at least with a high degree of cynicism' (p. 214).

- Use of trickery and deceit may encourage the police to lie in other contexts as well (Leo, 1992).

- Inbau *et al.* mention nonverbal cues of deception (postural shifts, self-manipulations, placing hand over mouth and eyes) which are not identified as such in the existing nonverbal behaviour and deception literature (see also Chapter 2).

- Inbau *et al.* rely heavily on nonverbal cues to detect deceit, probably more than is justified. As is described in Chapter 2, very few people are skilled at detecting deception on the basis of nonverbal behaviour.

An overview of tactics and techniques used to encourage uncooperative suspects to talk

To our knowledge, the most extensive review of the literature about police techniques is provided by Kalbfleisch (1994). She reviewed 80 books and articles about strategies used by practitioners to encourage uncooperative suspects to talk and distinguished 15 different strategies, which are listed in Table 6.1. Again, many tactics are based upon attitude-change techniques and are related to emphasizing positive aspects of making a confession and negative aspects of not making a confession.

TABLE 6.1 *Typology of 15 strategies used by practitioners to encourage uncooperative suspects to talk*

1. Intimidation
2. Situational futility
3. Discomfort and relief
4. Bluff
5. Gentle prods
6. Minimization
7. Contradiction
8. Altered information
9. A chink in the defence
10. Self-disclosure
11. Point out deception cues
12. Concern
13. Keeping the status quo
14. Direct approach
15. Silence

Intimidation includes accusing the individual of being a liar, laughing at the person, and hammering (a rapid fire of accusations and criticisms). This strategy is used to 'force' a suspect to reveal the truth. Examples of **situational futility** are telling the suspect that the truth will come out one day, presenting the situation as a *fait accompli* (there is nothing that can be done to make a bad situation better and that continued deceit may only make it worse), and pointing out various consequences that will result from continued deception. The 'no-win' situation and the consequences of continuous deceit will persuade a suspect to reveal the truth. **Discomfort and relief** indicate making clear to the suspect that denying and lying only creates discomfort and that, alternatively, 'confession is good for the soul'. **Bluff** means pointing out some fabricated evidence that suggests the person has lied. The absence of any prospects of being found innocent will break down the suspect's resistance. **Gentle prods** means coaxing a suspect to reveal information by encouraging him or her to continue speaking, making requests for further elaboration, and praising the suspect. **Minimizations** are attempts to facilitate any admission of committing the crime, for instance by providing an excuse for an individual's motivation to commit the crime, reducing the significance of an action, blaming someone else or indicating that anyone else would have done the same thing. The strategy is meant to play down the significance of the crime, which will facilitate a confession. **Contradictions** means pointing out any inconsistencies or contradictions in the account of the suspect. If they have not appeared in the initial story, the interrogator may attempt to elicit them by repeating a question and listening for significant differences between the speaker's response to these questions. The occurrence of inconsistencies will make clear to the suspect that there is no way left to escape. **Altered information** refers to asking a suspected deceiver a question containing incorrect information. The correction of this information may signal that a person is actually telling the truth. A **chink in the defence** is a two-stage strategy in which the interviewer first gains a foothold in the account presented by the suspect, and then uses this foothold to implicate a suspect as having deceived (e.g. 'If you lied about one thing, what guarantee do I have that you haven't lied about others?'). **Self-disclosure** means that an interviewer reveals things about him or herself and that, as a result of this self-disclosure, the suspect will, in turn, reveal personal information as well. This strategy relies on the norm of reciprocity. **Pointing out deception cues** refers to telling a person that he or she is exhibiting certain physical manifestations that are indicative of deception, such as sweating or voice change. This strategy does not rely on actual indicators of deception but instead relies on the suspected person's beliefs that these cues are correlated with lying. This tactic will lead suspects to believe that they are not successful liars. **Concern** means showing concern towards the suspect ('You are important to me', 'In some respects I admire you', 'I understand how you feel, I would probably be responding in a similar manner', and so on). This empathy will create an atmosphere that facilitates the suspect to reveal the truth. **Keeping the status quo** refers to telling suspects that their status is in danger if others find out that they have lied, or that it will lower their self-esteem if they continue lying. This strategy thus points out additional costs of hiding the truth and will therefore facilitate revealing the truth. **Direct approach** means that the interviewer tells the suspect straightforwardly to tell the truth. The underlying moral is that telling the truth is a desirable thing. **Silence** refers to maintaining silence after a person has said something. It is suggested that a suspect will find this uncomfortable and will attempt to fill the pause.

It is unknown how often these methods of interrogation are used. Leo (1996) described his own recent observations of 182 live and videotaped interrogations conducted in the state of California and found that detectives used a mean of 5.62 tactics per interrogation, including confronting the suspect with false evidence and minimizing the moral seriousness of the offence.

Concerns with these tactics and techniques

The central argument against these tactics is that they are not part of an 'information-gathering system'. These all have the implicit assumption that the suspect has indeed committed the offence. Moston, Stephenson and Williamson (1990) argue that interviewing merely to gain a confession can be counterproductive as the police then miss opportunities to secure good corroborative evidence. Some of these techniques here do not, however, seem problematic in that they do not induce the suspect to confess. Self-disclosure, for example, may put the suspect at ease and facilitate communication. However, the nature of the self-disclosure is all important as it may be possible to 'lead' the suspect into giving desired responses (as with leading questions).

HOW TO LET THE SUSPECT TALK

Baldwin (1992) described a less offensive approach to the interviewing of suspects. The use of trickery, deceit, and other methods to build up psychological pressure are no longer included, also nonverbal cues to deception are disregarded. Preparation/planning, rapport building and social skills of the interviewer are accentuated instead. Baldwin gives the following description of a good interviewer:

> The best interviewers appear to bring to interviews some natural social skills which they adapt as the circumstances demand...they had generally prepared carefully beforehand, they put the allegations clearly and calmly and made no assumptions about what the response to the allegations should be...they listened to what the suspects had to say, challenging denials that were made when they did not square with the available evidence and without harrying or bullying, retained a firm control of what was taking place. A good interviewer therefore has well-developed communicative and social skills, a calm disposition and temperament, patience, subtlety, and ability to respond quickly and flexibly, legal knowledge and some imagination' (p. 13).

The three major elements in Baldwin's definition: planning, rapport building and social skills, are emphasized more recently by different researchers. Cherryman and Bull (1996) and Williamson (1993) pointed out that preparation and planning are of considerable importance for the quality of investigative interviews. Köhnken (1995) also stressed the importance of planning. He considered planning as a method to reduce cognitive load on the interviewer during the interview, and as a result of this, more cognitive capacity is available for information processing during the interview. Moreover, Köhnken believes that rapport building is an important factor in the success of an interview, because it creates a more relaxing atmosphere in which people are more willing to talk (see also Chapter 8). After listening to 69 taped police interviews with suspects Bull and Cherryman (1996) concluded that differences between 'skilled' and 'not skilled' interviews could be attributed to the communication skills of the interviewer, particularly to showing flexibility, empathy and compassion. Stockdale (1993) mentioned that fairness, an open mind, listening skills and maintaining integrity are important elements of a good interview style.

At first sight, one might say that Baldwin's approach looks 'softer' than Inbau *et al.*'s technique, however, this is not necessarily the case. Also in Baldwin's approach a 'tough' interview is allowed, but the use of tricks is forbidden. It might be that suspects who decided not to talk during the interview will remain silent without the use of tricks. If this is true, Baldwin's approach will not be successful in interviewing uncooperative suspects. Whether this is a real disadvantage depends, of course, on the percentage of suspects that is unwilling to talk during police interviews: the higher this percentage is, the bigger the disadvantage will be. We will return to this issue later in this chapter.

Differences between Inbau *et al.* and Baldwin

Inbau's technique is aimed to impress the suspect and meant to break down the resistance of the suspect. In Baldwin's view, interviewing is essentially an information-gathering exercise and certain skills are needed to elicit relevant and accurate information. In fact,

Baldwin's police interviews do not differ substantially from interviews in other contexts, such as interviews with patients or selection interviews (Buckwalter, 1980; Stephenson, 1992). Patients may sometimes lie to their doctors about their symptoms or behaviour, and candidates for a job may have an incentive to be economical with the truth. In all these situations, the interviewer must try to find out the truth and must create an atmosphere in which the interviewee is willing to talk. Needless to say, Inbau's interrogation technique differs strongly from doctor–patient interviews and job interviews!

The different styles are, at least partly, influenced by cultural differences: Inbau *et al.* are Americans and Baldwin is British. Some tactics, apparently used in the USA (such as trickery and deceit) are not allowed in England and Wales since the introduction of the Police and Criminal Evidence Act (PACE) in 1986 (Baldwin, 1993; Moston and Stephenson, 1993b), the use of these tactics will make a confession inadmissible.[1] PACE included new legislation governing the way in which suspects were arrested, detained and interviewed by police officers. The Act was intended to provide safeguards for suspects (and also for police officers). For example a special code ensures that suspects are not subjected to undue police pressure, police tricks or oppression (Moston and Stephenson, 1993a). And, in case of vulnerable suspects, an independent and responsible third party (the 'appropriate adult', see below) has to be called in by the police to provide special assistance to the suspect during the police interview (though some appropriate adults seem unsure of their role (Pearse and Gudjonsson, 1996c)). Moreover, PACE prescribes that all police interviews with suspects in police stations are audiotaped. These audiotapes are accessible to solicitors, judges and juries, as a result, the use of unacceptable tactics are, in principle, easy to check.[2]

Gudjonsson (1992) believes that the British outcry for, and subsequent legislation of, less oppressive police investigative interview techniques is heavily influenced by cases such as 'The Guildford Four' and 'The Birmingham Six', well-known cases of British miscarriages of justice (both cases will be discussed in the false confessions part of this chapter).

Despite the fact that information-gathering interviews are advocated in England and Wales, research shows that such interview techniques are still relatively rare. The main objective in police interviews seems to be obtaining a confession. McConville and Hodgson (1993) judged 157 interviews with suspects and found that in 83 per cent of the interviews the objective of the police seemed to secure a confession from the suspect. After examining 1067 cases, Moston, Stephenson, and Williamson (1992) concluded that in 80 per cent of these cases the interviewer's main goal was to obtain a confession from the suspect. A possible explanation is that in England and Wales confession evidence is considered prime evidence and is sufficient to gain conviction even in the absence of any other corroborating evidence. Stephenson (1992) gives three reasons why police officers seek confessions. First, confessions save time that might otherwise be spent obtaining evidence by alternative and tedious means. Secondly, suspects who confess are much more likely to plead guilty. Thirdly, many prosecutions where a confession was made (about 25 per cent according to Baldwin and McConville (1980)) would have been unlikely to succeed had the confession not been given in evidence. Mortimer (1994) mentioned a fourth reason: confessions are a mark of personal and professional prowess if obtained in the face of resistance from the suspect. Finally, Underwager and Wakefield (1992) pointed out that confessions have a compelling influence on jurors and they are more likely to convict on the basis of a confession than anything else, including eyewitness identification. In many other European countries, confessions are not considered prime evidence, hence, further evidence is needed to solve the case. It would be interesting to see whether this influences police interview techniques. It is possible that in many continental European countries more information-gathering interviews take place in order to obtain more information about the crime. Unfortunately, reliable data about police interview styles in continental Europe are not available, because police interviews are usually not audiotaped or videotaped in these countries.

HOW MANY SUSPECTS CONFESS AND WHY?

Percentage of suspects that confess

Few recent studies have been published which provide estimates of confessions occurring at police stations during police interviews. However, these (all British) provide almost similar confession rates. Baldwin (1993) found that 39 per cent of suspects made full confessions and 16 per cent made partial admissions. Moston, Stephenson, and Williamson (1992) found that 42 per cent of suspects made full confessions and a further 13 per cent made some form of 'damaging statement' (1992, p. 35). Pearse and Gudjonsson (1996b) found that 58 per cent made a confession or admission. Softley (1980) found that 48 per cent of suspects made full confessions and 13 per cent made partial admissions. The comparison between the latter study and the three other studies is interesting because Softley's study was conducted before PACE was introduced in 1986. Apparently, the 'softening' of the interview technique, the result of PACE, did not result in a strong decrease in confessions. This is further supported by findings of Irving and McKenzie (1989). They concluded that, while the number of manipulative and persuasive tactics has declined in England and Wales as a result of PACE, the number of admissions remained relatively constant at 62 per cent in 1979 and 65 per cent in 1986. However, it is not possible to conclude on the basis of these findings that manipulative tactics 'do not work'. McConville (1992), for instance, pointed out that PACE resulted in 'off-the-record interviews' in which pressure still occurs. He gave examples of 'off-the-record' exchanges between the police and suspects (interviews which are not audiotaped and not registered) in which unallowed coercion (threats) or unallowed deals (promises) took place. These off-the-record interviews were held before the formal, audiotaped interviews, and led to confessions during the formal audiotaped interviews. This practice led McConville to conclude that 'tape recorders provide no protection for suspects against police wrongdoing' (p. 962). Also Gudjonsson (1995) and Moston and Stephenson (1993a,b) acknowledge that pressure on suspects outside the formal interview setting is a serious problem in England and Wales.

Reasons for making a confession

Moston, Stephenson and Williamson (1992) examined a random sample of 1067 interviews conducted in England and tried to find out which factors lead to a confession. They proposed four main sets of factors that may influence confessions, namely background characteristics of the suspect (age, sex, criminal history), characteristics of the offence (type of offence, offence severity), contextual characteristics (strength of evidence and legal advice) and the interviewer's questioning techniques. Their findings revealed that police interviewing techniques played a minor role in influencing confessions, that is, suspects mainly stuck to their starting position (whether admission, denial, or somewhere in between), there were only a few cases in which suspects were persuaded to deviate from their initial response to police questioning. Moreover, interviewers appeared to be very nervous, often more nervous than the suspects. Finally, police interviewing skills were, as Moston (1996) recently described, 'almost non-existent' (p. 92).[3] Moston et al.'s study revealed that there was only a limited degree of flexibility on the part of interviewers. In a large number of cases a single strategy was repeatedly used (for example listing the evidence against the suspect), even though it clearly failed to influence the suspect. Among the factors that influenced the tendency to admit offences were strength of evidence, legal advice, and severity of the offence. When there was strong evidence, confessions were more likely; with increasing offence severity, suspects were less likely to reply to an accusation, preferring instead to use their right to silence (i.e. to say nothing); and admissions were less likely when the suspect received legal advice (usually they were advised to remain silent).

Gudjonsson and Petursson (1991) examined why 74 offenders in Iceland had made a confession. The reasons were classified into three categories: internal pressure (the need to get it 'off the chest'), external pressure (police behaviour, custodial factors, protecting others) and proof (both real or fabricated evidence). They found that the majority of the offenders (55 per cent) confessed because they thought the police would eventually prove their involvement in the crime, 44 per cent confessed as a result of internal pressure and 15 per cent as a result of external pressure. Sigurdson and Gudjonsson's (1994) study, in which 359 Icelandic sentenced prisoners participated, confirmed that their perception of the evidence against them is the most important reason why they confessed.

Baldwin (1993) examined 600 taped police interviews of suspects in England and came to the following three conclusions. In the majority of these cases (80 per cent) suspects were thoroughly cooperative and answered police questions of any significance, a finding that is, according to Baldwin, usually overlooked in popular police culture, where attention is usually paid to the awkward individuals. Baldwin gave an example of a suspect who gave full details of a very serious assault on his girlfriend. The suspect said he was 'insane with jealousy' and was completely open about what happened. He was more concerned about the future of the relationship with his girlfriend than the legal consequences of the assault. Secondly, the great majority of suspects (90 per cent) stuck to their starting position – whether admission, denial, or somewhere in between – regardless of how the interview was conducted. Only two per cent denied at first, but subsequently admitted part of the allegation, four per cent remained denying but showed some shifting of position and three per cent showed a complete change of story through the course of the interview resulting in a confession. Hence, the interview technique only had a very minor impact on confession rates. Thirdly, similar to Moston (1996), Baldwin criticized the communication skills of the interviewers. Most attempts to build up a rapport were highly artificial. Some interviewers tried an approach on the lines of 'Tell me something about yourself' – an invitation that usually met with confusion and unease. Moreover, most officers appeared nervous, ill at ease, and lacking in confidence throughout the interview, and several interview styles were questionable and unprofessional (e.g. misleading the suspect, interrupting the suspect, terminating the interview as quickly as possible after an admission, and losing control of an interview, i.e., overreacting to provocations of the suspects).

Pearse and Gudjonsson (1996b) analysed 161 English police interviews with regard to the type of techniques employed and suspects' reactions. They found further evidence to support the conclusions drawn by authors in previous studies. The suspects were generally cooperative, in only two per cent of the cases did suspects react in an angry or suspicious manner, the vast majority of reactions were classified as polite (98 per cent), with 83 per cent as generally compliant, and 62 per cent as giving full answers. The interview techniques did not have much impact on the decisions of suspects, in only a few instances (three per cent) were suspects persuaded to deviate from their original response to police questioning. The interview techniques were rather poor, the officers appeared to have a somewhat limited repertoire of interview techniques. The authors speculate that officers may be unsure as to what is acceptable behaviour in the wake of new legislation (PACE).

In short, the English studies presented here indicate that police interview techniques have little influence on suspects' decisions whether or not to confess. These outcomes led Moston *et al.* (1992) to conclude that police officers probably think that suspects make admissions because of their skilled techniques, but that the reality is quite different. It is the suspects' perception of evidence which determines their willingness to confess.

One might argue that most of the studies presented were based upon English audiotapes, in which tactics such as trickery, deceit and other ways to exert psychological pressure do not occur. It is possible that this lack of tactics reduces the possibility that police officers will get uncooperative suspects to talk. Perhaps, if these tactics were used, police interview techniques would be more successful in breaking the resistance of guilty suspects who initially do not want to cooperate. We have no doubt that many practitioners will agree with this suggestion! However, as far as we know, the effectiveness of the variety of interview strategies, which are outlined in this chapter, has never been examined in any scientific study. Keeping in mind that suspects seem to be sensitive to perceived evidence, one might expect that tricks which are related to evidence will persuade a suspect to talk, such as presenting fictional evidence, pointing out to the suspect that 'there is already enough evidence for a conviction' and so on. The importance of evidence-related tricks in influencing suspects may also become clear when looking at the attitude-change model which was described previously. The major disadvantage of making a confession is the subsequent conviction. As soon as suspects believe that there is no possibility anymore to escape conviction (the result of real or fabricated evidence), this negative aspect of making a confession is eliminated, and a more positive attitude towards a confession is likely. As mentioned before, the use of tricks does not only make guilty suspects more cooperative, it may result in false confessions from innocent suspects as well, as will be shown in the next part of this chapter.

FALSE CONFESSIONS

The Guildford Four (Gudjonsson, 1992)

On 5 October 1974, members of the Irish Republican Army (IRA) planted, without giving a warning, bombs in The Horse and Groom and the Seven Stars, two public houses in Guildford (England). The bomb in the Horse and Groom exploded at about 8.50 p.m. Five people were killed and another 57 were injured. At 9.25 p.m., there was a massive explosion at the Seven Stars, which did not cause casualties among customers because the pub had been evacuated after the Horse and Groom bombing.

On 28 November 1974, Paul Hill, an Irishman, was arrested in Southampton. He was taken to Guildford Police Station and interviewed about the Guildford bombings. Within 24 hours he had made a written confession about his involvement in the Guildford bombings and had spoken about the involvement of his friend, Gerry Conlon. Mr Conlon was arrested in Belfast on 30 November and brought to Guildford for questioning. He confessed within two days and implicated a number of people, including Paddy Armstrong and Carole Richardson (Armstrong's 17-year-old girlfriend). They were both arrested on 3 December 1974, and made serious self-incriminating admissions within 48 hours.

On 16 September 1975 the trial of the Guildford Four opened and all four were charged with the Guildford bombings. The prosecution relied almost exclusively on the confessions (there was some circumstantial evidence produced in the case of Armstrong), there was no identification or forensic evidence ever produced to link them with the bombings. The Four maintained that the confessions were not obtained voluntarily but were the result of police pressure and coercion. The police denied any impropriety during the interviews. During the trial it was revealed that there were over 140 inconsistencies and inaccuracies between the statements of the four defendants. For example, Richardson had told that she was responsible for both bombings, the police's own time plans, however, showed that the people who bombed the Horse and Groom could never have planted the bomb in the Seven Stars. She further claimed to have *thrown* a bomb, which never happened. The prosecution argued that the inconsistencies were made by the defendants on purpose in order to confuse the police. The truth was that the inaccuracies were caused by a lack of knowledge among the defendants because they were in no way involved.

During the trial Richardson gave the strongest alibi evidence. It was clearly established that she was in south west London between 7.30 and 8.30 p.m. attending a concert. A photograph of her at the concert was available. The prosecution maintained that she could have travelled from south London to Guildford (40 miles), planted the bomb and returning to London within 50 minutes. A police driver claimed to have made the journey in about 45 minutes.

The jury took 27 hours to reach their unanimous verdict of 'guilty'. All four were sentenced to life imprisonment. At the end of October 1975, they began to serve their life sentences. In 1977 two other defendants admitted to the Guildford bombings and stated that, to their knowledge, the Guildford Four were innocent. Also in 1977, Paddy Armstrong was interviewed in prison by Professor Haward, a professor in clinical psychology. Professor Haward concluded that Armstrong had falsely confessed because of immense anxiety and fear of the police. This new evidence was presented at an appeal hearing in October 1977, but this appeal failed.

In 1989 the case was to be referred back to the Court of Appeal. The Avon and Somerset Police, who were appointed by the Home Secretary in 1987 to look at the confessions of the Guildford Four, discovered that crucial evidence concerning the confessions of Hill and Armstrong had been fabricated. Moreover, there were questions over the mental state of Carole Richardson at the time of her interrogation in 1974. Miss Richardson was arrested on 3 December 1974 and made a total of four statements to the police, dated 4, 5, 6 and 9 December 1974. She says she confessed falsely mainly out of fear. She found the police pressure unbearable (for days she was not allowed to notify anybody of her arrest and was not allowed to see a solicitor until 11 December) and decided to go along with the interviewer, all that she wanted was to be left alone. After several days in police custody, Miss Richardson began to believe that she had been involved in the Guildford bombings, due to the police officers' confidence in her involvement and the fact that she could not recall precisely where she had been on 5 October 1974. The convictions were quashed by the Court of Appeal. The Guildford Four were released from prison on 19 October 1989, after serving more than 15 years in prison for crimes they did not commit.

The Birmingham Six

On 21 November 1974, two public houses in Birmingham (England) were bombed by the IRA killing 21 people. Later that night five Irishmen were arrested as they were boarding a ferry to Ireland. They were subjected to a Greiss test, which was at that time thought to be a foolproof way of detecting nitroglycerine, a substance commonly found on people's hands after handling explosives. Nitroglycerine was supposedly found on the hands of two of the five men. After the test, the five men were subjected to interrogations in which three men made and signed a confession. One of these five men told the police that a sixth man was involved as well. This man was arrested at his home, and signed a confession after being interviewed by the police. In June 1975, the six men were charged with murder. Their trial lasted 45 days. The evidence against the six men consisted of evidence of the Greiss test and the written confessions of four of the men. The defence claimed that the confessions were given involuntarily and had been beaten out of the defendants. All six defendants were convicted and sentenced to life imprisonment.

In October 1985 the validity of the Greiss test was severely challenged. Further tests showed that a number of substances will give a positive reaction on a Greiss test, including a substance that is used in playing cards. The five men had been playing cards shortly before their arrest. Mullin (1989) claimed to have traced and interviewed three of the men who were responsible for the Birmingham bombings. They made it clear to him that none of the convicted men had been involved in any way in the bombings. The information that these people gave suggested insightful knowledge about the explosions. In October 1986 an ex-policeman told that he had been on night duty at the police station during the two nights that the Birmingham Six were held there. He gave accounts of ill-treatment of the men during their custody, including a dog handler encouraging a dog to bark throughout the night in an attempt to keep the six awake.

In August 1990 the case was referred back to the Court of Appeal. The Greiss test was totally criticized and it was revealed that the police had fabricated documentary evidence against the six men. The convictions of the six men were quashed and the men were released from prison on 14 March 1991, after being in prison for 17 years, convicted for murders they had not committed.

How often do false confessions occur?

The Guildford Four and Birmingham Six cases make clear that false confessions do occur. How often false confessions occur is unknown. Kassin (1997) reported that estimates range from 35 per year to 600 per year in the USA alone. Kassin (1997), Leo (1996) and Underwager and Wakefield (1992) state that enough cases have been documented to suggest that a concern over the risk of false confessions is justified. The problem is that police officers themselves are generally reluctant to accept that false confessions occur (Gudjonsson, 1992; McConville, 1992; Perske, 1994), as the following quote of (an American) police interviewer shows: 'There is a principle in interrogation. A person will not admit to something they haven't done, short of torture or extreme duress. No matter how long you are grilled, no matter how much you are yelled at, you are not going to admit to something you have not done' (Perske, p. 159). Unfortunately, this police officer was involved in interviewing Johnny Lee Wilson, a mentally disabled man who falsely confessed to have murdered a woman. Perske (1994), who had access to the audiotapes of that interrogation, gives a detailed description of this case. The interrogation was tough, Wilson initially denied but confessed later on. The police themselves helped Wilson to make his confession. For example, Wilson was asked what he used to bind the victim's ankles. 'I'm thinking...Handcuffs, I think' Wilson said. 'No. No. Wrong guess,' responded the officer. 'The victim's ankles had been bound with duct tape' (pp. 157–158). A couple of years later Wilson explained why he confessed. He became frightened when the officers grabbed his face and turned it toward them. 'A cop said: "Well if you confess...we can all go home". At that point I thought he meant me too' (p. 158).

Inbau *et al.* (1986) acknowledge the danger of false confessions. In their view three interview techniques lead to false confessions, namely inflicting physical force, a threat of physical harm and an interrogator's promise to a suspect that if he confesses he will go free or receive only a lenient penalty. These techniques should therefore never be used. They do not believe that their nine-steps approach will ever lead to false confessions, a statement described by Gudjonsson (1992) as 'naïve' (p. 323).

Why do false confessions occur?

The confession literature suggests three psychologically distinct types of false confession, namely voluntary false confessions, coerced-compliant false confessions and coerced-internalized false confessions (Gudjonsson, 1992; Kassin, 1997; Kassin and Wrightsman, 1985; Stephenson, 1992).

Voluntary false confessions

Voluntary false confessions are false confessions which are given without any external pressure from the police. Commonly people making these go voluntarily to the police station and inform the police that they have committed a crime they have seen on television or they have read about in the newspaper. There are several reasons why people give voluntary false confessions. First, people may falsely confess because of a 'morbid desire for notoriety', that is a pathological need to become infamous and to enhance self-esteem, even if it means the prospect of imprisonment. For example Huff, Rattner and Sagarin (1986) mentioned a case in which a man confessed to murder in order to impress his girlfriend. Secondly, people may falsely confess in an attempt to relieve guilt. Gudjonsson (1992) stated that this type of false confession is most likely in depressive people and he described the case of a depressive man who had a disturbed and turbulent childhood. As a result he tended to confess to murders which had taken place in a part of the country where he had been at some point in his life. Thirdly, people may falsely confess because they are unable to distinguish facts from fantasy. According to Gudjonsson (1992) schizophrenic people especially are prone to this type of confession. He described the case of a schizophrenic woman who heard conversation voices in a hospital ward about a murdered woman, and who subsequently thought that she was the murderer. Fourthly, people may falsely confess because they want to protect the real criminal. Fifthly, people may confess because they see no possible way of proving their innocence (after failing a polygraph test, after being accused by a psychological expert as being guilty) and confess in order to get a reduced punishment. Finally, suspects may confess to hide other, non-criminal facts. Huff *et al.* (1986) mentioned a case of an adulterous woman who falsely confessed to a murder in an attempt to hide the fact that she was with her secret lover at the time of the murder!

Coerced-compliant false confessions

Coerced-compliant false confessions result from the pressures of the interview process. People confess in order to escape from the stressful and intolerable interviews. Paddy Armstrong (one of the Guildford Four) made such a confession. The risk police officers run in obtaining false confessions due to police pressure and police tricks is at least acknowledged in England and Wales, which led to the PACE legislation (a safeguard for suspects and officers).

Coerced-internalized false confessions

Coerced-internalized false confessions occur when people come to believe, during police interviewing, that they have committed the crime they are accused of even though they have no actual memory of having committed the crime. Carole Richardson (one of the Guildford Four) reported such an experience. Moreover, Ofshe (1989) gives the following detailed description of a case in which a man, Tom Sawyer, finally believed he committed a crime which he, in fact, never had committed. Tom Sawyer's next-door neighbour was murdered by manual strangulation. The police became suspicious of Sawyer solely because he seemed to them to be nervous when they spoke with him during routine interviews of the murdered woman's neighbours. They were unaware of the fact that he suffered from severe social anxiety. His anxiety attacks caused him to blush a deep red and to sweat in response to the simplest social interaction. The detectives decided to lure Mr Sawyer to the police station in an attempt to let him make some form of admission. In response to questions about his general background, Mr Sawyer discussed both his social anxiety and the fact that he had been an alcoholic. In trying to engage Mr Sawyer in conversation about the crime, the detectives asked him to help them create a scenario of how the murder might have happened. Mr Sawyer, who loved to watch detective shows on television, was eager to help and joined in. The police let Mr Sawyer explain several scenarios and accused him at the end of having committed the murder. The police claimed that Mr Sawyer knew nine facts that only the killer could have known. Analysis of the interrogation transcripts afterwards showed that all the crucial information was introduced into the interrogation by the police. Following the accusation, Mr Sawyer strongly denied his guilt. The police obtained fingerprint and hair samples of Mr Sawyer and suggested a polygraph examination. Mr Sawyer believed that the polygraph examination would prove his innocence and agreed with the examination. After the test, the examiner told Mr Sawyer that the test proved he was lying (subsequent rescoring of the test by a polygraph expert later on revealed that the test outcome was inconclusive). Once told that the polygraph showed him to be lying, Mr Sawyer's confidence began to erode. He was no longer able to express firm denials of guilt, he could only say that he still didn't believe he had done it. His main defence against the police's demands to confess was his lack of memory of having committed the crime. The police replied by saying that he was blocking out his memory of the crime, that he had a black-out, just as he often had when he had been drinking. Mr Sawyer was vulnerable to this argument but was puzzled as to how, if he had committed the crime, he could have done so without memory. He introduced the possibility that perhaps because he had used an alcohol-based aftershave lotion he might have started to drink and subsequently blacked-out. At this point, Mr Sawyer still refused to fully accept that he had committed the crime and had hoped that the other tests (fingerprints and hair test) would reveal his innocence. The detectives decided to lie to him and told him that his hair samples matched hairs found on the victim's body. With receipt of this information, Mr Sawyer's resistance collapsed, he agreed that 'all the evidence was in' and that he must have committed the crime. During the next period of the interrogation the detectives wanted to get an accurate description of the crime, which was impossible for Mr Sawyer because he did not commit the crime. Ofshe describes this part of the interrogation as a 'guessing game' in which Mr Sawyer's story was continually shaped to conform to the facts the detectives knew or thought to know. For example, the police believed that the victim had been sexually assaulted. Mr Sawyer confessed, encouraged by the police detectives, to have raped the victim. When the medical examiner's report was received, no evidence of sexual assault was indicated.

The term 'internalized', by the way, is somewhat confusing because in social-psychological terms, internalized ideas persist over a period of time. This, however, is not necessarily the case in internalized false confessions. It is possible that suspects who make internalized false confessions in police interviews only believe during the police interview that they have committed the crime.

How to prevent false confessions

Several ways of preventing false confessions can be suggested.

■ Both coerced-compliant and coerced-internalized confessions are the result of police pressure and police tricks during interviews. Hence, an obvious way to prevent false confessions is to reduce such pressure. This could be established by utilizing more information-gathering techniques rather than techniques used to obtain confessions. Techniques meant to obtain confessions are, however, likely to occur because police officers usually assume guilt (Baldwin, 1993) and, as mentioned earlier, obtaining a confession has benefits for police officers.

■ It might be fruitful to audiotape all interviews. As we saw before, strong coercion seldomly occurs on audiotaped recordings. This may decrease the likelihood of false confessions. Essential, of course, is that in such a situation 'off-the-record interviews' do not take place.

Kassin (1997) reported that one-third of all large police and sheriffs' departments in the USA now videotape at least some interrogations. He also mentioned a potential danger of videotaping suspects, namely the point-of-view bias. Sometimes, the camera is stationed behind the police detective and focuses solely on the suspect. Research (Lassiter and Irvine, 1986) has shown that this camera position influences the judgements people make about the interview. In their study, Lassiter and Irvine taped mocked police interviews from different angles, so that the suspect, the police detective or both were visible to mock jurors. The result was that those who saw only the suspect judged the situation as less coercive than did those focused on the police detective: directing the visual attention toward the accused suspect led mock jurors to underestimate the amount of pressure actually exerted by the 'hidden' detective. Therefore, videotaped interrogations should provide a complete record of the police–suspect interrogation.

■ Gudjonsson (1992) suggested analysing the language structure used by false confessors and genuine confessors during interrogations to find out whether these two types of confessions linguistically differ from each other. Such analyses has not yet taken place.

■ Suspects are likely to retract or withdraw their coerced-compliant and coerced-internalized false confessions as soon as the immediate pressures are over (Kassin and Wrightsman, 1985). Withdrawn confessions should therefore be treated with prudence because they may indicate false confessions.

- Compare the details given in confessions with the facts known by the police. Inconsistencies may indicate false confessions.

- Identify individuals who are vulnerable or 'at risk', that is who are more likely to give false confessions. PACE introduced the concept of 'appropriate adult', an independent and responsible third party, called in by the police to provide special assistance to a vulnerable suspect during a police interview. Pearse and Gudjonsson (1996c) describe the purpose of the presence of an appropriate adult as follows: 'To advise the person being questioned and to observe whether or not the interview is being conducted properly and fairly, and... to facilitate communication with the person being interviewed' (p. 102). Police practice has shown that it is not easy to make this concept effective, partly because it is still not clear what the exact role of the appropriate adult is in a police interview and partly because there are instances where their role tends to be devalued. A situation bitterly encapsulated by one police officer's explanation of a social worker's expected role: 'You are wallpaper, pal' (quoted by Pearse and Gudjonsson, 1996a, p. 4). For this and other reasons Pearse and Gudjonsson (1997) recently suggested utilizing trained and experienced legal advisers instead of appropriate adults. This can be established by giving solicitors additional training in the recognition and management of mentally disordered suspects. Another alternative is to provide police officers with training in how to interview vulnerable people to maximize the relevance, completeness and reliability of the information obtained (Bull, 1995).

Gudjonsson's research deals with identifying people at risk. He claims that people with mental disorders (schizophrenia, depression, learning disabilities), abnormal mental state (phobias, high anxiety or recent bereavement), and personality characteristics such as suggestibility and compliance are more likely to give unreliable confessions (Gudjonsson, 1994b).

Gudjonnson (1984, 1987, 1989) developed scales to measure interrogation suggestibility and compliance. According to Gudjonsson (1992), in the case of suggestibility there is personal acceptance of the proposition offered by the interrogator, whereas a compliant response does not require personal acceptance of the proposition; people may disagree with the proposition or request made, but they nevertheless react in a compliant way. He claims that his scales are highly accurate in identifying interrogative suggestibility and compliance. For example, the four people who confessed in the Birmingham Six case had higher scores on the suggestibility and compliance scales than the two people who did not confess. However, as Gudjonsson (1992, p. 312) admits, a suspect's mood (anger, for example) influences their susceptibility to suggestion. This creates a problem. The suspect's mood during the interview that led to a confession can differ from his or her mood during completion of the test, leading to different scores of susceptibility to suggestion between the two occasions (Vrij, 1995). The problem, however, is that a proper identification of these people at risk is, even by trained clinicians, a very difficult task (Gudjonsson, 1993; Pearse, 1995). This problem is partly caused by the fact that at this moment no operational definition exists in relevant UK laws about what exactly constitutes 'mental disorder' (Pearse and Gudjonsson, 1996c).

■ Ask suspects about their own vulnerability. Clare and Gudjonsson (1992) asked suspects, who had already been independently established as vulnerable or not, whether they found themselves vulnerable. Results showed that 80 per cent of the suspects classified themselves correctly, that is, identified themselves as vulnerable. (Unfortunately, they didn't ask suspects who were objectively not vulnerable to estimate their own vulnerability. It is therefore unknown to what extent these suspects find themselves vulnerable.)

CONCLUSION

This chapter reveals a dilemma. Some people (particularly Inbau and colleagues) claim that they have developed a highly effective interview technique, that is, a technique that makes even the most uncooperative suspect likely to confess to a crime he or she has committed. Unfortunately, the technique has several disadvantages. One of these disadvantages is that the interview methods are unethical. Inbau *et al.* acknowledge this problem but state that the serious crimes, committed by these suspects, justify these unethical police methods. Probably, both arguments pro and contra this point of view are imaginable. A second problem is that not all suspects interviewed by the police are guilty, some are innocent, and exposing innocent suspects to trickery and deceit may result in false confessions. In our view, interview methods which may easily cause false confessions are never justifiable. An alternative approach, in which trickery and deceit are no longer allowed, is advocated in England and Wales. The disadvantage of this approach is that it seems to be unsuccessful in persuading uncooperative suspects to confess. Despite this problem we are in favour of the latter approach for two reasons. First, research has indicated that the majority of suspects are willing to cooperate during police interviews and therefore the use of trickery and deceit is redundant in the vast majority of police interviews. Secondly, when trickery and deceit are not allowed thus ensuring the suspect can no longer be forced to confess, the police have no other alternative than finding other sorts of evidence in order to solve the case. This is a major advantage, because the presence of such evidence excludes the possibility of false confessions. Detectives should bear in mind that although one reason why suspects are uncooperative may be that they are not willing to admit the crime they have committed, an alternative reason may be that they are innocent!

The issue of false confessions makes clear that even in cases in which suspects give voluntary confessions searching for evidence remains necessary as research has revealed that some innocent suspects make voluntary false confessions.

NOTES

1. We don't suggest that all Americans are in favour of Inbau *et al.*'s approach. On the contrary, American authors such as Kassin, Leo and Ofshe criticize this approach.
2. However, Pearse and Gudjonsson (1996b) pointed out that in the first decade after the introduction of PACE only a handful of tapes have actually been listened to in courts so far, the tapes are mostly used for research! Moreover, as will be mentioned later,

audiotaping interviews has resulted in 'off-the-record' interviews in which the use of tricks still occurs.
3. McGurk, Carr and McGurk (1993) claim that police interviewing skills in England and Wales have increased in recent years as a result of training courses.

REFERENCES

Ajzen, I. and Madden, T.J. (1986). Prediction of goal-directed behavior: attitudes, intentions, and perceived behavioral control. *Journal of Experimental Social Psychology*, **22**, 453–474.

Baldwin, J. (1992). Videotaping of police interviews with suspects: an evaluation. *Police Research Series*, Paper No. 1. London, England: Home Office.

Baldwin, J. (1993). Police interview techniques. *British Journal of Criminology*, **33**, 325–352.

Baldwin, J. and McConville, M. (1980). Confessions in Crown Court trials. The Royal Commission on Criminal Procedure, Research Study No. 5. London, England: HMSO.

Buckwalter, A. (1980). *Interviews and Interrogations*. London, England: Butterworth.

Bull, R. (1995). Interviewing people with communication difficulties. In R. Bull and D. Carson (eds), *Handbook of Psychology in Legal Contexts*. Chichester, England: Wiley.

Bull, R. and Cherryman, J. (1996). Helping to identify skill gaps in specialist investigative interviewing: enhancement of professional skills. London, England: Home Office Police Department.

Cherryman, J. and Bull, R. (1996). Investigative interviewing. In F. Leishman, B. Loveday and S.P. Savage (eds), *Core Issues in Policing* (pp. 147–159). London, England: Longman.

Clare, I.C.H. and Gudjonsson, G.H. (1992). Devising and piloting an experimental version of the 'Notice to detained persons'. The Royal Commission on Criminal Justice, Research Study No. 7. London, England: HMSO.

Gudjonsson, G.H. (1984). A new scale of interrogative suggestibility. *Personality and Individual Differences*, **5**, 303–314.

Gudjonsson, G.H. (1987). A parallel form of the Gudjonsson Suggestibility Scale. *British Journal of Clinical Psychology*, **26**, 215–221.

Gudjonsson, G.H. (1989). Compliance in an interrogation situation: a new scale. *Personality and Individual Differences*, **10**, 535–540.

Gudjonsson, G.H. (1992). *The Psychology of Interrogations, Confessions and Testimony*. Chichester, England: Wiley.

Gudjonsson, G.H. (1993). Confession evidence, psychological vulnerability and expert testimony. *Journal of Community and Applied Social Psychology*, **3**, 117–129.

Gudjonsson, G.H. (1994a). Investigative interviewing: recent developments and some fundamental issues. *International Review of Psychiatry*, **6**, 237–245.

Gudjonsson, G.H. (1994b). Psychological vulnerability: suspects at risk. In D. Morgan and G. Stephenson (eds), *Suspicions of Silence*. London, England: Blackstone Press.

Gudjonsson, G.H. (1995). The effects of interrogative pressure on strategic coping. *Psychology, Crime, and Law*, **1**, 309–318.

Gudjonsson, G.H. and Petursson, H. (1991). Custodial interrogation: why do suspects confess and how does it relate to their crime, attitude and personality? *Personality and Individual Differences*, **12**, 295–306.

Huff, C.R., Rattner, A. and Sagarin, E. (1986). Guilty until proven innocent: wrongful conviction and public policy. *Crime and Delinquency*, **32**, 518–544.

Inbau, F.E., Reid, J.E. and Buckley, J.P. (1986). *Criminal Interrogation and Confessions*. Baltimore, MD: Williams and Wilkins.

Irving, B. and McKenzie, I.K. (1989). *Police Interrogation: The Effects of the Police and Criminal Evidence Act 1984*. London, England: Police Foundation.

Kalbfleisch, P.J. (1994). The language of detecting deceit. *Journal of Language and Social Psychology*, **13**, 469–496.

Kassin, S.M. (1997). The psychology of confession evidence. *American Psychologist*, **52**, 221–233.

Kassin, S.M. and McNall, K. (1991). Police interrogations and confessions: communicating promises and threats by pragmatic implication. *Law and Human Behavior*, **15**, 233–251.

Kassin, S.M. and Wrightsman, L.S. (1985). Confession evidence. In S.M. Kassin and L.S. Wrightsman (eds), *The Psychology of Evidence and Trial Procedure* (pp. 67–94). London, England: Sage.

Köhnken, G. (1995). Interviewing adults. In R. Bull and D. Carson (eds), *Handbook of Psychology in Legal Contexts* (pp. 216–233). Chichester, England: Wiley.

Lassiter, G.D. and Irvine, A.A. (1986). Videotaped confessions: the impact of camera point of view on judgments of coercion. *Journal of Applied Social Psychology*, **16**, 268–276.

Leo, R.A. (1992). From coercion to deception: the changing nature of police interrogation in America. *Crime, Law and Social Change*, **18**, 33–59.

Leo, R.A. (1996). Inside the interrogation room. *Journal of Criminal Law and Criminolgy*, **86**, 266–303.

McConville, M. (1992). Video taping interrogations. *New Law Journal*, **10**, 960–962.

McConville, M. and Hodgson, J. (1993). Custodial legal advice and the right to silence. The Royal Commission on Criminal Justice Research, Research Study No. 16. London, England: HMSO.

McGurk, B. Carr, J. and McGurk, D. (1993). Investigative interviewing courses for police officers: An evaluation. Police Research Series: Paper No. 4. London, England: Home Office.

Mortimer, A. (1994). Cognitive processes underlying police investigative interviewing behaviour. Unpublished PhD thesis. Portsmouth, England: University of Portsmouth, Psychology Department.

Moston, S. (1996). From denial to admission in police questioning of suspects. In G. Davies, S. Lloyd-Bostock, M. McMurran and C. Wilson (eds), *Psychology, Law, and Criminal Justice: International Developments in Research and Practice* (pp. 91–99). Berlin, Germany: Walter de Gruyter.

Moston, S. and Stephenson, G.M. (1992). Predictors of suspect and interviewer behaviour during police questioning. In F. Lösel, D. Bender and T. Bliesener (eds), *Psychology and Law: International Perspectives* (pp. 212–219). Berlin, Germany: Walter de Gruyter.

Moston, S. and Stephenson, G.M. (1993a). The changing face of police interrogation. *Journal of Community and Applied Social Psychology*, **3**, 101–115.

Moston, S. and Stephenson, G.M. (1993b). The questioning and interviewing of suspects outside the police station. The Royal Commission on Criminal Justice, Research Study No. 23. London, England: HMSO.

Moston, S., Stephenson, G.M. and Williamson, T.M. (1990). Police interrogation styles and suspect behaviour. Summary report to Police Requirements Unit. London, England: Home Office.

Moston, S., Stephenson, G.M. and Williamson, T.M. (1992). The effects of case characteristics on suspect behaviour during police questioning. *British Journal of Criminology*, **32**, 23–40.

Mullin, C. (1989). *Error of Judgment: The Truth About the Birmingham Bombers*. Dublin, Ireland: Poolberg Press.

Ofshe, R. (1989). Coerced confessions: the logic of seemingly irrational action. *Cultic Studies Journal*, **6**, 1–15.

Pearse, J. (1995). Police interviewing: the identification of vulnerabilities. *Journal of Community and Applied Social Psychology*, **5**, 147–159.

Pearse, J. and Gudjonsson, G.H. (1996a). How appropriate are appropriate adults? Unpublished manuscript.

Pearse, J. and Gudjonsson, G.H. (1996b). Police interviewing techniques at two south London police stations. *Psychology, Crime, and Law*, **3**, 63–74.

Pearse, J. and Gudjonsson, G.H. (1996c). Understanding the problems of the appropriate adult. *Expert Evidence*, **4**, 101–104.

Pearse, J. and Gudjonsson, G.H. (1997). Police interviewing and mentally disordered offenders: changing the role of the legal adviser. *Expert Evidence*, **5**, 49–53.

Perske, R. (1994). Johnny Lee Wilson did not kill anybody. *Mental Retardation*, **32**, 157–159.

Sigurdsson, J.F. and Gudjonsson, G.H. (1994). Alcohol and drug intoxication during police interrogation and the reasons why suspects confess to the police. *Addiction*, **89**, 985–997.

Softley, P. (1980). *Police Interrogation: An Observational Study in Four Police Stations*. London, England: HMSO.

Stephenson, G.M. (1992). *The Psychology of Criminal Justice*. Oxford, England: Blackwell.

Stockdale, J. (1993). Management and supervision of police interviews. *Police Research Series*, Paper No. 5. London, England: Home Office.

Underwager, R. and Wakefield, H. (1992). False confessions and police deception. *American Journal of Forensic Psychology*, **10**, 49–66.

Vrij, A. (1995). The psychology of interrogations, confessions and testimony (book review). *Criminal Justice Review*, **20**, 99–101.

Williamson, T. (1993). From interrogation to investigative interviewing: strategic trends in police questioning. *Journal of Community and Applied Social Psychology*, **3**, 89–99.

Williamson, T. (1994). Reflections in current police practice. In D. Morgan and G.M. Stephenson (eds), *Suspicion and Silence: The Right to Silence in Criminal Investigations*. London, England: Blackstone Press.

RECOVERED MEMORIES: PSYCHOLOGICAL ISSUES AND LEGAL QUESTIONS

Amina Memon

INTRODUCTION

In the 1990s we have seen a startling rise in reports of memories of childhood sexual abuse from adults alleging that the memories were previously 'unavailable' to them. Such memories are often 'recovered' during psychotherapy and have resulted in fierce debate concerning the veracity and reliability of such memories. It is a debate that has elicited considerable controversy in the courts, in academic circles and in professional practice due to its personal, social and political implications. A criminal case based on the recovered memory of a murder was instrumental in bringing the debate to the attention of the public and courts. In 1990, George Franklin was convicted for the murder of Susan Nason (who died in 1969) based primarily on evidence from his daughter Eileen who claimed she had repressed the murder of her little friend for 20 years (Maclean, 1993). The conviction was overturned following a successful appeal in 1995 but the case nevertheless remains a poignant example of the impact of a recovered memory in the legal context. In the academic domain, recovered memories have presented memory researchers with some challenging questions (see below), and the focus on conditions under which memories are recovered, and the power of suggestion has brought the practices of psychotherapists under close scrutiny. Unfortunately some have interpreted this as an invasion of the therapists' domain and as an attempt to undermine the credibility of therapists and victims. This has resulted in a needless polarization of the debate, the consequences of which are well illustrated by recent reviews (Loftus and Ketcham, 1994; Ofshe and Watters, 1994, Lindsay and Read, 1995; Pendergrast, 1995, Conway, 1997). This chapter will show how scientific research can inform the debate.

Defining terms

One of the major problems in working in the area of recovered memories is that of defining terms such as memory, amnesia, recovery, repression, trauma, therapy and even forgetting. Steven Rose (1992) in his discussion of artificial intelligence makes the fundamental point that the mind doesn't work with information in the computer sense but with meaning. The latter is shaped by our interactions with our environment and history. Rose points out that this is what makes the study of memory so difficult. Each time we remember we recreate our memories; memories are not simply called up from store, consulted and put away unchanged. Instead they may be modified and reconstructed over time. The term amnesia is terribly confusing since not only does it refer to memory problems in brain damaged individuals (organic amnesia) but it is also used in cases of psychogenic amnesia or functional amnesia which refers to 'a temporary loss of memory precipitated by a psychological trauma' (Schacter, 1996).

The term recovered memories broadly refers to the reporting of memories of childhood events for the first time by adults who have previously been unable to recall or report these events or the circumstances surrounding them. The definition of 'repression' is crucial in establishing whether or not there is supporting evidence for recovered memories. Unfortunately, Freud was inconsistent in his use of this term. In his early writings he clearly stated that repression involved the intentional rejection of distressing thoughts and memories from conscious awareness (also referred to in the literature as 'suppression' or 'repression proper'). Over time, he began to use the term repression in reference to unconscious defense mechanisms designed to exclude threatening material from protruding into conscious awareness (referred to as 'primary repression'). The assertion that this is involuntary distinguishes repression from suppression (see Erdelyi, 1990 for a full discussion of Freud's writings on the subject). Finally, it is helpful to define what is meant by the term 'trauma' since there is an implicit assumption in the literature that a traumatic experience may be remembered in a different way from a non-traumatic one (evidence pertaining to this is considered later). Brewin, Dalgleish and Joseph (1997) define 'trauma' as 'any experience that by its occurrence has threatened the health or well being of the individual.' So what are the most interesting psychological questions in the recovered memory debate?

Questions

Do recovered memories require special mechanisms to explain their existence and quality? This is a central question since it is the assumption that such memories are 'special' that makes them stand apart from 'normal' everyday memories in the eyes of the courts.[1] If traumatic memories are no different from other types of memories, then data from the study of autobiographical memories and eyewitness memory may provide some useful answers. Before reviewing the literature, it may be useful to summarize how the courts treat evidence based on a recovered memory claim.

The statute of limitations

In the USA statutes of limitations usually require that if someone wishes to take legal action for damages or harm suffered (say as a result of a car accident) she or he has to begin proceedings within one to three years of the event but if the individual is a minor or has learning disabilities the commencement of limitations is postponed until she or he reaches the age of majority or recovers from disability (see Taub, 1996 for a review). However, with respect to child sexual abuse (CSA) claims there are any number of pressures that may have prevented legal proceedings being initiated within the statutory period such as bribes and threats, dependency of the child on the adult and ignorance about harm being done (Bulkley and Horowitz, 1994).

Related to the statute of limitations is the 'delayed discovery' doctrine. This doctrine originated in medical malpractice cases (one of the most famous cases was when the drug Thalidomide was administered to pregnant women in the 1960s to prevent polio. Only years later was this linked to the disabilities seen in the offspring of the women). The discovery rule was soon extended to encompass other forms of professional malpractice. Two positions have been put forward by plaintiffs who have wished to apply the discovery rule in repressed memory claims. One position is that memories of abuse were repressed beyond the period covered by the statute of limitations. Another position is that the plaintiff was unable to link present psychological problems to initial abuse until after the statute of limitations expired (see Eisenberg, 1995 for examples). The statutory period of limitation in civil cases has now been extended in many states in the USA and Canada (see Lindsay and Read, 1995; Eisenberg, 1995 for details).

In the UK, the statute is applied loosely in criminal cases. In civil cases there are two periods, when suing for negligence, action should normally begin within three years of discovery, for trespass it is six years. The European Court of Human Rights recently rejected a plea from alleged sexual abuse victims that the statute of limitations (that civil suites be brought within six years of reaching the age of 18 years) breaches the European Convention on Human Rights. The basis for the plea was that abuse victims may not appreciate the extent of their psychological scars until later life but lose the right to sue at the age of 24. 'The European Court said that there was no uniformity on time limits in Europe and it was not commonly accepted in European states that time should only start to run when material facts were known to the victim' (*The Guardian*, 23 October 1996).

Having identified some of the relevant questions in the recovered memory debate, we will now take a look at the relevant literature in order to develop an understanding of some of the processes that may underlie memories for traumatic events. We will begin by looking at evidence for repression and related mechanisms. The evidence here comes primarily from recent studies of clinical samples. We will then turn our attention to the large body of experimental data on autobiographical memory and eyewitness recall to explore forgetting in normal populations. Finally, we will review the literature on the malleability of memory during retrieval and consider under what conditions a false memory may occur.

RECOVERING MEMORIES OF PAST EVENTS: MECHANISMS UNDERLYING FORGETTING

Searching for evidence of repression

A review of 60 years of experimental tests of 'repression proper' led to the conclusion that at this time there is no controlled laboratory evidence supporting repression (Holmes, 1990). This review of research is often cited in the recovered memory literature as evidence against the Freudian interpretation of repression as an unconscious mechanism without any clarification of what these null effects mean: are we to conclude from that there is no evidence for repression? Can we generalize from these laboratory studies (which for example use threatening words as emotional stimuli) to real trauma? A scientist should answer 'no' to both these questions but proceed to see if evidence can be obtained from other sources of data.[2] Currently substantive efforts are being directed towards the study of adult clients who have recovered memories of childhood abuse (primarily in a therapy context) in an attempt to provide some retrospective data on repression and recovery.

The typical method for documenting actual forgetting of trauma has been to identify individuals on the basis of trauma and ask whether they can remember it. This research provides us with an interesting insight into the nature of previously inaccessible memories but does not allow us to determine whether we are dealing with primary repression, repression proper or merely forgetting due to lack of retrieval cues and the passage of time. For example Briere and Conte (1993) asked their 450 clients (selected from therapists specializing in sexual abuse treatment) whether there were any conditions under which they could not remember the experience. Now this is a difficult question, does it mean was there a time when you couldn't remember, had not thought about the event. It is not clear what a 'yes' answer to this question means. The memory status of these patients prior to entering therapy is not clear either and the fact that the patients were already in survivor groups is problematic. Recent surveys (e.g. Poole, Lindsay, Memon and Bull, 1995) indicate that a significant minority of clients in therapy may have undergone some form of memory recovery therapy such as hypnosis. (See Yapko, 1997 for a discussion of the dangers of hypnosis in therapeutic contexts.)

Williams (1994) asked 129 adult women (who had been abused in childhood) during the course of a single interview whether they had been abused. No specific technique was used to help them remember and the interviewer's question did not allude to a specific episode of abuse. Hence when 38 per cent denied abuse it is not clear whether they were referring to a particular instance. Williams suggests that her respondents indicated that they were referring to periods of time during which they avoided thinking about the abuse. However, this does not constitute evidence for primary repression but is more consistent with suppression of the memory.

Repression or infantile amnesia?

Infantile amnesia refers to the inaccessibility for verbal recall of events occurring before 20–24 months of age (Fivush and Schwarzmueller, 1996). This may contribute to failures of memory in some of the clinical case studies reviewed although the work of Robyn Fivush and colleagues would caution us from specifying a childhood amnesia barrier for preschoolers. As indicated in a recent review children's earlier memories are highly dependent on social context and the extent to which adults can help children structure their experiences (Fivush, Pipe, Murchver and Reese, 1997). This may account for individual differences in memories for early childhood traumas (see Howe, Courage and Peterson, 1994; Peterson, 1996). Fivush *et al.* (in press) make the interesting observation that in the Williams (1994) study the women who always remembered the abuse recalled more supportive interactions surrounding their abuse experience from their mothers than those claiming to have forgotten for a period of time. As pointed out by Fivush and colleagues the effects of social variables on children's recall of early childhood events is only beginning to be studied but it does suggest the possibility that 'the absence of discussion may contribute to the forgetting of traumatic experiences.' They conclude that even if early memories are accessible in adulthood they are 'likely to be unorganized and quite sparse.'

Repression or dissociation?

Dissociation may also explain the gaps in memory noted in studies of recovered memory clients. Spiegel and Cardena (1991) define dissociation as 'a structured separation of mental processes (e.g. thoughts, emotions, connotation, memory and identity) that are ordinarily integrated'. Dissociation may take many different forms such as Multiple Personality Disorder (MPD), a condition in which an individual develops a separate personality or personalities and experiences a lack of memory for events experienced in different states. Perhaps the most well-known case is that of 'Sybil'who was reported as taking on some 16 different personalities following persistent sexual abuse by her sadistic mother (Schreiber, 1973). The extent to which MPD is a genuine condition and the extent to which it is manufactured during therapy is fiercely debated (e.g. Ofshe and Watters, 1994). Moreover, as Mulhern (1996) has so eloquently illustrated social and cultural forces have played a major part in shaping MPD as an idiom of distress.

Hunter, Andrews and Brewin (1996) conducted in-depth interviews with women who had recovered memories in therapy and noted partial/profound amnesia evidence in 12 of their 16 cases with a slight tendency for amnesia to be associated with earlier onset of abuse and more severe episodes. Dissociative strategies were seen in these women and they took various forms including (i) an out-of-body experience during which the assault was described as happening to someone else, (ii) an imaginary world was created in order to escape, and (iii) conscious attempts were made to block memories of the experience. These data need to be treated with caution, however, since the number of cases falling into these categories are small (three in each example). As more data are collected it may be possible to obtain better insight into the different mechanisms that may account for the forgetting of traumatic experiences and the way in which these mechanisms interact with other variables.

Psychogenic amnesia and fugue states

Studies of psychogenic amnesia suggest that traumatic experiences can lead to extensive memory loss and sometimes 'fugue' states in which a person is completely unaware of having lost all knowledge of personal identity. Schacter (1996) gives the example of a wartime fugue, an Australian soldier serving in Africa during the Second World War became traumatized supposedly when a German fighter plane swooped down towards him. He recalled trying to fire at the plane before blacking out. He became aware of his memory loss when he came to in a Syrian hospital about a month later. He had wandered in fugue in the intervening period focused on seeking refuge near a camp he had heard about in Syria. While it is not possible to conduct controlled tests of the conditions under which fugue occurs, it does provide us with another illustration of apparently sudden and severe disturbance in memory functioning in response to a threatening situation. The literature on psychogenic amnesia is reviewed by Kihlstrom and Schacter (1995).

The verification of repressed memories: new directions

Much of the evidence discussed so far has been covered in earlier reviews of the literature (e.g. Lindsay and Read, 1994; 1995). As the pace of research on recovered memories increases and research methodology improves we are beginning to see some promising lines of investigation for the future. In this final section on evidence for repression, we will take a brief look at some new avenues of research.

Systematic studies of clinical cases

The clinical psychologist and researcher Constance Dalenberg has developed multiple methods for examination of recovery and amnesia. She lists single clinical case studies of recovered memories, surveys of clinicians' behaviour, clinical group comparisons between recovered and nonrecovered memory cases and studies of eyewitness memory including the memories of holocaust survivors (Dalenberg, 1996). Dalenberg is currently undertaking a study of her former clients recruited after their therapy was completed. She draws a distinction between continuous memories of sexual abuse and recovered memories of sexual abuse (thereby making a within-subject comparison of the reliability of the recovered memories of a patient with that patient's other memories). Clients were asked to rate the truth value of each memory and a record was made of the point at which the memory emerged, whether it was continuous or recovered, and whether it emerged in or out of therapy. Clients were asked to track down any physical evidence supporting their memories and Dalenberg interviewed the fathers who were the alleged perpetrators of the abuse. Independent raters assessed the evidence which included some confessions from fathers. Two-thirds of the sample were able to locate evidence confirming or disconfirming their memories. The percentage accurate ranged from 32 to 96 per cent with four clients with more accurate continuous memories and four clients with more accurate recovered memories (for nine clients accuracy of continuous/recovered memories was identical). Dalenberg concludes that this constitutes some evidence for recovered memories but does it tell us about the mechanisms underlying the prior unavailability of these memories? Nine of the father/daughter pairs stated they had never discussed the abuse in their lives suggesting that the memories may have been suppressed. As pointed out by Dalenberg, the question of what constitutes accuracy is critical here. All the clients were accusing their fathers and in 10 cases corroboration came from confessions or medical evidence. Not all recovered memories were corroborated, however, and Dalenberg presents two cases of false memories. Dalenberg speculates that the women here are likely to have had violent and sexually provocative fathers but they probably did not abuse their daughters. Here is an example from Dalenberg (1996):

> Stephanie recovered a memory of her father grabbing and shaking her. He was nude in the flashback and she was convinced it was a post-sexual abuse experience. She gradually recalled the where – a houseboat – her age – 16 and the type of abuse – oral sex. In the investigation, the divorce report told an interesting story. Stephanie couldn't have interacted in this way with her father at age 16, since the divorce occurred at age 12 and she no longer saw him. At age 12, Stephanie walked in on her father while he was having sex with a 16-year-old. He did chase her and admits threatening her. The family believe Stephanie placed herself in the role of the other child. Social services did investigate and no evidence emerged. Stephanie did have nightmares...one route to partially false memories.

This is a good example of a case where the description of an event may contain some accurate details and some confabulations. It is also an example of how easily memory may be distorted and source confusions occur (see below).

Cases histories of recovered memories: non-therapy samples

In addition to improved studies of clinical populations, there has been an effort to obtain non-clinical examples of recovery from repression in order to come up with data on the veracity of recovered memories that occur outside the therapy domain. The technique is to undertake a detailed analysis of case studies. Schooler has provided us with some scholarly reviews of this work (Schooler, 1994; Schooler, Bendiksen and Ambadar, 1997). There are two public cases of delayed discovery of sexual abuse that are described by Schooler *et al.* In the first case, that of Ross Cheit, the corroboration came from newspaper report articles. In the second, the case of Commonwealth of Massachusetts *v.* Porter in 1993, the corroboration came from multiple sources including suspicions of Porter's improper behaviour and allegations which followed from others who knew him or of him. More convincing is the case of JR who was allegedly repeatedly abused on camping trips by a parish priest. JR denies having any recollection of the history of the abuse prior to the recovery experience (which began when he watched a movie where the main character was subject to memories of sexual abuse) despite having been in therapy discussing intimate life events several years earlier. Corroboration came from several 'reputable' sources including a colleague of Schooler who maintained regular contact with JR throughout the recovery process. As indicated by Schooler and colleagues it is not possible to check the authenticity of this recovered memory account and one cannot rule out the possibility that repression was being used as a means of overturning statute of limitation laws. They conclude, however, that this is not a case where repression was being feigned. In our opinion this does not rule out other explanations for the delayed discovery or the possibility that corroborating evidence (including the reports of JR) were uncontaminated. Several other cases are detailed by Schooler *et al.* and again the evidence is carefully documented but is in need of unbiased external corroboration (in one such case the victim acknowledged that she had not disclosed due to embarrassment). While the case studies offer a fascinating insight into the processes which may underlie recovery of memories of trauma, they do not in themselves offer adequate scientific support for repression as a mechanism underlying delayed discovery of abuse.

Repression: the role of cognitive mechanisms

So far, we have sought evidence for primary repression and other unconscious defensive mechanisms as explanations for memory loss. Brewin (1996) draws to our attention the cognitive psychology literature which suggests that repression and dissociation imply the presence of cognitive mechanisms that inhibit the activation of representations of traumatic events. He argues that these mechanisms have parallels in everyday cognitive processing thus providing us with yet another interpretation of repression. Relevant research reviewed by Brewin (1996) includes studies of retrieval-induced forgetting where subjects are typically presented in the study phase with categories of words and exemplars of them. In the next phase they have to practise retrieval of some items from the studied categories by completing words that formed part of the category exemplars (e.g Animal–Ho– – –). In a subsequent recall test subjects' recall more of the practised items but recall of unpractised items is impaired relative to recall of items from control (baseline) categories in which no items were rehearsed. This is taken as evidence of 'active inhibitory processes' (see Anderson and Spellman, 1995).

Brewin *et al.* (in press) elaborate on inhibitory mechanisms in the discussion of their dual processing model of post-traumatic stress disorder (PTSD) which according to the authors is characterized by 'an alternation between reexperiencing and avoiding trauma related memories' (p. 4). It is proposed that traumatic memories are represented in two ways: (i) a conscious experience of the trauma (verbally accessible memories) which can be deliberately retrieved from the memory store, (ii) a non-conscious processing of the traumatic situation resulting in automatic activation of memories in specific contexts (referred to as specific situationally accessible knowledge). The dual representation theory predicts that the latter would remain intact even when verbal memories are incomplete. Brewin *et al.* (in press) argue that various 'inhibition strategies' may be employed to avoid thinking about the trauma and intrusive memories will be prevented from surfacing but this does not mean that the memories cannot be reactivated later in life. While this theory remains to be systematically tested it may be useful in understanding how individual differences in coping strategies may contribute to memory deficits and other symptoms in trauma victims.

SUMMARY

The evidence reviewed in this section suggests that it is possible for deficits in memory functioning and memory loss over time, but the available evidence does not provide unequivocal support for the theory that this is a result of primary repression. On the other hand what has been referred to as suppression (repression proper), dissociation and inhibition could be coping strategies for dealing with the discomfort caused by the memories of the trauma. Perhaps these strategies are a response to the intrusive memories of traumatic experiences rather than a response to the threatening elements of the trauma itself (Creamer, Burgess and Pattison, 1992). Studies of PTSD victims lend support to this hypothesis. Indeed the intrusive thoughts reported by such victims go against the theory of repression. There are clearly individual differences in reactions to traumatic experiences as revealed by some of the evidence considered above. Moreover, case studies show how complex it is to check the validity of these memories. As the quality of research with clients in therapy continues to improve we may be able to develop a better understanding of the contribution of the different mechanisms, and new theoretical developments in the study of the reactions of trauma victims may further improve our understanding. In the next section we turn our attention to the literature on the effects of emotional arousal on memory in order to focus more on the question of recall accuracy of emotionally arousing events. Are memories of such events resistant to forgetting and distortion? In this section we begin to address the question of how memory distortions may come about.

THE EFFECTS OF EMOTIONAL AROUSAL ON MEMORY

A recurring conclusion throughout the early literature (e.g. Clifford and Hollin, 1981; Kuehn, 1974) was that the accuracy and completeness of testimony (either of victim or witness) are adversely affected by the presence of emotion or violence experienced during an event. The field research of Yuille and his colleagues (Yuille and Cutshall, 1986; Yuille and Tollestrup, 1992) led them to take issue with this conclusion. Yuille and Cutshall (1986) studied reports of a real-life shooting incident and found unusually high accuracy and completeness of testimony over a five-month period. Although some specific aspects of the event were forgotten, the authors maintain that these did not affect the overall accuracy of the rest of the account. A model of the diverse effects of event impact on memory was proposed by Yuille and Tollestrup (1992) based on attention and rehearsal. 'Remarkable' (i.e. distinctive) events of great impact – not achieved in the laboratory – tend to be rehearsed frequently and hence memories for such are well maintained. (Howe, Courage and Peterson, 1994, concur that stress is just one factor which makes an event unique.) Furthermore, Yuille and Tollestrup (1992) posit that attention may be focused either internally or externally during an emotional event. An internal focus may be on emotions, and consequently few event details will be stored; while an external focus (i.e. on the event itself) leads to the retention of central thematic elements. Thus it can be assumed that the extent of memory for details is a function of emotional impact, a conclusion that is supported by data from recent studies of arousal on memory for detail (e.g. Libkuman, Nichols-Whitehead, Griffith and Thomas, 1996).

Thus we begin to see the complexity of the association between emotion and memory. Certain elements of a traumatic event may be remembered well, while others display quite poor retention. One group of researchers (e.g. Christianson, 1992a; 1992b; Kebeck and Lohaus, 1986) suggests that the centrality of details may predict whether or not they are recalled. Central details such as the emotional event itself tend to be well retained; while background information (peripheral details) is more susceptible to forgetting. Despite its circularity, the central/peripheral dichotomy may plausibly account for the discrepancies in the effects of emotion on recall. Moreover, Christianson (1992b) has applied Easterbrook's

(1959) cue utilization theory to the current domain. The latter predicts that arousal affects memory by redirecting attention or reducing attentional resources, such that gist or central information is well retained at the expense of peripheral details. Recent tests of this hypothesis have produced mixed results. For example Wessel and Mercelbach (in press) exposed spider phobics and low-fear controls to a large live spider and tested their memory afterwards. The phobics displayed a poorer memory for peripheral detail information but there were no group differences with respect to central memory details. While this only provided partial support for the attention narrowing hypothesis, it does fit with the theory proposed by Yuille and Tollestrup (1992) considered earlier. If the phobics directed part of their attention inwardly (on their emotions) then memory for peripheral details would have suffered.

Emotional focus and source memory

Locating the source of an event (initial experience of the event) and distinguishing it from memories of largely internal experiences (thoughts about the event, the reading of written information about it and what others have said about it) is essential in order to arrive at an accurate memory of an experienced event. This has been referred to as source monitoring (Johnson, Hashtroudi and Lindsay, 1993).

Johnson, Nolde and Leonardis (1996) have recently looked at the role of emotional focus in source monitoring. They argue that insofar as peripheral details are critical in identifying source of information, an internal focus on emotions may occur at a cost to the processing of external perceptual information (information about source). Johnson *et al.* reason that 'Self-focus should have a negative impact on source monitoring because it reduces the chances that a listener will bind features of a speaker (e.g. voice quality, inferred attitudes, etc.) to the semantic content of what was said' (Johnson *et al.*, 1996, p. 138). In support of their hypotheses, Johnson *et al.* (1996) found when students focused on their own feelings (self-focus) about statements on 'emotional' topics heard on tape relative to how the speakers felt (other focus) they were better at recognizing the statements but worse at identifying the source. Moreover, subjects who focused on their emotions were less accurate at identifying the source on the more emotion-evoking statements.

The neat thing about source monitoring theory is that it can account for accurate recall and false recall. In terms of the effects of emotion on source monitoring, Johnson *et al.* (1996) argue that when emotion induces 'reactivations' of events that took place it should result in accurate recall, but when it induces embellishments false memories may occur (see the final section of this chapter for a discussion of conditions under which source confusions may result in false memories).

Repressed memories and flashbulb memories

So far it appears that attentional mechanisms at encoding act to preserve some details in memory while not preserving others. Thus, intensity of emotion is not a safeguard against forgetting. However, there remains a debate in the applied domain as to the effects of emotion, whether it is facilitative or detrimental to memory. Both schools of thought employ a special mechanism to explain their phenomenon – in the former case, flashbulb memories are formed; in the latter, repression occurs. In actual fact, the experimental evidence described above suggests that emotion may be both facilitative and detrimental to memory, depending on circumstances and that a special mechanism is not required to explain these effects. Take the literature on 'flashbulb' (FB) memories (apparently vivid and confidently held memories of significant events, such as the *Challenger* spacecraft explosion, or the assassination of John F. Kennedy). The term 'flashbulb' is misleading since it implies a photographic reproduction when it has been found that even these highly lucid memories can be in error (Neisser and Harsch, 1992).

Terr (1996) interviewed children (aged 8 and 15) about their memories of the *Challenger* spacecraft explosion of January 1986. The interviews took place five to seven weeks after the explosion and again at 14 months. While such memories were clear, consistent and detailed they were not without errors. Some 30 per cent of children had misunderstood something about the explosion and incorporated the misinformation into their memories of the event. In other words, clarity and detail cannot guarantee accuracy.

So what impact does trauma have on memory for an event? Terr's work shows that it is possible for children to recollect traumatic details albeit with some inaccuracies. Terr (1991) attempted to come up with a theory of when traumatic memories may be repressed and when they are retained. She maintained that while a single event produced a flashbulb type memory, a multiple incident would result in dissociation or repression. This theory has met with much criticism and the limitations of Terr's theorizing are best summed up by Schacter (1996, p. 256):

> Terr's ideas are provocative but hundreds of studies have shown that repetition of information leads to improved memory, not loss of memory, for that information. To produce profound amnesia, the repression mechanism would have to be so effective as to succeed despite the normal tendency for repeated experiences to enhance memory. People who live through repeated traumas in war generally remember these terrifying experiences only too well. An individual experience or trauma may be set aside, especially when much time has passed, but with rare exceptions such as fugue states – which are generally of short duration – people do not forget an entire set of repeated traumas.

SUMMARY

There has been much controversy in the literature about how accurately people remember emotionally significant information. The research presented here suggests that the effects of emotional arousal on memory are complex. Central details of a traumatic event may be remembered well, while peripheral information is sometimes poorly retained. Moreover, attending to one's emotional reactions may occur at the expense of identifying the source of the remembered information (Johnson *et al.*, 1996).

While studies of flashbulb memories initially suggested that such memories are accurate and persistent, it is clear that even when memories are vivid and compelling they are susceptible to distortion in the same way that normal memories are. Such memories do not warrant any special mechanisms (a conclusion echoed by Hyman and Loftus, in press). Normal processes imply that normal errors may occur, and in the next section it will be shown that the conditions that influence veridical remembering map closely onto conditions that result in the creation of false memories.

RETRIEVAL OF INFORMATION FROM MEMORY

It has been well established through decades of careful research that forgetting can occur over short and long delays through deficits in encoding, storage or retrieval processes, or a combination of these (see Brainerd, Reyna, Howe and Kingma, 1990 for a review). Encoding specificity theory (see Chapter 8) highlights the role of retrieval cues which match conditions at encoding in facilitating access to memory. Indeed recollection of an experience is likely to be most successful when a retrieval cue reinstates a person's subjective perception of an event, including any thoughts, fantasies and inferences (Schacter, 1996). Schacter and colleagues have recently completed research in their laboratory that provides a good illustration of how properties of retrieval cues can influence what is recalled about the past. In their experiments, college students looked at photos of people (in which they were slightly smiling or frowning) and heard them speak in either a pleasant or irritating tone of voice. Later, when trying to recall the tone of voice they saw the same photos again (as cues). Those cue faces seen with a slight smile tended to be attributed a pleasant voice and vice versa (when in fact there had been no relationship originally between facial expression and tone of voice). Schacter (1996) concludes from this: 'the memories that people reported contained little information about the event they were trying to recall (the speaker's tone of voice) but were greatly influenced by the properties of the retrieval cue that we gave them (the positive or negative facial expression)' (p. 71). The relevance of this study to the current discussion about recovered memories is that questioning strategies and techniques used in memory recovery therapy may influence what a person remembers about her or his past (see Lindsay and Read, 1994 for a review of memory recovery therapies).

THE RECONSTRUCTIVE NATURE OF MEMORY

We know that false recollections increase with the passage of time (e.g. Barclay and Wellman 1986). There are now several types of research that inform us about the mechanisms underlying memory distortions. The first type dates back to 1932 when Bartlett so tacitly demonstrated the effects of pre-existing knowledge and reconstructive processes in story memory. Another type of evidence comes form the work of Loftus and colleagues over the last two decades (Loftus, 1974 to present) showing how easily it is to bias recollection through subtle changes in wording of questions (see Schacter, 1995 for a historical review). This work has resulted in a wealth of literature on a phenomenon which has become known as 'suggestibility' (but also includes compliance with experimenters' demands). The vulnerability of child and adult witnesses to suggestion was discussed in Chapter 9. In the present chapter we examine the relevance of this research to the debate about the accuracy of recovered memories.

Source monitoring and false memories

The role of source confusions in creating false memories was alluded to earlier in our discussion of the effects of emotional focus on source memory. Zaragoza and Mitchell (1996) highlight some of the conditions under which source monitoring failures may lead to eyewitness memory distortions in their work on repeated suggestions. In their study participants viewed a video of a burglary and immediately afterwards answered questions about the event, some of which contained misleading suggestions. Some suggestions appeared once and others three times in the written post-event questionnaire. Participants were tested on their memory for the source of the suggested items (after 10 minutes, 48 hours or one week). A false memory was defined as one where a suggested item (by the questionnaire) was attributed to the video. In all three groups there was a progressive increase in false memories from no exposure to suggestion to one exposure and most markedly from one exposure to suggestions to three exposures. The authors conclude that 'what is striking about the present results is that repetition produced a marked increase in high confidence misattribution errors even though it served to preserve subjects' memory for the source of the suggestions' (p. 12).

The role of source monitoring in the creation of false memories about a real-life event (the crashing of El AL Boeing 747 onto apartment buildings in Amsterdam) was examined by Crombag, Wagenaar and Van Koppen (1996). They misled adults (including a large number of law students) into believing they had witnessed (seen on television) the plane crash when in reality they had only heard about the crash from media reports and seen the effects of the aftermath (no film of the crash exists). Crombag *et al.* argue that the ease with which participants were fooled about such a serious event questions the 'supposedly indelible' nature of flashbulb memories. Furthermore, a significant number answered detailed visual questions about the crash. The effects are attributed to source monitoring problems, a confusion of what they had read and heard about with what they had seen on the television. The authors go on to point out: 'Conflicting and implausible information typically occurs in court cases; one witness contradicts another.... Then all of a sudden "source monitoring" becomes of the essence, and that is why the law of evidence in many countries forbids or at least limits, the use of hearsay information in court' (p. 103). Crombag *et al.* stress that witnesses in legal trials need to be explicitly reminded that they should only report what they know first-hand.

The studies reviewed in this section concur with the conclusion that memory distortions involve source monitoring failures.

The false memory paradigm

As a direct result of concerns about the possibility that false memories can be created, several laboratories have developed paradigms to study systematically whether or not it is possible to implant an entire false memory in the mind of an adult. This work is of great importance because it looks at the cognitive and social factors that can influence memory. There are two strands of studies here. The first set provides a demonstration of false recall in a verbal paradigm, the second set provides a demonstrate how it is possible to implant an entire false memory about a childhood event in the mind of an adult. We will review the latter in more detail than the former given its more direct relevance.

Following a procedure that was pioneered by Deese (1959) several researchers have presented subjects with a list of words all associated to a single non-presented word (e.g. slumber, doze, nap, bedtime). After studying the word list, subjects complete recognition tests with the common finding that the common non-presented word *sleep* is recognized with as much confidence as are the presented words (e.g. Roediger and McDermott, 1995). The effects have been replicated in a cued recall paradigm (McDermott, 1996) and the false memory has been shown to increase over successive recall tests (a hypermnesia false recall effect) even when subjects were warned about guessing on recall tests (Payne, Elie, Blackwell and Neuschantz, 1996). Schacter and colleagues have recently completed a study in their laboratory using neuroimaging techniques called positron emission tomography (PET scanning), this allows the scientist to see the brain in action while people remember. PET scans have shown that medial temporal lobes close to the left hippocampus become active during both 'true' recognition of previously studied words and during the 'false' recognition of non-studied but associated words. Moreover, areas in the temporal and parietal lobes that store information about word sounds became active following recognition of words that had been heard in the experiment but did not become active during the false recognition of non-presented associates (Schacter, Reiman, Curran, Yun, Bandy, McDermott and Roediger, 1996 cited in Schacter, in press).

Implanting entire false memories in adults

The typical procedure in the memory implantation studies is described by Loftus and Pickrell (1995). In the first part of their study, participants receive a booklet containing four stories about events from their childhood (provided by an older relative). Three stories are 'true' and one is a 'false' event (e.g. lost in a shopping mall). All participants are interviewed twice and asked to recall as much as they can. Loftus and Pickrell report that 68 per cent of the true events are remembered while 25 per cent of false events are fully or partially recalled at the first and second interview. Apparently, people can be led to believe that entire events happened to them after suggestions to that effect. These findings have been replicated. For example Hyman, Husband and Billings (1995, experiment 2) implanted childhood memories of an accident at a wedding reception which resulted in a punch bowl being overturned on the parents of the bride. Memory for true events was highly accurate over their three separate interviews. For the false punch bowl event, no participants provided false recollections during the first interview whereas 25.5 per cent did so by the third interview. (The false recalls varied in clarity, with six of the 23 rated as 'very clear'.) Interestingly, subjects who incorporated script-relevant details of the punch bowl event into their first or second interview were more likely to have false recollections by interview three. The extent to which one has some prior knowledge of, or a script for the implanted event may determine the likelihood that the event will be suggestively implanted into memory. Payne *et al.* (1996) believe that the conceptual framework provided by fuzzy trace theory (Brainerd and Reyna, 1990) offers a useful perspective from which to evaluate false memory effects. Basically fuzzy trace theory would lead us to predict there are two separate representations at encoding: (i) verbatim (information itself) and (ii) gist (semantic content) and that the latter is more accessible than former. This fits with the hypothesis that people may be more likely to introduce false memories in situations where they have a script of the target episode (Pezdek, 1995).

Hyman and Pentland (1996) were interested in whether guided imagery type procedures resembling the ones sometimes used in therapy would increase the recall of true and false memories and whether 'hypermnesia' (or net increases in recall) would occur over repeated interviews. Students were interviewed three times about a series of 'true' events (based upon information supplied by their parents) and a false event (the accident with the punch bowl). They were given basic cues (their age, nature of event, locations). When participants in the imagery condition failed to recall the time of the event, they were asked for detailed descriptions (and asked questions about what happened). The control group were asked to sit quietly and think about the event for a minute. There were no significant differences in the imagery versus control condition in the percentage of true events recalled but there was a tendency for additional information to be reported following the first interview (this is most marked in the imagery condition) suggesting a form of hypermnesia. Not surprisingly, memories provided by participants in the imagery condition were rated as higher in image clarity than memories provided in the control condition. Turning to the false events, these were scored as 'clear false memory', 'partial', 'no memory' and 'no but trying' (a memory recovered from the first to the third interview was referred to as a recovered memory). The number of clear false memories increased across interviews in both conditions (there were no differences in partial memories although some individuals went from partial to clear memories). By the third interview, experimental condition was related to the creation of a false memory. 37.5 per cent in the imagery condition versus 12.4 per cent in the control condition had created a false memory. Those who created a false memory in the imagery condition tended to rate their image as clearer and were more confident. The data are compatible with source monitoring theory (see above).

Garry *et al.* (1996) have demonstrated that imagery increases confidence and likelihood that a false event occurred. In a three-stage procedure, participants first completed a life events inventory (LEI) where they rated the likelihood of a series of true and false events on an eight-point scale. Two weeks later they returned and were asked to produce an image of some of these events as having happened to them. They were also asked questions about the images to cue them further. Note that there were eight critical events, split into two groups of four, one set to be imagined and one to serve as control (the items were varied across participants). Following this the experimenter asked them to complete the LEI once more, on the pretense that their earlier scores had been misplaced. The majority of participants did not change their confidence scores for the critical events in the imagine/non-imagine condition. Analysis of individual items did reveal significant differences in the confidence of events in the imagined condition. For example 24 per cent of subjects who had imagined the false event 'put hand through glass and broke window' increased their subjective confidence as compared to 12 per cent who had not imagined the event. Interestingly, there was a general increase in subjective confidence among items regardless of whether they had been imagined. (The authors suggest this could reflect regression towards the mean or be an effect of hypermnesia.) This is in keeping with the finding that illusions of familiarity can be created by manipulating the *ease* with which items to mind (see work of Lindsay and Kelley, 1996 and Jacoby *et al.*, 1989).

Relevance to the therapy context

Guided imagery or visualization techniques may be used successfully in therapeutic contexts in the relief symptoms of post-traumatic stress disorder in rape victims (e.g Foa, Rothbaum, Riggs and Murdock, 1991). After all the basic aim of much therapy is to discharge emotion and not to enhance better recall of the episode as such. However, there are occasions when 'memory recovery techniques' may be used to elicit memories from adults (see Lindsay and Read, 1994; Poole *et al.*, 1995). If anything, the therapist is more likely to have enlisted the trust and confidence of clients than is an experimenter (after all this is an essential part of the client–therapist relationship). This means that demand characteristics may have a greater impact in the real world.[3] Trauma patients in therapy may hold the belief that abuse occurred in very early childhood and this is why they do not remember it. Kihlstrom (1995) argues that under these circumstances, memories may be based on attributional processes and not on retrieval.

SUMMARY

The focus of this section has been on the impact of retrieval conditions on remembering. A number of different paradigms have been used to demonstrate how over repeated suggestive questioning a false memory may occur. At the same time the term 'false memory' ought to be used carefully. As pointed out by Winograd and Killinger (1983) there is an important sense in which no memory is false, if information is part of the cognitive system and an individual's beliefs about what happened then its presence needs to be explained. Moreover, we cannot take for granted that people really report what was originally encoded. As noted by Schacter (1995) our 'subjective experience of remembering does not correspond in any simple way to the reawakening or reactivation of a dormant picture in the mind' (p. 24).

It has been shown how readily false suggestions may be incorporated into an individual's memory beliefs. Therapists need to exercise caution in the techniques used to facilitate memory recovery so that the truth can be reached without contaminating it. While some clinicians maintain that the accuracy and detail with which an account is recalled is not critical (e.g. Olio and Cornell, 1994), we would argue that knowing whether abuse has truly occurred may well help therapy progress (see Pennebaker and Memon, 1996). In the forensic context, not only is it important to establish whether or not an event has occurred but to determine precisely what happened. In the final section of this paper, we illustrate the significance of accuracy and memory for details with reference to some recent cases of recovered memory that have gone to trial (see also Chapter 10).

Verifying the accuracy of recovered memories in the courtroom

Willem Wagenaar, who has often served as an expert witness in the Netherlands, recounts (1996) the case of Yolanda who accused her parents and others of continual abuse and the murder of her unborn babies. Wagenaar was asked to review the reliability of the witness evidence (autobiographical memories) in this case which came to trial in 1991. He noted how difficult this was to do given that some suspects had been questioned around 20–30 times and had changed their accounts. This together with the 'gaps' and inconsistencies in information about what had transpired made it impossible to ascertain the accuracy of information with the degree of precision required by the court. One of the critical questions in the case was when Yolanda's pregnancy had been terminated. Abortion is defined as the termination of a pregnancy that lasted less than 24 weeks while the termination of a pregnancy that lasted over 24 weeks is technically a murder. Specifying when the termination occurred was critical in terms of deciding whether a crime had been committed, but as Wagenaar discovered this was impossible to find out given that the first pregnancies supposedly occurred around 1980 and the memories of witnesses for dates were so hazy.

In the case of George Franklin cited in the opening paragraph of this chapter, the expert witnesses (Lenore Terr for the prosecution and Elizabeth Loftus for the defence) could not comment on the precision of the details reported by Eileen Franklin but only on the conditions under which memory is likely to be accurate or inaccurate. Corroboration of Eileen's account came from police files and media reports of the case and we can only assume that the information obtained was accurate.

As an increasing number of cases of recovered memories are proceeding to litigation the evidence for such recovered memories is likely to be subject to increasing scrutiny to see whether or not it meets scientific standards (see Chapter 10). It would help if sceptics and advocates of repressed memories could agree on what constitutes sufficient evidence. The courts are clear on this point with respect to criminal trial: guilt has to be proven beyond reasonable doubt.

Extreme caution is required when trying to judge the accuracy of recovered memories. Ross and Newby (1996) argue that rememberers and observers will invoke a variety of truth criteria to assess the validity of recollections, and that they will often be wrong. They illustrate this with reference to memories of alien abductions where a rememberer may use as verifying criteria context, vividness, memorability and originality to support the validity of these accounts, in the absence of external evidence. Of course the same criteria could be used by observers to discredit the memory. Thus if someone truly believes her or his memory of an event then what we as scientists ought to be able to do is to study the conditions under which it was obtained and be able to comment on the accuracy of the report. However, according to Ross and Newby trying to distinguish true and false memories on the basis of truth criteria is not going to tell us much about the accuracy of the memory. Unless external corroboration is available, neither cognitive nor clinical psychologists are able to distinguish between false memories on the one hand and genuine memories on the other. This is the major area where the results of future research are awaited.

CONCLUSION

The aim of the research reviewed in this chapter has been to review some of the mechanisms that may account for recovered memories and to examine their likely accuracy in relation to the literature on the encoding and retrieval of traumatic events. It was concluded that evidence for primary repression is sparse and that intentional forgetting or suppression may account for the previous unavailability of childhood memories. A similar conclusion was reached in a case filed by the Court of Appeal of Maryland in July 1996 (Jane Doe *et al. v.* A. Joseph Maskell, *et al.*). In this case the court was asked to decide whether the discovery rule was applicable. The details of the case are relevant to the present discussion. Jane Doe and Jane Roe were students at a parochial school in Baltimore in the late 1960s. During their time there they had individually been referred for counselling to the school chaplain Father A. Joseph Maskell. It is alleged that Maskell subjected the girls to repeated sexual, physical and psychological abuse. Both girls were allegedly threatened with punishments if they told and they claimed to have ceased to recall the abuse after they left school in 1971/72. The girls filed suits in 1994 claiming that in order to avoid the pain associated with recalling the abuse they had 'repressed' their memories and then later 'recovered' them. According to their claim they were 'blamelessly ignorant' and thus could not have filed suit earlier. The Court of Appeal posed two questions: (i) is there is a difference between repression and mere forgetting and (ii) is the difference of a sufficient quality to operate the discovery rule. The Court reviewed the scientific literature on repression and forgetting (including some of the studies described earlier in this chapter) and concluded that repression and forgetting could not be distinguished scientifically and thus should be treated the same legally. The Court concluded therefore that the plaintiffs' suits were barred by the statute of limitations three years after they reached their eighteenth birthdays (1974/75).

There is no doubt that sexual abuse is a serious problem, the contexts in which it occurs and fear of consequences of reporting makes it very difficult for victims to come forward (Browne and Finkelhor, 1986; Beitchman, Zucker, Hood, da Costa, Akman and Cassavia, 1992). Indeed false denials are likely to exceed false memories for this reason. Ethical constraints prevent researchers from simulating the threat experienced in real-life situations. We therefore have to rely on what we know from research about the vulnerability of memory and the power of suggestion. Even Freud modified his theories when he discovered that some of the early memories his patients retrieved were fantasy-based confabulations (Freud, 1910). We (researchers and practitioners) should aim to create conditions where accurate recollections can be fostered while being cautious that we may be fostering inaccurate recollections under the same conditions.

NOTES

1. This chapter should be read in conjunction with Chapter 10, the latter provides a more detailed review of the role of expert witnesses in court with respect to evidence involving recovered memories.
2. As indicated by Bowers and Farvolden (1996) scientific claims are always underdetermined by the available evidence.
3. A poignant example of the power of suggestion comes from the work on facilitated communication, a procedure that is used to help people with severe learning disabilities to communicate. The facilitators takes charge of the client's wrist while the client points to what he or she wishes the facilitator to type. Early reports showed remarkable advances in the communication abilities of clients. More stringent tests of the procedure

revealed the facilitator was the source of the clients' communication – putting words into the hands of the client (see Hastings, 1996 for a review of the literature).

REFERENCES

Anderson, M.C. and Spellman, B.A. (1995). On the status of inhibitory mechanisms in cognition: memory retrieval as a model case. *Psychological Review*, **102**, 68–100.

Barclay, C.R. (1986). Schematization of autobiographical memory. In D.C. Rubin (ed.), *Autobiographical Memory*. Cambridge: Cambridge University Press.

Barclay, C.R. and Wellman, H.M. (1986). Accuracies and inaccuracies in autobiographical memories. *Journal of Memory and Language*, **25**, 93–103.

Bartlett, F.C. (1932). *Remembering: A Study in Experimental and Social Psychology*. Cambridge: Cambridge University Press.

Beitchman, J.H., Zucker, K.J., Hood, J.E., da Costa, G.A., Akman, D. and Cassavia, E. (1992). A review of long-term effects of child sexual abuse. *Child Abuse and Neglect*, **16**, 108–118.

Bowers, K.S. and Farvolden, P. (1996). Revisiting a century-old Freudian slip – From suggestion disavowed to the truth repressed. *Psychological Bulletin*, **199**, 355–380.

Brainerd, C.J. and Reyna, V.F. (1990). Gist is the gist: the fuzzy trace theory and new intuitionism. *Developmental Review*, **10**, 3–47.

Brainerd, C.J., Reyna, V.F., Howe, M.L. and Kingma, J. (1990). The development of forgetting and reminiscence. *Monographs of the Society for Research in Child Development*, **55**, 3–4 Serial No. 222.

Brewin, C.R. (1986). Clinical and experimental approaches to understanding repression. Paper presented at the NATO Advanced Study Institute on Recollections of Trauma, France, 15–25 June.

Brewin, C.R., Dalgliesh, T. and Joseph, S. (in press). A dual representation theory of post-traumatic stress disorder. *Psychological Review*.

Briere, J. and Conte, J. (1993). Self-reported amnesia for abuse in adults molested as children. *Journal of Traumatic Stress*, **6**, 21–31.

Browne, A. and Finkelhor, D. (1986). The impact of child sexual abuse: a review of research. *Psychological Bulletin*, **99**, 66–77.

Bulkley, J.A. and Horowitz, M.J. (1994). Adults sexually abused as children: legal actions and issues. *Behavioural Sciences and the Law*, **12**, 65–86.

Christianson, S. (1992a). Do flashbulb memories differ from other types of emotional memories? In E. Winograd and U. Neisser (eds), *Affect and Accuracy in Recall: Studies of 'Flashbulb' Memories* (pp. 191–211). New York: Cambridge University Press.

Christianson, S. (1992b). Emotional stress and eyewitness memory: a critical review. *Psychological Bulletin*, **112**(2), 284–309.

Clifford, B.R. and Hollin, C.R. (1981). Effects of the type of incident and the number of perpetrators on eyewitness memory. *Journal of Applied Psychology*, **66**, 364–370.

Conway, M.A. (1997). *Recovered Memories and False Memories*. Oxford: Oxford University Press.

Creamer, M., Burgess, P. and Pattison, P. (1992). Reaction to trauma: a cognitive processing model. *Journal of Abnormal Psychology*, **101**(3), 452–459.

Crombag, H.F.M., Wagenaar, W.A. and Van Koppen, P.J. (1996). Crashing memories and the problem of source monitoring. *Applied Cognitive Psychology*, **10**, 95–104.

Dalenberg, C. (1996). The prediction of accurate recollections of trauma. Paper presented at the NATO Advanced Study Institute on Recollections of Trauma, France, 15–25 June.

Deese, J. (1959). On the prediction of occurrence of particular verbal intrusions in immediate recall. *Journal of Experimental Psychology*, **58**, 17–22.

Easterbrook, J.A. (1959). The effect of emotion on cue utilization and the organization of behavior. *Psychological Review*, **66**, 183–201.

Eisenberg, M.J. (1995). Recovered memories of childhood sexual abuse: the admissibility question. *Temple Law Review*, **64**, 249–280.

Erdelyi, M.H. (1990). Repression, reconstruction and defense: history and integration of the psychoanalytic and experimental frameworks. In J.L. Singer (ed.), *Repression and Dissociation: Implications for Personality Theory, Psychopathology and Health*. Chicago, IL: University of Chicago Press.

Fivush, R., Pipe, M-E., Murachver, T. and Reese, E. (1997). Events spoken and unspoken: implications of language and memory development for the recovered memory debate. In M.A. Conway (ed.), *Recovered Memories and False Memories*. Oxford: Oxford University Press.

Fivush, R. and Schwarzmueller, A. (1996). Children remember childhood: implications for childhood amnesia. Paper presented at the Second International Conference on Memory, Padua, Italy.

Foa, E.B., Rothbaum, B.O., Riggs, D. and Murdock, T. (1991). Treatment of post-traumatic stress disorder in rape victims: a comparison between cognitive behavioral procedures and counseling. *Journal of Consulting and Clinical Psychology*, **59**, 715–723.

Freud, S. (1910). Leonardo da Vinci and a memory of his childhood. In J. Strachey (ed.), *The Standard Edition of the Complete Psychological Works of Sigmund Freud*. London: Hogarth Press.

Garry, M., Loftus, E.F. and Sherman, S.J. (1996). Imagination inflation: imagining a childhood event inflates confidence that it occurred. *Psychonomic Bulletin and Review*, **3**(2), 208–214.

Hastings, R. (1996). Does facilitated communication free imprisoned minds? *The Psychologist*, **9**, 19–24.

Holmes, D.S. (1990). The evidence for repression: an examination of sixty years of research. In J.L. Singer (ed.), *Repression and Dissociation: Implications for Personality Theory, Psychopathology and Health*. Chicago, IL: University of Chicago Press.

Howe, M.L., Courage, M.L. and Peterson, C. (1994). How can I remember when I wasn't there: long-term retention of traumatic experiences and convergence of the cognitive self. *Consciousness and Cognition*, **3**, 327–355.

Hunter, E., Andrews, B. and Brewin, C. (1996). Memory loss for childhood sexual abuse – distinguishing between encoding and retrieval factors. Paper presented at the International Conference on Memory, Padova, 14–19 July.

Hyman, I.E. and Loftus, E.F. (in press). Memory: modern conceptions of the vicissitudes of early childhood memories. In D.A. Halperin (ed.), *False Memory Syndrome: Therapeutic and Forensic Perspectives*. American Psychiatric Press.

Hyman, I.E. and Pentland, J. (1996). The role of mental imagery in the creation of false memories. *Journal of Memory and Language*, 35, 101–117.

Hyman, I.E., Husband, T.H. and Billings, J.F. (1995). False memories of childhood experiences. *Applied Cognitive Psychology*, 9, 181–197.

Jacoby, L.L., Kelley, C.M. and Dywan, J. (1989). Memory attributions. In H.L. Roediger and F.I.M. Craik (eds), *Varieties of Memory and Consciousness: Essays in Honor of Endel Tulving* (pp. 391–422). Hillsdale, NJ: Lawrence Erlbaum.

Johnson, M.K. (1996) Identifying the origin of mental experience. In M.S. Myslobodsky (ed.), *Mythomanias*. Hillsdale, NJ: Lawrence Erlbaum.

Johnson, M.K., Hashtroudi, S. and Lindsay, D.S. (1993). Source monitoring. *Psychological Bulletin*, 114, 3–28.

Johnson, M.K., Nolde, S.F. and De Leonardis, D.M. (1996). Emotional focus and source monitoring, *Journal of Memory and Language*, 35, 135–156.

Kebeck, G. and Lohaus, A. (1986). Effect of emotional arousal on free recall of complex material. *Perceptual and Motor Skills*, 63, 461–462.

Kihlstrom, J.F. (1995). The trauma memory argument. *Consciousness and Cognition*, 4, 63–67.

Kihlstrom, J.F. and Schacter, D. (1995). Functional disorders of autobiographical memory. In A. Baddeley, B. Wilson and F. Watts (eds), *Handbook of Memory Disorders* (pp. 337–364). Chichester: Wiley.

Kuehn, L.L. (1974). Looking down a gun barrel: person perception and violent crime. *Perceptual and Motor Skills*, 39, 1159–1164.

Libkuman, T., Nichols-Whitehead, P., Griffith J. and Thomas R. (1996). Source of arousal and memory for detail. Manuscript submitted for publication.

Lindsay, D.S. and Kelley, C.M. (1996). Creating illusions of knowing in a cued recall remember know paradigm. *Journal of Memory and Language*, 35, 197–211.

Lindsay, D.S. and Read, J.D. (1994). Psychotherapy and memories of child sexual abuse: a cognitive perspective. *Applied Cognitive Psychology*, 8, 281–338.

Lindsay, D.S. and Read, J.D. (1995). Memory work and recovered memories of childhood sexual abuse: scientific evidence and public, professional and personal issues. *Psychology, Public Policy and Law*, 1, 846–908.

Loftus, E. (1974). Reconstructing memory: the incredible witness. *Psychology Today*, 8, 116–119

Loftus, E. and Ketcham, K. (1994). *The Myth of Repressed Memory*. New York: St Martins Press.

Loftus, E.F. and Pickrell, J.E. (1995). The formation of false memories. *Psychiatric Annals*, 25(12), 720–725.

Maclean, H. (1993). *Once Upon a Time*. New York: Harper Collins.

McDermott, K.B. (1996). The persistence of false memories in list recall. *Journal of Memory and Language*, 35, 212–230.

Memon, A., Wedge, G. and Beese, R. (1996). Juror perceptions of recovered memories: does prior knowledge influence decision making? Poster presented at the NATO Advanced Study Institute on Recollections of Trauma, France, 15–25 June.

Mulhern, S. (1996). The socialisation of altered states of consciousness. Paper presented at the NATO Advanced Study Institute on Recollections of Trauma, France, 15–25 June.

Neisser, U. and Harsch, N. (1992). Phantom flashbulbs: false recollections of hearing the news about challenger. In E. Winograd and U. Neisser (eds), *Affect and Accuracy in Recall: Studies of 'Flashbulb' Memories* (pp. 9–31). Cambridge: Cambridge University Press.

Ofshe, R. and Watters, E. (1994). *Making Monsters: False Memories, Psychotherapy and Sexual Hysteria*. New York: Scribner.

Olio, K. (1989). Memory retrieval in the treatment of adult survivors of sexual abuse. *Transactional Analysis Journal*, **19**, 93–100.

Olio, K. and Cornell, W.F. (1994). Making meaning not monsters: reflections on the delayed memory controversy. *Journal of Child Sexual Abuse*, **3**(3), 77–93.

Payne, D.G., Elie, C.J., Blackwell, J.M. and Neuschatz, R. (1996). Memory illusions: recalling, recognizing and recollecting events that never occurred. *Journal of Memory and Language*, **35**, 261–285.

Pennebaker, J.W. and Memon, A. (1996). Recovered memories in context: thoughts and elaborations on Bowers and Farvolden. *Psychological Bulletin*, **119**(3), 381–385.

Pendergrast, M. (1995). *Victims of Memory: Incest Accusations and Shattered Lives*. Hinesburg, VT: Upper Access.

Peterson, C. (1996). The preschool child witness: errors in accounts of traumatic injury. *Canadian Journal of Behavioural Science*, **28**, 36–42.

Pezdek, K. (1995). What types of childhood event are not likely to be suggestively planted? Paper presented at the Annual meeting of the Psychonomic Society, Los Angeles.

Poole, D.A., Lindsay, D.S., Memon, A. and Bull, R. (1995). Psychotherapy and the recovery of memories of childhood sexual abuse: US and British practitioners' opinions, practices and experiences. *Journal of Consulting and Clinical Psychology*, **63**(3), 426–437.

Roediger, H.L. and McDermott, K.B. (1995). Creating false memories: remembering words not presented in lists. *Journal of Experimental Psychology: Learning, Memory and Cognition*, **21**, 803–814.

Rose, S. (1992). *The Making of Memory*. New York: Anchor Books.

Ross, M. and Newby, I.R. (1996). Distinguishing memory from fantasy. Commentary on Newman and Baumeister. *Psychological Inquiry*, **7**(2), 173–177.

Schacter, D.L. (in press). Illusory memories: a cognitive neuroscience analysis. *Proceedings of the National Academy of Science*.

Schacter, D.L. (1996). *Searching for Memory: The Brain, the Mind and the Past*. New York: Basic Books.

Schacter, D.L. (1995). Memory distortion: history and current status. In D.L. Schacter, J.T. Coyle, G.D. Fishbach, M-M. Mesulam and L.E. Sullivan (eds), *Memory Distortion: How Minds, Brains, and Societies Reconstruct the Past*. Cambridge, MA: Harvard University Press.

Schreiber, F.R. (1973). *Sybil*. New York: Warner Books Inc.

Schooler, J. (1994). Cutting towards the core: the issues and evidence surrounding recovered accounts of sexual trauma. *Consciousness and Cognition*, **3**, 452–469.

Schooler, J.W., Bendiksen, M. and Ambadar, Z. (1997). Taking the middle line: can we accommodate both fabricated and recovered memories of sexual abuse? In M.A. Conway (ed.), *Recovered Memories and False Memories*. Oxford: Oxford University Press.

Spiegel, D. and Cardena, E. (1991). Disintegrated experience: the dissociative disorders revisited. *Journal of Abnormal Psychology*, **100**, 366–378.

Taub, S. (1996). The legal treatment of recovered memories of child sexual abuse. *Journal of Legal Medicine*, **17**, 183–214.

Terr, L. (1996). Children's memories in the wake of Challenger. *American Journal of Psychiatry*, **153**, 618–625.

Terr, L. (1991). Childhood traumas: an outline and overview. *American Journal of Psychiatry*, **148**, 10–20.

Wagenaar, W. (1996). Autobiographical memory in court. In D.C. Rubin (ed.), *Remembering Our Past*. New York: Cambridge University Press.

Wessel, I. and Mercelbach, H. (in press). The impact of anxiety on memory for details in spider phobics. *Applied Cognitive Psychology*.

Williams, L. (1994). Recall of childhood trauma: a prospective study of women's memories of child sexual abuse. *Journal of Consulting and Clinical Psychology*, **62**, 1167–1176.

Winograd, E. and Killinger, W.A. Jr. (1983). Relating age at encoding in early childhood to adult recall: development of flashbulb memories. *Journal of Experimental Psychology: General*, **112**, 413–422.

Yapko, M. (1997). The troublesome unknown about trauma and recovered memories. In M.A. Conway (ed.), *Recovered Memories and False Memories*. Oxford: Oxford University Press.

Yuille, J.C. and Cutshall, J.L. (1986). A case study of eyewitness memory of a crime. *Journal of Applied Psychology*, **71**, 291–301.

Yuille, J.C. and Tollestrup, P.A. (1992). A model of the diverse effects of emotion on eyewitness memory. In S-A. Christianson (ed.), *The Handbook of Emotion and Memory: Research and Theory* (pp. 201–215). Hillsdale, NJ: Lawrence Erlbaum.

Zaragoza, M.S. and Mitchell, K.J. (1996). Repeated exposure to suggestion and the creation of false memories. *Psychological Science*, **7**, 294–300.

CHAPTER 8

TELLING IT ALL: THE COGNITIVE INTERVIEW

Amina Memon

INTRODUCTION

The cognitive interview (or CI) is one of the most exciting developments in forensic psychology in the last 10 years and it is a much cited technique in the field of eyewitness memory. The CI is a forensic tool that comprises a series of memory retrieval techniques designed to increase the amount of information that can be obtained from a witness and may help police officers and other professionals obtain a more complete and accurate report from a witness. The CI can only be used with a cooperative interviewee and therefore may be most suitable in interviews where the interviewee is not a suspect. The effectiveness of the CI in improving the quality and quantity of information from an eyewitness and as a way of improving the skills of interviewers has been empirically tested. To date some 45 studies have been conducted. This includes two studies conducted in the field using real-life witnesses and police officers trained in the CI technique.

The CI was initially developed by the psychologists Ed Geiselman (University of California, Los Angeles) and Ron Fisher (Florida International University) in 1984 as a response to the many requests they received from police officers and legal professionals for a method of improving witness interviews. The CI is based upon known psychological principles of remembering and retrieval of information from memory. Police detectives trained to use this technique enabled witnesses to produce over 40 per cent more valid information than detectives using their traditional interviewing techniques (Fisher, Geiselman and Amador, 1989).

This chapter will provide a critical review of research on the CI and will highlight methodological and theoretical issues that have arisen during the course of relevant research. Two key questions will be addressed throughout: (1) Has the CI been adequately tested in laboratory research? (2) Does the CI work because of the cognitive techniques or are we instead seeing an effect of improved communication or rapport between interviewer and witness? Practical issues and directions for future research will also be reviewed. Before describing the procedure and reviewing the empirical research, it is useful to understand *why* a procedure such as the CI is necessary.

WHAT LED TO THE DEVELOPMENT OF THE COGNITIVE INTERVIEW?

The ability to obtain full and accurate information from a witness is critical in an investigation, it may determine whether or not a case is solved, yet the eyewitness literature reveals that such recall is difficult to achieve (e.g. Goodman *et al.*, 1987). An empirical study of the techniques used by untrained police officers working in a police department in Miami, Florida (Fisher *et al.*, 1987a), however, suggested that improving witness memory was only part of the story. There existed some fundamental problems in the conduct of police interviews that were leading to ineffective communication and poor memory performance. Fisher *et al.* (1987a) documented several characteristics of the 'standard police interview' among which were constant interruptions (when an eyewitness was giving an account), excessive use of question–answer format and inappropriate sequencing of questions. George (1991) studied the techniques typically used by untrained officers in London and found a remarkably similar pattern among that group. This led to the characterization of a 'standard police interview' as being one of poor quality and stressed the need for an alternative procedure for interviewing witnesses. Such calls have now begun to be answered and a number of innovative procedures have been developed for use by professionals who interview witnesses in Britain (Bull, 1992; Bull, 1995). However, the focus has tended to be on child witness interviews, while there is much room for improving the quality of investigative interviews with adult witnesses including interviews with suspects (see Cherryman and Bull, 1995; Gudjonsson, 1994 for reviews).

The CI represents the alliance of two fields of study. The original version drew heavily upon what psychologists know about the way in which we remember and recall things. Revisions of the procedure focused more heavily on the practical considerations for managing a social interaction and this was led by a desire to improve communication in police interviews and alleviate some of the problems described above. Obviously the 'cognitive' and 'communication' components work in tandem, however, for the purposes of describing the procedure as it has been depicted in the published literature, the 'cognitive' and 'communication' components will be outlined separately in our description of the CI.

The original cognitive interview: theoretical principles

The 'cognitive' components of the CI draw upon several theoretical perspectives on memory. First, a retrieval cue is effective to the extent that there is an overlap between the encoded information and the retrieval cue (Flexser and Tulving, 1978). Reinstatement of the original encoding context increases the accessibility of stored information (Tulving and Thomson's Encoding Specificity Hypothesis, 1973). Secondly, Multiple Trace Theory (Bower, 1967) contends that our memories are made up of a network of associations and consequently, there are several means by which a memory could be cued. It follows from this that information not accessible with one technique may be accessible with another (Tulving, 1974) and this is one of the guiding principles that led to the development of multiple techniques for retrieving information in the CI. Finally, the development of the CI was influenced by Schema Theory (Schank and Abelson, 1977) according to which familiar events have a schema or script (based upon prior experience) and this guides the encoding of the event by organizing information into a hierarchy of slots. Schema guide retrieval of information by providing an organized information system to search and a witness's prior experience may allow him or her to fill empty slots with information that fits the schema. This may sometimes result in recall of schema-consistent information (e.g. the magician was wearing a hat) that was not present in the event (see below). Schema-guided retrieval also results in the filtering out at recall of details that do not fit the schema or are incongruent with expectations although situational circumstances at the time of a crime will determine what information is processed (see Koehnken, 1995). Let us look at the applications of these theoretical principles and the specific 'cognitive' techniques in some depth.

Context reinstatement

The first technique, drawing upon notions of encoding specificity, encourages the witness mentally to reconstruct the physical and personal contexts which existed at the time of the crime. Although this is often not an easy task the interviewer can help witnesses by asking them to form an *image* or *impression* of the environmental aspects of the original scene (e.g. the location of objects in a room), to comment on their emotional reactions and feelings at the time (surprise, anger, etc.) and to describe any sounds, smells and physical conditions at the time (hot, humid, smoky, etc.). Geiselman and his colleagues (Saywitz *et al., 1992*) have suggested that it may be helpful for child witnesses to verbalize out aloud when mentally reinstating context. For example to describe the room as the image comes to mind, to describe smells, sounds and other features of the context. The following is an example of how the instructions to reinstate context were administered in a study where adult witnesses were interviewed about a photography session (Memon, Wark, Holley, Koehnken and Bull, 1997):

> Interviewer: *First of all I'd like you to think back to that day. Picture the room in your head as if you were back there .... Can you see it?* (pause for reply) *Think about who was there* (pause). *How you were feeling?* (pause) *What you could see?* (pause) *What you could hear?* (pause) *Could you smell anything?* (pause). *Now I want you to tell me as much as you can about what happened when you came to get your photograph taken.*

It should be noted that the effectiveness of context reinstatement depends not only on reinstating physical conditions but also on the compatibility of affective states at the time of encoding and testing. As pointed out by Schacter (1996) in his book *Searching for Memory* what matters most is a person's subjective experience at the time they experienced the event. The latter may comprise their thoughts, feelings and inferences about the event. We cannot assume that all experiences are preserved intact and are potentially recallable. Sometimes we forget because the relevant cues are unavailable, but sometimes we forget 'because the relevant engrams (the representations of memory in the brain) have become weakened or blurred' (Schacter, 1996). This is an important point with respect to the issue of recovery of childhood memories (see chapter on recovered memories for a further discussion).

Report everything

A second CI technique is to ask the witness to *report everything*. This may well facilitate the recall of additional information, perhaps by changing the criteria we use when deciding what details to report. We may only choose to report information that we think is salient, relevant and that is remembered well. Fisher and Geiselman (1992) argue that witnesses should be encouraged to report in full without screening out anything they consider to be irrelevant or for which they have only partial recall. In addition to facilitating the recall of additional information, this technique may yield information that may be valuable in putting together partial information from different witnesses to the same crime. An eyewitness who provides more details may also be judged to be a more credible witness in the courtroom (Bell and Loftus, 1989), although the overall accuracy of these details rather than the amount of information that is reported should be the major question in this context. We will expand on this point later.

Change perspective

A third technique used in the CI is to ask for recall from a variety of perspectives. This technique tries to encourage the witnesses to place themselves in the shoes of the victim (if the witness is not a victim) or of another witness who was present and to report what they saw or would have seen. The aim is to increase the *amount* of detail elicited by reducing the extent to which prior knowledge and expectations (schema) limit memory search. Geiselman *et al.* (1990) report that changing perspectives can be particularly helpful for child witnesses if the following instructions are given: 'Put yourself in that other person's body and describe what they would have seen.' However, in our research with young children we have found that children have difficulty with the change perspective instruction as illustrated by the following quotation from Memon *et al.* (1993):

> Interviewer: *What I'd like you to try and do is imagine that you are the nurse and that you can see the room from where she was standing, by the wall chart. Just tell me what you can see.*

> Child: *Umm..Did you see the letters, can you see the letters good and I said yes and that's all she said to me.*

Evidence obtained using this particular technique may not be easily accepted in legal procedures where it is likely to be seen as subjective information or as an inference (see Memon and Koehnken, 1992 for a discussion of this).

Reverse order

The fourth component of the CI is the instruction to make retrieval attempts from different starting points within the event. Witnesses usually feel that they have to start at the beginning and are usually asked to do so. However, the CI encourages extra focused and extensive retrieval by encouraging witnesses to recall in a variety of orders from the end, or from the middle or from the most memorable event. This technique also draws upon schema theory, the change in temporal perspective may cause witnesses to recall information that may not necessarily fit the schema. Geiselman and Callot (1990) found that it was more effective to recall in forward order once followed by reverse order than to make two attempts to recall from the beginning. There are some problems associated with the use of this technique, however. Alterations of the temporal order of recall operates in opposition to the strategy of context reinstatement in which the sequencing of details matches that at the time of encoding. This may account for the recent finding that reverse order recall is relatively ineffective in yielding additional information when used in conjunction with the context reinstatement technique (Memon, Wark, Bull and Koehnken, 1997a).

Tests of the original 'cognitive' CI procedure

Between 1984 and 1990 several 'simulation' studies of CI were undertaken employing staged and filmed scenarios of forensic relevance including Los Angeles Police Department training films which depicted 'realistic' criminal events. The interviews in some of these studies were conducted by trained and experienced police officers. For example Geiselman *et al.* (1985) compared the cognitive interview with the interviews more usually conducted by experienced police officers (the 'standard' interview procedure described earlier). The participants (witnesses) were undergraduate students and the interviewers were experienced law enforcement professionals (e.g. police investigators, members of the CIA and private detectives). The training films used in this study were simulations of life-threatening situations which depicted a number of scenarios modelled on real-life events. Witnesses were interviewed by the interviewers (who had *not* seen the training films) approximately 48 hours after viewing the film. Three weeks prior to the interview the interviewers received instructions to follow one of two procedures: (i) *standard interview* or (ii) *the cognitive interview*. Geiselman *et al.* (1985) coded the witnesses' recall information as pertaining to information about 'persons' or 'objects' or 'events' and found that the CI elicited 35 per cent more correct information than did a standard control interview (SI) without increased errors or confabulations (the reporting of things not in the event). Subsequent studies conducted in the Geiselman laboratory extended the earlier findings and suggested that witnesses interviewed with the CI were less likely to be misled (by earlier suggestive questions) than those interviewed with a standard interview (Geiselman *et al.*, 1986, see also Milne *et al.*, 1995).

Revisions of the CI: improving communication and retrieval

The original version of the cognitive interview resulted in substantial gains in the amount of correct information that was elicited from eyewitnesses without any apparent increases in errors. However, in order to be able effectively to implement the use of the 'cognitive' components of the CI, it is necessary to provide interviewers with the necessary social skills and communication strategies that are required in order to build rapport with a witness (Fisher *et al.*, 1987b). As indicated earlier, research with police officers has suggested that this was something they lacked. The revised version of the CI (also referred to as the enhanced version) incorporated the following techniques.

Rapport building

This is an attempt to get to know the witness a little to clarify what the interviewer and interviewee expectations are and generally to put them at their ease. An important component of rapport building is for the interviewer explicitly to 'transfer control' to the witnesses by (a) making it clear to witnesses to do the work and (b) allowing them time to think and respond. Interviewees tend incorrectly to assume that it is the interviewer who is the most active participant in an interview and accordingly adopt a passive role. The CI makes the witness an active participant in the interview process. The interviewer is assigned the role of facilitator. The interviewer can do this by effective transfer of control to the witness. For example by making sure that the questions asked are guided by the retrieval process of the interviewee (see below). The advice to interviewers is to keep the number of questions to a minimum, let the witness do the talking and follow-up with specific questions where clarification or probing is required, as illustrated in the next section.

Focused retrieval

While the CI encourages the witness to structure his or her own recall, it also emphasizes the need for the interviewer to facilitate witness retrieval using *focused* memory techniques. One of the techniques used in conjunction with the context reinstatement is the instruction to form an image of the various parts of the witnessed event. Fisher and Geiselman (1992) draw a distinction between conceptual image codes (an image stored as a concept or dictionary definition) and pictorial codes (the mental representation of an image). The notion is that images create dual codes or more meaningful elaborations (Paivio, 1971). The 'imaging' part of the CI usually occurs in the questioning phase of the interview and assumes that the witness has effectively recreated the context in which an event occurred. The instruction could take the following form: 'Concentrate on the picture you have in your mind of the suspect, focus on the face and describe it.' While this technique has the potential to increase the amount of detail a witness provides, it may also be responsible for some increases in errors (see below).

Witness compatible questioning

As indicated earlier, allowing a witness to guide the retrieval process is an important element of the CI. The timing of the interviewer's questions is critical (deemed witness compatible questioning). Following principles of encoding specificity and feature overlap, questions should be guided by the witness' pattern of recall rather than by adhering to a rigid protocol. For example if a witness is describing a suspect's clothing the interviewer should not suddenly switch the line of questioning to the actions of the suspect.

Supportive interviewer behaviour

The CI interviewer does not simply attend to the verbal interaction between interviewer and witness but also concentrates on the nonverbal components of the interaction. Koehnken (1995) directs us to the most important elements of an interviewer's nonverbal behaviour. In order to facilitate recall, the interviewer should create a relaxed atmosphere. We know from the 'principle of synchrony' that the interviewer's behaviour will shape the interviewee's mood and behaviour. Therefore the interviewer should sit in a relaxed manner, avoiding sudden movements, express attention, support and interest by listening carefully to what the witness says without interrupting.

Testing the CI: an effective control group

From a practical perspective, it is important to show that the CI is more effective than the techniques previously in use by police officers and others. The selection of untrained police interviewers in the Geiselman *et al.* (1985) study was a sensible, practical control. However, a theoretical perspective, an experimental control is needed to demonstrate that the techniques themselves are causing the effects and not some aspect related to training such as motivation, quality of questioning or rapport-building skills. The use of the term 'standard' in earlier studies itself implies inferiority and police officers are sensitive to this and may sometimes take it to imply that their experience is worthless (Memon, Bull and Smith, 1995). However, it may be that the positive effects of their job experience are offset by the negative effects of their poor interview techniques. Thus the standard interview may not be a good procedure with which to compare the CI. The issue of experimental control has become even more important in testing the revised version of the CI given that it combines the cognitive techniques with some general strategies for improving communication. This raises another question: What evidence is there that the gains in information elicited are not merely due to the improved communication?

In order to address some of the concerns outlined above, more recent tests of the CI have compared the CI with a procedure known as the structured interview (SI) procedure where the quality of interviewer training in communication and questioning techniques is comparable to the CI procedure. The training of the structured group follows a procedure that is recommended to professionals who interview children (the Home Office Memorandum of Good Practice, Home Office and Department of Health, 1992). The essence of the Memorandum is to treat the interview as a procedure in which a variety of interviewing techniques are deployed in relatively discrete phases proceeding from general to open, to specific, closed-form questions. Rapport-building and active listening, are also important components.

The techniques used in the original, enhanced, standard and structured interviews are indicated in Table 8.1.

Is it possible for an interviewer armed (merely) with a range of 'good' interviewing techniques and effective communication skills to achieve the same effects as a CI-trained interviewer? This question was first addressed by Guenter Koehnken and colleagues in their studies conducted in Germany (Koehnken *et al.* 1994; Koehnken *et al.* 1995; Mantwill *et al.* 1995). In these studies the cognitive interview was compared with a structured interview. The structured group received training in basic communication skills of comparable quality and length to that received by the cognitive interviewers. This included instruction on rapport building and use of various types of questioning. The training of the cognitive group in addition involved the use of the various cognitive techniques. The cognitive and structured interviewers received a written sample of questions and sample interviews (transcripts) were fully discussed and critically evaluated on the basis of techniques used. While the CI group focused on the retrieval aids used by the interviewer and the specific question types (open, closed, leading, etc.), the SI group focused on questioning strategy and types of questions only. The interviewers then watched a

TABLE 8.1 *Components of the CI, ECI, standard and structured interviews*

	Original CI	ECI	Standard	Structured
Rapport and transfer control		×		×
Supportive interviewer behaviour		×		×
Context reinstatement	×	×		
Report everything and in detail	×	×		
Free recall (FR)	×	×	×	×
Questions related to what was said in FR and follow-up questions		×		×
Use your usual technique (e.g. who, what, when, why, how . . .)			×	
Activate/probe images		×		
Change perspective	×	×		
Witness compatible questioning		×		
Reverse order recall	×	×		

Note: × indicates the technique emphasized in the training of interviewers. The standard group are typically untrained but may be experienced police officers.

videotaped interview. Finally each interviewer took part in a role play and received feedback on her or his performance. The training session lasted between four and five hours.

In these German studies, the to-be-remembered event was a video recording showing a blood donation. Participants were tested a week after viewing the event. In the Koehnken *et al.* (1994) study the participants (witnesses) and interviewers were non-psychology students without any prior experience in investigative interviewing. Each interviewer conducted one interview. The CI resulted in an average of 52 per cent more correctly recalled information without increasing the number of errors and confabulated (i.e. made-up) details. The interviewers' memories were also tested by asking them to prepare from memory written accounts of the event. The superiority of the CI was noted in the interviewer accounts with an average of 42 per cent more correct details as compared to the structured interviewers.

So far the evidence suggests that the enhanced CI effects are due to the use of the cognitive techniques rather than merely a result of enhanced communication. However, this does not fit with the results of a series of studies conducted in England as part of a project funded by the Economic and Social Research Council in the UK (Memon *et al.*, 1997a, 1997b; 1996b, 1996c). Memon *et al.* (1997b) directly examined whether the source of the CI advantage was due to facilitated communication arising from the use of the 'communication' components of the enhanced CI or a result of the 'cognitive' components of the enhanced

CI (context, imagery, reverse order and reporting in detail). Following Koehnken, CI and SI interviewers received a similar quality of training. The interviewers were psychology undergraduates who had no previous experience of interviewing and the interviewees were college students. All interviewers were trained separately over a period of two days in basic communication techniques such as building rapport, in types of questions to ask, and they had the opportunity to conduct role plays and receive feedback on practice interviews. In order to examine the effects of training and motivation, we also included an untrained group in the study.

To our surprise we found that the cognitive interviews and structured interviews did not differ in terms of the overall amount recalled, the accuracy of recall, the number of errors or the number of confabulations. Both groups of trained interviewers elicited more in the way of overall information and amount of correct information than did the untrained group. However, this was offset by their producing a significantly higher number of errors and confabulations than the untrained group. These findings are important in themselves but they also raise the question of what is the appropriate control group. Clearly, if the CI is compared to an untrained group it produces some advantages. However, if the cognitive interviewers are compared to a group matched for everything but the cognitive techniques (namely the structured interview) then the advantage of the CI is reduced. This finding is at odds with the studies conducted in Germany and suggests that the effects of the cognitive interview depend on the standard of comparison that is used (Memon and Stevenage, 1996). The discrepancy in results could be due to sampling differences and interviewer differences (Memon's interviewers were psychology graduates and were possibly more motivated). It should be pointed out that while the structured interviewers in the Memon *et al.* study (in press b) were behaving more like cognitive interviewers they did not use any of the cognitive techniques. Of course this does not rule out the possibility that the non-CI interviewees were spontaneously using CI techniques. Memon *et al.* (1996a) found that college students frequently report the use of context reinstatement and imagery as aids to recall. Indeed such techniques are also reported to be used by older participants drawn from the general population (Harris, 1980). Future studies may benefit from collecting data not only on the techniques that interviewers use but also on the techniques used by witnesses.

A second explanation for the results of the Memon *et al.* studies (1996b, 1996c, 1997a, 1997b) is that the primary effect of the CI is that it enhances communication. It is possible that the most effective component of the enhanced CI is the 'transfer of control' instruction. Moreover, this facilitates the use of techniques such as context reinstatement. Koriat and Goldsmith (1996), however, put forward an alternative explanation. They suggest that the CI may achieve its effects by improving self-monitoring (or screening of memory) and strategic regulation. In other words the 'meta-cognitive' decisions made by the interviewee during memory reporting are critical. Koriat and Goldsmith indicate that these may constitute 'covert attributions' about what an interviewee believes he or she remembers. The extent to which it may be possible, by improving monitoring effectiveness, to increase the amount and accuracy of reported information in witness interviews presents itself as a fruitful area for future research (cf. Ross and Newby, in press). We would, however, need to find a way of improving self-monitoring in the CI without interfering with the cognitive mnemonic techniques such as the instruction to 'report everything'.

It would be premature to conclude from the Memon *et al.* (1997b) that untrained interviewers are the best ones for a number of reasons. First, the study was limited in ecological validity. The interviewers were not police officers but college students. Moreover, they were intelligent and motivated students who had been asked by an authority figure to collect some data for a research project and they knew that the interviews were being recorded. It is unlikely that they could be compared to typical police officers (Memon *et al.*, 1994). Indeed the quality of interviews of the Memon *et al.* untrained group were quite different from what is found with police officers using the standard procedure. In other words, Memon *et al.*'s interviewers tended to ask fewer questions, did not interrupt the witness when they were speaking and did not ask leading questions (cf. Fisher *et al.*, 1987a; George, 1991). The untrained student interviewers in our study also made fewer inaccuracies. This again suggests the effects observed in the laboratory depend on the standards of comparison. It would be interesting to compare student and police interviewers in a single study holding interview training constant. At this point it may be helpful to turn to field research on the cognitive interview to see if the picture is any clearer there.

Field tests of the cognitive interview

A field study is one where data are collected in the 'real world' by eliciting the support of those who would collect the data as part of their job and allow it to be subject to experimental analyses. The results of the field studies conducted to date, while based upon small samples, are promising.

The first field test of the CI was conducted by Fisher, Geiselman and Amador (1989) with the help of police detectives in Miami, Florida. In the pre-training stage of the study sample interviews were collected from police detectives using their usual interview techniques. Half of the group were then selected for training in the CI which took place over four one-hour sessions and covered principles of cognition as well as all the elements of the enhanced CI. The detectives received feedback on a practice interview before using the CI in the field when interviewing real witnesses. Two measures of the effects of training were taken: (i) the number of facts elicited before and after training (comparing each officer's technique before and after the training) and (ii) number of correct facts elicited by trained as compared to untrained (standard) interviewers. The CI was found to be effective in both comparisons.

One of the difficulties of conducting field research on memory is that of corroboration of memory reports. In the Fisher *et al.* study (1989) the accuracy of witness reports was checked by comparing them to the reports of other witnesses, forensic evidence, etc. It is reported that where corroboration was possible, 90 per cent of the witness recall was corroborated and there was no difference in corroboration rates between the cognitive and standard interviews. While the sample size is small and select, the fact that six of the seven trained detectives improved has important practical implications for training.

Richard George, a British police officer replicated and extended the findings of the US field study. George (1991) constructed an elaborate training programme for his police officers in the CI and in a technique known as Conversation Management (a procedure based on the use different conversation styles, verbal and nonverbal skills to enhance interviewer–interviewee communication). The CI elicited significantly more information than the standard interview and more so than conversation management.

The field studies raise questions about how much training is required to produce effective use of the CI, an important question given that resources for training are often limited. George (1991) trained his officers over two days and commented that the training went down well given his police background. Memon *et al.* (1994) trained officers for four hours and found that this was insufficient to motivate them to use the CI techniques. Moreover, the trainees commented on the fact that a police officer would have more experience of interviewing witnesses than a psychologist! Turtle (1995) evaluated several one-week training courses in Canada and he found that such training had little effect on the frequency with which CI techniques were used. Clearly the effects of training are complex and are likely to be influenced by who does the training, attitudes to training and its perceived applicability in the field.

THE CI AND CHILD WITNESSES

Research in this area has been timely given recent developments concerning laws and procedures involving child witnesses (see Chapter 9 for a review).

There is now strong evidence to suggest that usually younger children (ages 6–7) will often recall *less* information than do older children (ages 10–11 e.g. Davies *et al.*, 1989). Given that the primary aim of CI is to increase the *amount* of information retrieved it may be a most effective procedure to use with young children. Saywitz *et al.* (1992) attempted to evaluate and refine the CI for children (ages 7–8 and 10–11) using a live event. The event was a game where children dressed up, interacted with, and were photographed by a stranger. The CI significantly increased correct facts recalled across both age groups by 26 per cent. The interviews in this first study were conducted by students. In a second study, a CI 'practice session' was included, the aims of which were to familiarize the children with the cognitive interview techniques and to give feedback on their performance. The interviewers in the main study were experienced police officers who received written instructions and a two-hour training session during which they were informed about child-appropriate language, rapport building, interview preparation and procedure. The CI interviewers received additional information on the use of the four original CI techniques. The standard interview group were instructed to use the techniques they would normally use. The CI led to more correct details being recalled than did the SI (20 per cent increase for the 8–9 year olds and 44 per cent for the 11–12 year olds). Furthermore, collapsing across age levels, a practice cognitive interview prior to the main interview improved performance by an additional 25 per cent. No increase in the amount of incorrect or confabulated details was observed. Thus it appears to be an efficient strategy to familiarize children with the CI before they are questioned about the event (cf.

Memon *et al.*, 1996). Interestingly it was the older children whose performance improved most with a practice interview which is the opposite to what we would expect based on our understanding of children's development of memory strategy usage (Ornstein *et al.* 1985). An analysis was conducted to look at the frequency with which interviewers used the four CI techniques. It was apparent that the student interviewers (in the first study) were more likely to use each of the four techniques compared to the experienced detectives. For example only half of the detectives used the 'change perspective' instruction as compared to 94 per cent of the student interviewers. George (1991) in the British field study and Turtle (1995) also found police officers did not use this technique even though they had been trained to do so.

The Saywitz *et al.* study provides a powerful demonstration of the effectiveness of a CI with children over the age of eight. There are, however, several concerns. First the CI interviewers received training while the standard interviewers did not. This may affect the motivation of the CI interviewers. Secondly while the authors of this study did attempt to correlate use of each CI technique with overall memory scores we have no information about the types of details elicited with the various CI techniques. A related point is that the details about errors are not provided. Thirdly, while the CI practice group had an opportunity to rehearse and become familiar with the task of retrieval, the control group did not. Despite these shortcomings, this study has been supported by the findings produced in Germany by Koehnken and colleagues. Koehnken *et al.* (1992) investigated the effectiveness of the enhanced CI with 9- and 10-year-old children who had been shown a short film. After a delay of three to five days, they were questioned by trained psychology students about the film using either an enhanced CI or an SI (structured) interview. In this study great care was taken to ensure that the SI interviewers were trained in the same way as CI interviewers save for using the special CI techniques. The enhanced CI produced a 93 per cent increase in the amount of correct information recalled compared to the SI. The number of confabulations (the reporting of details not present in the event) increased, however, and this has been found in several studies where the CI had been used with child witnesses (e.g Fisher and McCauley, 1995; Mantwill *et al.*, 1995).

Memon and colleagues attempted to isolate the effects of the individual components of the original CI (Memon *et al.*, 1996d) and have tested the effectiveness of the CI with younger children (aged 6–7). In the Memon *et al.* (1996d) study, each of the four mnemonic techniques of the CI (recreate context, report in detail, change order and change perspective) was compared with an instruction to 'try harder'. Prior to each interview there was a practice session in which each child described a familiar activity using the relevant one of the four CI techniques e.g. context reinstatement. There were no significant differences in correct recall or errors as a function of instruction condition. A qualitative analysis of the interview transcripts suggested that the children did not fully understand all the techniques and had difficulty using the change perspective instruction. This suggests that refinement of the CI is needed for younger children. As Ornstein (1991) points out, a good interviewer should tailor the interview so that it takes into consideration the cognitive and linguistic capabilities of an individual child.

Finally, Memon *et al.* (1997a) tested the revised version of the CI using 8- and 9-year-old children who were witnesses to a live magic show. The CI was found to significantly increase correct and incorrect (errors) in an interview two days (but not 12 days) after the event while accuracy was unaffected. The increases in information were isolated to the questioning phase of the interview. The CI interviewers asked significantly more questions than the structured interviewers but this was because they were getting more information and probing for details with specific questions. It is well established in the literature that questions may serve as prompts and that they may also increase errors (e.g. Davies *et al.*, 1989; Gee and Pipe, 1995). In the Memon *et al.* (in press) study further investigation of the errors revealed that they were associated with particular types of details namely descriptions of persons. Again previous research suggests children have difficulty with person details (Davies *et al.*, 1989). It should be noted, however, that the specific questioning in the Memon *et al.* study followed the witnesses' use of imagery techniques and the latter could also be responsible for the increase in errors. Unfortunately, the Memon *et al.* data do not allow us to isolate the cause of the errors other than to specify where they occurred in the interview and the types of details that tended to be erroneously reported (see Memon and Stevenage, 1996 for a more extensive discussion on errors).

It is possible to glean some information about errors by looking at the nature of the to-be-remembered event, however. The magic show is an event for which children have a schema and there is some evidence to suggest such an event elicits a high number of schema consistent details (Milne *et al.*, 1995).

Limitations of the use of CI with child witnesses

Several problems in applying the CI with children have been identified. First, younger children (ages 6–7) have difficulty understanding the CI techniques in the form developed for adults (Memon *et al.*, 1993; 1996). Secondly, CI when used with children can increase errors (Memon *et al.*, 1997a; Milne *et al.*, 1995) and confabulations (Koehnken *et al.*, 1992). Thirdly, the CI procedure may also increase demand characteristics in that children respond in a way they think may please the interviewer. This is illustrated in the following transcript taken from the Memon *et al.* (1993) child witness study.

Interviewer: *OK, but what about the day the nurse came, can you tell me about that? I know you've told me already, but I need to find out more.*

Child: *Yes, just in case I am saying the right things.*

Interviewer: *Well no, not exactly, but just in case you remember any more.*

Child: *Yes, some different things that I forgot to say at all.*

Interviewer: *Yes. The best thing to do is to start again and tell me everything again.*

Child: *Well, I can't tell you the same things.*

It is apparent from the above example, that the success of the technique relies to a large extent on the interviewers' abilities effectively to communicate techniques to the children and this may in part be related to the quality of training received. At the same time individual qualities of the interviewee may also contribute to the successful use of the CI techniques and this is an area where there is a dearth of research.

INTERVIEWER VARIABLES

It is generally accepted that interviewee performance varies with the quality of the interviewer and vice versa. Given that the CI is a interactive process between the interviewer and witness aiming to facilitate recall, it is surprising that such little attention has been paid to interviewer behaviour in the CI. It could be argued on the basis of the research by Fisher and Geiselman that the original CI procedure could be applied with relatively little training whereas the enhanced CI procedure, which places far greater demands on the interviewer, may well require more extensive training (Fisher *et al.*, 1987b). In addition, since the revised version places more emphasis on social skills it is reasonable to expect more variation between interviewers in their use of the techniques.

A quantitative analysis of interviewer behaviour (i.e. use of the various techniques and questioning style) in cognitive and structured (control) interviews was undertaken in the Memon *et al.* (in press a) experiment and some preliminary data were collected on interviewer variability (Memon *et al.*, in press d). There were differences among the individual CI interviewers in the number and type of questions asked (e.g. open ended versus closed). Analysis of the structured interviewers in the Memon *et al.* (in press a) study revealed that they were a more homogenous group when it came to their use of questions and interview style although there was some variability in performance. This suggests that perhaps the cognitive interviewers were utilizing more cognitive resources than the structured interviewers and therefore found it more difficult to keep their interview procedure on track. The solution to this problem is more extensive practise in the use of CI techniques. According to Koehnken (1995) when an interviewer has achieved a level of expertise that allows them to conduct a CI without having constantly to check guidelines (regarding interview procedure) and attend to appropriate behaviours, the cognitive load on the interviewer is likely to be reduced. This should enable the techniques to be used more efficiently.

CONCLUSION

The cognitive interview (CI) emerges as probably the most exciting development in the field of eyewitness testimony in the last 10 years. It is a technique to facilitate recall and initial tests show consistent gains in the amount of information that can be gathered from a witness with a cognitive interview. The early work, however, was limited in conclusions due to the use of an untrained control group. In other words it is not possible to conclude that the CI effects reflect the use of cognitive techniques or some aspect of interviewer behaviour that has changed as a result of training. More recent studies have remedied this by including trained control groups and at the same time have scrutinized revised versions of the CI to determine the effects of improved communication skills on witness' memory performance. Such studies suggest the CI may be more effective than a structured interview but in some studies the latter appears to be as effective as the CI. In other words, the CI and the SI have the potential to yield more detailed information without jeopardizing the accuracy of that information. The only area of concern is that more errors are sometimes elicited but progress has recently been made in identifying where in the interview these occur. Obviously, the benefits of any innovative technique need to be carefully weighed up against any costs. In a forensic investigation an increase in number of details could be especially helpful at the information-gathering stage in providing new clues that could lead to a successful conviction. It is up to the investigator to consider when a CI may or may not be helpful and to take particular care when probing the witness with specific questions.

Future research

While much research has already been conducted on the CI, there are some questions that remain unanswered. What are the qualities that make a good interviewer? Researchers could consider the effects of interviewer variables either by including interviewers as factors in the design of experimenters and/or by collecting baseline data on interviewer performance prior to training. In a related vein, the effects of training need to be monitored over a reasonable period of time in order to assess the effects of feedback and experience in use of the techniques on performance. Another worthwhile line of research is to see how the CI fares across repeated testing and when memory is tested after a long delay. We know that context reinstatement can be a powerful cue to recognition when memory is tested after a five-month delay (Malpass and Devine, 1981). How does the memory fare with the CI after such a delay? Can the CI be used to aid the recollection childhood memories? Finally, we suggest that more research attention be given to the impact of individual differences in witness factors (such as age, gender, personality, affect) and characteristics of the to-be-remembered event on performance in a cognitive interview.

REFERENCES

Bell, B. and Loftus, E.F. (1989). Trivial persuasion in the courtroom: the power of a few minor details. *Journal of Personality and Social Psychology*, 56(5), 669–679.

Bower, G. (1967). A multicomponent theory of memory trace. In K.W. Spence and J.T. Spence (eds), *The Psychology of Learning and Motivation, vol. 1*, New York: Academic Press.

Bull, R. (1992). Obtaining evidence expertly: the reliability of interviews with child witnesses. *Expert Evidence: The International Digest of Human Behaviour, Science and Law*, 1(1), 5–12.

Bull, R. (1995). Innovative techniques for the questioning of child witnesses especially those who are young and those with learning disability. In M. Zaragoza, J.R. Graham, G.C.N. Hall, R. Hirschman and Y.S. Ben-Porath (eds), *Memory and Testimony in the Child Witness*. Thousand Oaks, CA: Sage.

Cherryman, J. and Bull, R. (1995) Investigative interviewing. In F. Leishman, B. Loveday and S. Savage (eds), *Core Issues in Policing*. London: Longman.

Davies, G., Tarrant, A. and Flin, R. (1989). Close encounters of the witness kind: children's memory for a simulated health inspection. *British Journal of Psychology*, 80, 415–429.

Fisher, R.P., Geiselman, R.E. and Raymond, D.S. (1987a) Critical analysis of police interviewing techniques. *Journal of Police Science and Administration*, **15**, 177–185.

Fisher, R.P., Geiselman, R.E., Raymond, D.S., Jurkevich, L.M. and Warhaftig, M.L. (1987b) Enhancing eyewitness memory: refining the cognitive interview. *Journal of Police Science and Administration*, **15**, 291–297.

Fisher, R.P., Geiselman, R.E. and Amador, M. (1989) Field test of the cognitive interview: enhancing the recollection of actual victims and witnesses of crime. *Journal of Applied Psychology*, **74**(5), 722–727.

Fisher, R.P. and Geiselman, R.E. (1992). *Memory Enhancing Techniques for Investigative Interviewing: the Cognitive Interview*. Springfield IL: Charles C. Thomas.

Fisher, R.P. and McCauley, M. (1995). Improving eyewitness testimony with the cognitive interviews. In M. Zaragoza., J.R. Graham., G.C.N. Hall, R. Hirschmann and Y.S. Ben-Porath (eds), *Memory and Testimony in the Child Witness*. Thousand Oaks, CA: Sage.

Flexser, A. and Tulving, E. (1978) Retrieval independence in recognition and recall. *Psychological Review*, **85**, 153–171.

Gee, S. and Pipe, M-E. (1995). Helping children to remember: the influence of object cues on children's accounts of a real event. *Developmental Psychology*, **31**(5), 746–758.

Geiselman, R.E. and Callot, R. (1990). Reverse versus forward recall of script based texts. *Applied Cognitive Psychology*, **4**, 141–144.

Geiselman, R.E., Saywitz, K.J. and Bornstein, G.K. (1990). Cognitive interviewing techniques for child witnesses and witnesses of crime. Report to the State Justice Institute.

Geiselman, R.E., Fisher, R.P., MacKinnon, D.P. and Holland, H.L. (1985). Eyewitness memory enhancement in the police interview: cognitive retrieval mnemonics versus hypnosis. *Journal of Applied Psychology*, **70**, 401–412.

Geiselman, R.E., Fisher, R.P., Cohen, G., Holland, H.L. and Surtes, L. (1986). Eyewitness responses to leading and misleading questions under the cognitive interview. *Journal of Police Science and Administration*, **14**, 31–39.

George, R. (1991). A field evaluation of the cognitive interview. Unpublished Masters Thesis, Polytechnic of East London.

Goodman, G.S., Aman, C. and Hirschman, J. (1987). Child sexual and physical abuse: children's testimony. In S.J. Ceci, M.P. Toglia and D.F. Ross (eds), *Children's Eyewitness Memory* (pp.1–23). New York: Springer-Verlag.

Gudjonsson, G. (1994) Investigative interviewing: recent developments and some fundamental issues. *International Review of Psychiatry*, **6**, 237–245.

Harris, J.E. (1980). Memory aids people use: two interview studies. *Memory and Cognition*, **8**(1), 31–38.

Koehnken, G. (1995). Interviewing adults. In R. Bull and D. Carson (eds), *Handbook of Psychology in Legal Contexts*. Chichester: Wiley.

Koehnken, G., Finger, M., Nitschke, N., Höfer, E. and Aschermann, E. (1992). Does a cognitive interview interfere with a subsequent statement validity analysis? Paper presented at the Conference of the American Psychology-Law Society in San Diego.

Koehnken, G., Schimmossek, E., Aschermann, E. and Höfer, E. (1995). The cognitive interview and the assessment of the credibility of adults' statements. *Journal of Applied Psychology*, **80**, 671–84.

Koehnken, G., Thurer, C. and Zorberbier, D. (1994). The cognitive interview: are interviewers' memories enhanced too? *Applied Cognitive Psychology*, **8**, 13–24.

Koriat, A. and Goldsmith, M. (1994). Memory in naturalistic and laboratory contexts: distinguishing accuracy oriented and quantity oriented approaches to memory assessment. *Journal of Experimental Psychology*, **123**, 397–415.

Malpass, R. and Devine, P. (1981). Guided memory in eyewitness identification. *Journal of Applied Psychology*, **66**, 343–350.

Mantwill, M., Koehnken, G. and Aschermann, E. (1995). Effects of the cognitive interview on the recall of familiar and unfamiliar events. *Journal of Applied Psychology*, **80**, 68–78.

Memon, A. and Bull, R. (1991). The cognitive interview: its origins, empirical support, evaluation and practical implications. *Journal of Community and Applied Social Psychology*, **1**, 291–307.

Memon, A. and Koehnken, G. (1992). Helping witnesses to remember more: the cognitive interview. *Expert Evidence: The International Digest of Human Behaviour, Science and Law*, **1**(2), 39–48.

Memon, A. and Stevenage, S.V. (1996) Interviewing witnesses: what works and what doesn't? Psycholoquy. 96.7.06.witness–memory.1.memon

Memon, A., Bull, R. and Smith, M. (1995). Improving the quality of the police interview: can training in the use of cognitive techniques help? *Policing and Society*, **5**, 53–68.

Memon, A., Cronin, Ó., Eaves, R. and Bull, R. (1996a). An empirical test of the mnemonic components of the cognitive interview. In G.M. Davies, S. Lloyd-Bostock, M. McMurran and C. Wilson (eds), *Psychology and Law: Advances in Research*. Berlin: De Gruyter.

Memon, A., Milne, R., Holley, A., Bull, R. and Koehnken, G. (1994). Towards understanding the effects of interviewer training in evaluating the cognitive interview. *Applied Cognitive Psychology*, **8**, 641–659.

Memon, A., Cronin, Ó., Eaves, R. and Bull, R. (1993). The cognitive interview and child witnesses. In G.M. Stephenson and N.K. Clark (eds), *Children, Evidence and Procedure. Issues in Criminological and Legal Psychology*. No. 20. Leicester, UK: British Psychological Society.

Memon, A., Wark, L., Holley, A., Koehnken, G. and Bull, R. (1997). Context effects and event memory: how powerful are the effects? In D. Payne and F. Conrad (eds), *Intersections in Basic and Applied Memory Research*. New York: Lawrence Erlbaum Associates.

Memon, A., Wark, L., Holley, A., Bull, R. and Koehnken, G. (1996b). Reducing suggestibility in child witness interviews. *Applied Cognitive Psychology*, **10**, 503–518.

Memon, A., Wark, L., Holley, A., Bull, R. and Koehnken, G. (1996c). Interviewer behaviour in cognitive and structured interviews. *Psychology, Crime and Law*, **3**, 181–201

Memon, A., Cronin, Ó., Eaves, R. and Bull, R. (1996d). An empirical test of the mnemonic components of the cognitive interview. In G.M. Davies, S. Lloyd-Bostock, M. McMurran and C. Wilson (eds), *Psychology and Law: Advances in Research*. Berlin: De Gruyter.

Memon, A., Wark, L., Bull, R. and Koehnken, G. (1997a). Isolating the effects of the cognitive interview techniques. *British Journal of Psychology*, **88**(2), 179–198.

Memon, A., Wark, L., Holley, A., Bull, R. and Koehnken, G. (1997b). Eyewitness performance in cognitive and structured interviews. *Memory* (in press).

Milne, R., Bull, R., Koehnken, G. and Memon, A. (1995). The cognitive interview and suggestibility. In G.M. Stephenson and N.K. Clark (eds), *Criminal Behaviour: Perceptions, Attributions and Rationality*. Division of Criminological and Legal Psychology Occasional Papers, No. 22. Leicester, UK: British Psychological Society.

Ross, M. and Newby, I.R. (1996). Distinguishing memory from fantasy. Commentary on Newman and Baumeister. *Psychological Inquiry*, **7**(2), in press.

Ornstein, P.A. (1991). Putting interviewing in context. In J. Doris (ed.), *The Suggestibility Of Children's Recollections: Implications For Eyewitness Testimony*. Washington DC: American Psychological Association.

Ornstein, P.A., Stone, B.P., Medlin, R.G. and Naus, M.J. (1985). Retrieving for rehearsal: an analysis of active rehearsal in children's memory. *Developmental Psychology*, **21**(4) 633–641.

Paivio, A. (1971). *Imagery and Verbal Processes*. New York: Holt, Rinehart and Winston.

Saywitz, K.J., Geiselman, R.E. and Bornstein, G.K. (1992). Effects of cognitive interviewing and practice on children's recall performance. *Journal of Applied Psychology*, **77**, 744–756.

Schacter, D.L. (1996). *Searching for Memory: The Brain, the Mind and the Past*. New York: Basic Books.

Schank, R.C. and Abelson, P. (1977). *Scripts, Plans, Goals and Understanding*. Hillsdale, NJ: Erlbaum.

Tulving, E. (1974). Cue-dependent forgetting. *American Scientist*, **62**, 74–82.

Tulving, E. and Thomson, D.M. (1973). Encoding specificity and retrieval processes in episodic memory. *Psychological Review*, **80**, 353–370.

Turtle, J. (1995, July). Officers: What do they want? What have they got? Paper presented at the 1st biennial meeting of the Society for Applied Research in Memory and Cognition, University of British Columbia.

9 OBTAINING INFORMATION FROM CHILD WITNESSES

Ray Bull

INTRODUCTION

On 14 June 1996 the weekly magazine *Private Eye* contained the following brief item:

> Orkney islands' social services department still faces problems despite the compensation to four families whose children were seized after allegations of satanic abuse. In the case of the W family the mother is still fighting to reunite her family following abuse allegations. The accommodation costs for the six W children in care last year have now been revealed as £120,000. Three years' lack of contact between mother and children prompted a recent Orkney hearing to recommend long-term rehabilitation. Two W children still remain in care. One of them was only seven years old when she was taken from home for questioning sessions which left her suffering repeated nightmares. Two months later she 'confessed' to being abused (p.13).
>
> (Private Eye, 1996, p.13)

This magazine item relates to an incident in February 1991 when a number of children were ordered to be removed by the local social services department from their homes on the Scottish island of Orkney and flown to the mainland. Accusations of sexual and satanic abuse had been made. These children were then interviewed by various professionals. In the light of complaints about the removal of the children the Secretary of State for Scotland set up an official Inquiry chaired by Lord Clyde. In October 1992 Her Majesty's Stationery Office published this Inquiry's report. Among the recommendations made were several concerning how to interview children. In *The Independent* newspaper (28 October 1992) it was stated that: 'A Scottish Office spokesman said it was widely accepted that this was a difficult area "What we don't know about interviewing children would fill books" he said'. The main aim of this chapter is to provide an account of what psychologists now know about the investigative interviewing of children.

Most of the research on the investigative interviewing of child witnesses/victims has been published in the last 10 years. This is an exciting, developing area of psychology. This chapter will focus on changes in England and Wales in the law and court practice, on developments in guidance for investigative interviewers, and on a major recent court case to illustrate the substantial contribution of psychology in this legal arena. Similar but as yet less substantial changes and developments have recently occurred in several other countries such as the USA, Canada, Australia, New Zealand, South Africa, Scotland and Denmark. (For reviews of these see Bottoms and Goodman, 1996.)

Need for corroboration?

In many countries one of the first major changes in criminal law in recent times has been concerned with the issue of whether a child's evidence needs to be corroborated by some other type of evidence before a person can be found guilty. In England and Wales according to the Children and Young Person's Act 1993 the evidence of child witnesses/victims too young to be sworn (i.e. too young to understand the meaning of the oath) had to be independently corroborated. A major problem with this was that those who wished to abuse children could focus on the young ones (whose evidence would need corroboration) and commit their crimes (e.g. oral sex) in a way that would make any type of corroboration (e.g. from the child's body or an adult eyewitness) impossible. (Note that an account of one unsworn child could not corroborate the account of another unsworn child.) The criminal law's inability to convict the perpetrators of such crimes led many people in the 1980s to call for reform, especially in the light of society's sad but important, growing realization that the abuse of young children was, and is, much more prevalent than many think.

In 1987 the Home Office (the relevant government department) published a report which addressed this issue of corroboration. Instead of relying solely on the opinions of politicians, pressure groups and so on, the Home Office commissioned an overview of psychological research on relevant issues. This report (by Carol Hedderman of the Home Office Research and Planning Unit) was an important first step in the subsequently growing contribution of psychology to law concerning children's evidence.

In the introduction to her report Hedderman made the crucial point that the evidence which is presented to a criminal court needs to meet certain standards of reliability and veracity. She stated that the sexual abuse of young children is a heinous crime deserving of severe legal and social censure. However, for this very reason she stated that it is fair that the rules of evidence be applied stringently to reduce the rate of which innocent people are wrongly convicted. Her report focused on whether young children were likely to be the very inadequate witnesses that some lawyers in the 1980s believed (e.g. Heydon, 1984, p. 84).

Hedderman noted that many people in the 1980s (and perhaps today?) thought (i) that children may lie more frequently than adults (but we could ask how often adults lie to courts and to the police), and (ii) that children are unable to distinguish fact from fantasy. She noted that 'these stereotypical assumptions have been given greater credibility in relation to children who claim to be abused by reference to Freud (1959) who interpreted the fact that so many of his female patients reported being abused as children as examples of childhood fantasies' (p. 5).

The longest chapter in Hedderman's report is entitled 'Empirical Research'. This demonstrates how much her report's recommendation (see below) relied upon the published psychological research available at the time. She began this chapter by noting that the 1972 Criminal Law Revision Committee recommended retention of the requirement that children's evidence be corroborated regarding alleged sexual abuse victims 'on the grounds that under the age of fourteen children's poor memories make them unreliable witnesses' (p. 8). In 1972 there existed and therefore was available to this committee little recently published research on the likely abilities of child witnesses. Work much earlier this century could be taken to suggest that children make poor witnesses (see below for criticism of this work), but it is to the discredit of psychologists that we had not more recently conducted good, relevant research that the 1972 committee could have referred to. Fortunately, for Hedderman in the late 1970s and early 1980s research psychologists had become brave enough to begin to conduct ecologically more relevant research rather than hide in the laboratory doing easier research. In her chapter Hedderman said that: 'The need for independent corroboration should be determined on the basis of what we know about child witnesses and not what is assumed about them' (p. 8).

Children's memory

Hedderman noted that psychological research which had examined adults' recall and recognition performances had demonstrated that these can be poor and susceptible to suggestion, as can those of children, and that very few studies have compared adults and children. (This is one of the reasons why we conducted a study of children's and adults' recall of the same event after a five-month delay – Flin, Boon, Knox and Bull, 1992.) She reviewed recent relevant research on children's memory and susceptibility to suggestion (e.g. Cohen and Harnick, 1980; Davies and Flin, 1987; Dent, 1982; Goodman and Reed, 1986; Marin, Holmes, Guth and Kovac, 1979; Parker, Haverfield and Baker-Thomas, 1986) and came to the view that: 'On balance, ... the available evidence does support the view that accuracy and reliability of recall are related to a certain level of cognitive maturity' (p. 15), and that 'Memory capacity does not appear to be a function of age. However, the acquisition and orchestration of techniques for operating the memory system appear to be related to other forms of cognitive maturation, such as the ability to think conceptually. Estimates of the age at which children begin to think conceptually vary between five and seven ... whilst children younger than five may have some stored information about an abusive experience, the question of whether they can be reliable witnesses depends on whether their memories are robust and whether it is possible to compensate for their lack of deliberate recall skills by external cues' (pp. 24/28). (For more on interview procedures to help children recall see below.)

Fantasies and fabrication

Hedderman came to the view that 'The question of whether children do lie more than adults cannot be answered from existing empirical evidence' (p. 21). She noted that Feldman's research (Feldman, Jenkins and Popoola, 1979; Feldman and White, 1980) suggested that as children grow older they (like adults) have learned how to deceive. She also noted the work of Johnson and Foley (1984) which suggested that even six-year-olds seemed able to distinguish between what they had only thought and what they had actually done. However, in her report she said that their work did not examine whether young children can equally make this distinction regarding their recall of the actions (real or imagined) of other people. Hedderman noted that 'One group of Freudian psychiatrists (Rosenfeld *et al.*, 1979) do claim that allegations of abuse made by children under the age of nine should be carefully scrutinized. They say that children aged eight or less are often less able to distinguish between fantasy and reality than older children' (p. 21). (For more recent work on this topic see the section below on source monitoring.)

Overall, on the question of lies/fantasies Hedderman came to the view that: 'There is virtually no evidence available on which to judge whether children are prone to fantasise about abuse.... This question really needs much more rigorous and thorough investigation' (p. 27).

In the light of the available research studies (some briefly mentioned above) Hedderman concluded that 'A general legal requirement that children's evidence be corroborated does not appear to be necessary' (p. 34). However, she also concluded that 'Most of the studies were experiments which, with a few recent exceptions, were carried out in unrealistic, oversimplified stimuli which were of no interest to the subjects' (p. 37). She quite rightly called for more realistic/ecologically valid studies to be carried out. (In the 1990s some psychologists have risen to this challenge.) Hedderman also called for much more research to be conducted on interviewing techniques. The government took Hedderman's report seriously and the statutory ban on convicting on the uncorroborated evidence of unsworn children was abolished by the 1988 Criminal Justice Act.

Use of closed-circuit television

In England and Wales another part of the 1988 Criminal Justice Act permitted for the first time child witnesses to give their evidence in criminal trials not in the actual courtroom but from another room in the court building, linked to the courtroom by a closed-circuit live television link (CCTV). This was done in an attempt to reduce the stresses that testifying in the courtroom might cause children. For example Flin, Davies and Tarrant in a 1988 survey confirmed the view that fear of seeing the accused and giving evidence in the formality of a large courtroom were believed to be major sources of stress for child witnesses. However, there has not been a lot of research conducted on whether actually testifying in a real courtroom trial is typically overwhelmingly stressful for children. Indeed in Flin, Bull, Boon and Knox's (1993) observations of children testifying in criminal courtrooms in Glasgow it was found that by no means did all children find it difficult to testify in the courtroom.

Psychological researchers have been used to evaluate the effects of the provision of CCTV for child witnesses in England and Wales, in Scotland (Murray, 1995), and in Australia (Cashmore, 1992). In England and Wales, Davies and Noon (1991) were commissioned by the Home Office to examine the effectiveness of the 'live link' for child witnesses which had been introduced into some courts in 1989. Overall, their conclusion was that the live link 'has been demonstrated to have positive and facilitating effects on the courtroom testimony of children and to have widespread acceptance among the various professional groups involved in the processes of justice' (p. 138). However, in the USA there is great concern that shielding the child witness from the defendant may not be appropriate (Montoya, 1993, 1995), given the constitutional right there for defendants to confront their accusers. (See Chapter 10 for more on the issue of children's testimony in court.)

The government in England and Wales in 1988 not only brought in the Criminal Justice Act which dispensed with the corroboration requirement for younger children's evidence and which permitted testimony by the 'live video link' (see above), but it also set up a committee chaired by Judge Pigot to consider the question of whether future legislation should go even further and permit children's video-recorded evidence to be shown in criminal trials. This committee (which reported to the Home Office) was very willing to receive evidence from psychologists. Most members of the committee took the trouble to attend the whole of a three-day conference on children's evidence which we organized at Cambridge where most of the speakers were psychologists from several different countries (see Spencer, Nicholson, Flin and Bull, 1990).

In the light of the psychological research evidence (plus other matters) put to the Pigot Committee it recommended that video recordings of children making their witness statements should be shown in criminal trials. This would (i) preserve on tape the child's statement which might otherwise suffer from the passage of time between being interviewed about an event and later testifying about it in court (typically such delays exceed five months – see Flin *et al.*, 1992), and (ii) reduce the effects upon the child of giving testimony in court (or via the live video link).

The government acted on some of the Pigot Committee's recommendations. In the 1991 Criminal Justice Act it was proposed that a video recording of an interview with a child could act as the child's evidence-in-chief (i.e. the evidence the child gives for the 'side' that called the witness, usually the prosecution). To be cross-examined (usually by the defence) the child would still have to be present at court during the trial and give live evidence (often via the live video link).

Memorandum of Good Practice

The Pigot Committee realized that if video recordings of earlier interviews with children were to replace their evidence-in-chief, these interviews (likely to be conducted by social workers and police officers) would have to be conducted in line with the rules of evidence that apply in criminal proceedings (Birch, 1992) and in line with what was known about how best to interview children to help them give full and accurate accounts of what they may have witnessed. Furthermore, the extent to which the interviewers succeeded in this would be very open to scrutiny via the videotaped recordings of their interviews. Only if an interview was conducted appropriately would the judge allow the video recording of it as evidence. Therefore, the Committee recommended that a document be written giving interviewers guidance on these matters. The government accepted this recommendation and the Home Office set up in 1991 a Policy Steering Group to advise it on this matter. A psychologist (myself) and a lawyer (Professor Diane Birch) were commissioned by the Home Office to write the first working draft of this document. This version was revised by the Home Office and then sent to members of the Policy Steering Group (e.g. representatives of the Law Society, the Criminal Bar Association, the National Society for the Prevention of Cruelty to Children, the Association of Chief Police Officers, the Association of Directors of Social Services, the Royal College of Psychiatrists, the British Psychological Society, Childline, the National Children's Bureau, the Crown Prosecution Service). In light of the feedback received from these representatives (and others) the Home Office revised the document and sent it out again. It was then revised again, and again, each time the Policy Steering Group (plus myself and Professor Birch) meeting at the Home Office. Eventually, the Policy Steering Group having been made aware of the findings of relevant psychological research, a finalized version (now called the 'Memorandum of Good Practice On Video Recorded Interviews With Child Witnesses For Criminal Proceedings') was published by Her Majesty's Stationery Office in August 1992. This Memorandum advocates (as did our very first working draft of it) a phased approach within the interview involving (i) rapport, (ii) free narrative, (iii) questioning (in various forms in sequential order), and (iv) closure. This advice is closely based on the relevant psychological research available at the time. (For more on this see Bull, 1992; 1995a; 1996; see also Yuille, Hunter, Joffe and Zaparniuk, 1993.)

In 1996 Professor Graham Davies and his colleagues from the psychology department at the University of Leicester (Davies, Wilson, Mitchell and Milsom, 1996) reported their evaluations, commissioned by the Home Office, of video-recorded interviews in criminal trials and the usefulness of the Memorandum. Their research largely found the Memorandum to be well received.

Suggestibility

A number of lawyers (e.g. Heydon, 1984) have voiced their concern that children may be suggestible in that their accounts can be biased by suggestions put to them, either purposely or unwittingly. Some psychologists have found children to be very resistant to suggestion, whereas others have found suggestions to have a strong biasing influence on children's responses to questions and on their subsequent accounts. Suggestibility can be the result of alterations of memory or of social pressure to say something counter to that in memory, or both. In order to try to arrive at a consensus view on what psychological research can reveal about the suggestibility of children, Professor Stephen Ceci of Cornell University co-organized a conference there in 1989 to which leading, world, psychological researchers on children as witnesses were invited. This conference was sponsored by the American Psychological Association which subsequently published a book (Doris, 1991) containing the major papers presented at the conference and commentaries upon these.

This conference and the book did achieve a measure of consensus among the international delegates and book chapter authors. The point was also made (e.g. Bull 1991) that what the general public, juries, police, lawyers, judges, etc. believe about the suggestibility of child witnesses was more important than any disagreements among psychologists.

What became apparent at the conference (and after the publication of the related book) was the need for a full overview of the psychological research (and theory) relevant to this topic. Stephen Ceci and Maggie Bruck undertook this task. They wrote a draft overview which they then sent for comment to a number of interested parties (e.g. psychologists researching on children as witnesses, including the present author). A final version of their overview was then published in the prestigious journal *Psychological Bulletin* in 1993. In this (appropriately) long paper Ceci and Bruck noted that on the issue of suggestibility: 'The field of children's testimony is in turmoil...' (p. 403). In their review and synthesis of the research they particularly focused on two types of factors that need to be considered, these being (i) cognitive, and (ii) social. They concluded that age differences exist in suggestibility, but also that 'even very young children are capable of recalling much that is forensically relevant' (p. 403).

The effects of suggestion on children's accounts

Ceci and Bruck (1993) pointed out that for nearly a century researchers have tried to study the effect of suggestion upon children's accounts. They noted that since 1983 more research had been conducted on this topic than in all the previous decades combined, and that this had been prompted by the fact that in several countries young children were increasingly being called upon to give accounts as witnesses or victims. Much of the research conducted prior to the 1980s was of poor quality, and little of it had compared the suggestibility of children with the suggestibility of adults. This latter point, which even today is still under-researched, assumed greater significance with the seminal research of Elizabeth Loftus who showed (e.g. Loftus, 1979) that some adults' accounts could be manipulated by the experimenter's use of suggestion.

The dilemma facing experts whose opinions were sought on child witness suggestibility was that, as Ceci and Bruck noted:

> On the one hand, children are described as highly resistant to suggestion, as unlikely to lie, and as reliable as adult witnesses about acts perpetrated on their own bodies (e.g. Berliner, 1985; Goodman, Rudy, Bottoms and Aman, 1990; Jones and McGraw, 1987). On the other hand, children are described as having difficulty distinguishing reality from fantasy, as being susceptible to coaching by powerful authority figures, and therefore as potentially being less reliable than adults (e.g. Feher, 1988; Gardner, 1989; Schuman, 1986; Underwager and Wakefield, 1990).
>
> (Ceci and Bruck, 1993, p. 403)

Their overview sought to reconcile these apparently opposing views, though they were aware that 'both camps express the belief that children are capable of high levels of accuracy, provided that adults ... do not attempt to bias their reports' (p. 403). This last point, about the influence of adults, is a crucial one. It is absolutely essential that people are made aware of how the interviewer can unwittingly or purposely make suggestions to the child. Both adults' (e.g. Gudjonsson, 1992) and children's (Carter, Bottoms and Levine, 1996) accounts can be biased by the interviewer's behaviour. To realize this and to be fully aware of it is even more important than any differences which may, or may not, exist between children's and adults' suggestibility.

In fact, some measure of suggestibility may be found in the adults who conduct research and write on the topic of children's suggestibility. Though psychologists put great effort in endeavouring that their research studies follow the established principles of science, they always have to interpret the meaning of the data they collect. To some of them their own data can appear to support their theory, whereas to others (e.g. in opposing 'camps') this may not appear to be the case. As Ceci and Bruck pointed out '... although there is controversy, it is less the result of inconsistent data than of how the data are interpreted' (p. 403).

Early research on suggestibility

The Salem witch trials at the end of the seventeenth century resulted in defendants being executed based, at least partly, on the testimony of child witnesses. However, some years later these witnesses changed their stories. Cases such as this, and European research early this century, had a great influence on people's beliefs, especially lawyers', concerning children's suggestibility. The European research was taken by many to suggest that young children are highly suggestible. However, as Ceci and Bruck noted, close examination of the published reports of this 'early' research does not readily result in the simple conclusion that children are very suggestible. In some of these early research studies children's responses to adults' questions did contain incorrect information. However, this was very largely the result of the experimenters' purposive attempts to influence the children's replies. For example, Binet (1900) and Stern (1910) found that asking children misleading questions occasioned more incorrect information than asking children to provide their own accounts (i.e. by using free recall). The subsequent mistake some lawyers and other adults made was to take such research to suggest that children are somehow inherently suggestible, irrespective of the way in which they are interviewed. In assessing this early research we must be aware of the very important point hinted at by Donaldson (1978) that when children are asked a question by an adult, if they have no information in memory as a response to that question, in order to 'answer' the question they may 'translate' or 'gloss' the question into ever distant versions of the original question until they find a version which can actually occasion 'correct' recall from their memory. They then provide in their response a 'true' answer to a 'translated' question, which is not a correct answer to the original question.

Varendonck (1911) in one study asked children in his class for descriptions of a person whom Varendonck said had gone up to him in the school playground earlier that morning during playtime. Around 70 per cent of the children then provided details of the person. However, no such event took place. The apparently worthless nature of children's accounts was underlined by the (very limited amount of) research conducted in the next 70 years. In such studies (see Ceci and Bruck, 1993 for a review) the effects of adult interviewers providing misleading information was found to be greater on the responses of younger children than on older children or adults. However, few of these studies focused on what young children could provide when questioned/interviewed appropriately.

More recent research on suggestibility

There has been an immense increase in research on children's suggestibility since 1980, and Gudjonsson (1992) noted a similar trend in research on adults' suggestibility. Ceci and Bruck (1993) reported that since 1979 more than 100 studies have been reported on children's suggestibility, and they noted that several issues may account for this immense increase. First, in some countries at least, there was in the 1980s an increasing willingness by courts (especially civil ones) to admit the expert testimony of psychologists. Secondly, research psychologists were becoming more willing 'to apply their scientific training to socially relevant issues' (p. 408) (see also Bull, 1982). Thirdly, more and more research studies focused on the exciting topic of witness testimony, partly because some lawyers called for this (Devlin, 1976; Bull and Clifford, 1976) and partly because such research was seen to be at the crossroads of 'science' and 'usefulness'. Fourthly, in many countries there was an increasing awareness of the frequency of child abuse. Until the 1980s most people seemed unaware that child abuse was a fairly common occurrence (Spencer and Flin, 1993). Of late, more and more data suggest that a significant proportion of children are abused (physically and/or sexually). The increasing awareness of the abuse of children ran counter to the belief (e.g. based on some interpretations of Freudian theory) than children fantasize about sex and make up allegations of sexual abuse. Governments commissioned overviews of the relevant research and came to the view that legislation was needed to remove the barriers to children's testimony leading to convictions in criminal trials. This increased the call (and the funding) for research relevant to obtaining reliable evidence from child witnesses.

The research conducted since 1980 has not only usually been methodologically more sophisticated than that which preceded it, it has also often tried to be more relevant to the needs of interviewers and of legal procedures. Also, instead of merely trying to establish that children can be highly suggestible, modern research has been attempting to determine whether this occurs only under certain (possibly extreme) conditions or whether it happens in most situations in which young children are called upon to give accounts of what they have witnessed. If it happens only under certain conditions then perhaps we can avoid those conditions. If it is likely to be a common occurrence we must devise investigation and interviewing procedures to reduce it.

Ceci and Bruck (1993) provided a review of research on the questions of (a) whether children are more suggestible than adults, and (b) whether young children are more suggestible than older children (see also Ceci, 1994). In their 1995 book they also focus on the conditions under which suggestibility effects are likely to occur (Ceci and Bruck, 1995). Several years ago the work of Elizabeth Loftus (e.g. 1979) demonstrates that some adults will answer 'yes' to the question 'Did you see a barn?' when this is posed after they heard the suggestive/misleading question 'How fast was the car going as it passed the barn and approached the traffic lights?' – when there was no barn, but there was a car and traffic lights in the event presented to them. More recently Cassell and Bjorklund (1995) found somewhat similar effects with children.

Sue White (1990) pointed to the undesirable effects that misleading questions could have on children's later recall.

> A serious situation may occur when the child denies the leading information, but does not provide spontaneous data in return. In such circumstances, it may be argued that this child may assimilate the leading information and may subsequently incorporate it into a statement concerning the allegation, a statement which, at a later point, might be considered a true disclosure. By that stage, tracing the path of such information from the interviewer through the child's memory is very difficult.
>
> An even more serious problem may arise when the child affirms the leading information by answering in a positive manner (head shake or verbalization). If the interviewer then takes the child's affirmation as support for the leading material, the interviewer is compounding the error of leading with providing an interpretation of the child's behaviour without supportive data supplied by the child. At that point, it may be difficult to know if some, all, or none of the affirmed information is true.
>
> (White, 1990, p. 382)

Do adults know everything?

Why should a witness give a response to a misleading question that is not, in fact, in accord with the real facts? The suggestibility of (child) witnesses results from a combination of social and memorial effects. As children grow older they come more and more to appreciate the rules that usually govern conversations. Most adults appreciate that when a person asks a question in everyday conversation (even a misleading/ suggestive one), that person does not already know (for sure) the answer. However, young children may well believe that adults already know most things, if not everything (Fielding and Conroy, 1995; McGurk and Glachan, 1988; Menig-Peterson, 1975). Therefore, if a child is of the opinion that the questioner already knows the answer the child may be willing to go along with the suggestion made in a misleading question, when the child in fact has no recall of the relevant information. Furthermore, even when the child does have some (correct) recall of the relevant information, if this is contrary to the suggestion in the question the child may 'trust' the adult's suggestion more than his or her own memory. For example, Ceci, Ross and Toglia (1987) found that preschool children were more affected by the misleading information provided by adults than by seven-year-old children. Children readily learn that adults (e.g. parents, teachers) know much more than they do. Unfortunately, they do not readily learn (i) that adults' questions to them can include incorrect information, and (ii) that, sadly, some adults' questions can purposely contain deceptive, even purposely untruthful information. (For more on this topic see Gaffam Walker and Warren, 1995.) The credibility of the adult can affect the impact on children's accounts of her or his misleading information. Lampinen and Smith (1995) found a misinformation effect only for adults who were perceived as being credible.

An extension of this notion could be used to explain the widely cited finding of Hughes and Grieve (1980) that five- and seven-year-old children often replied 'yes' or 'no' to what we might deem bizarre questions. If children assume that adults only ask *sensible* questions, then children might not have sufficient confidence in their own abilities (even if they think that the question is bizarre) to tell the adult that the question is nonsensical. Instead, they may well, as Donaldson (1978) could be taken to suggest, make the assumption that the question must (somehow) be sensible to the adult and thus guess 'yes' or 'no'. In fact, in certain circumstances adults respond in a similar way to bizarre questions (Pratt, 1991). But clearly the person at fault is the questioner rather than the responder. It is a false conclusion that because people provide answers to purposely bizarre questions in experiments, such people cannot be relied on as witnesses.

Lepore and Sesco (1994) found that young children produced misleading reports about events when prompted in a biased way by 'an opinionated adult interviewer' (p. 108). They concluded that: 'There is a great danger of evoking false information and misleading reports from 4- to 6-year-old children when they are engaged in a negatively charged, incriminating interview ... interviewers of child witnesses must be sensitised to the manner in which they conduct their interviews. Future research on child witnesses should explore further the social and motivational factors that might moderate children's susceptibility to suggestions' (p. 118). Mulder and Vrij (1996) found that explaining to children that 'I don't know' is an acceptable answer reduced suggestibility (see also Bull, 1992; 1996) as did explaining that the interviewer had not witnessed the event.

Children are not always misled

However, Siegal and Peterson (1995) found that children's recollections are not always biased by misinformation provided by adults. When Siegal and Peterson gave some of the young children in their study a reason for discounting the misinformation provided by an adult, these children's recollections were less biased by the misinformation than were other children's. Similarly, Newcombe and Siegal (1996) have found that the effect on children's recollections of subsequent biased information is reduced if the interviewer makes it clear to the child that recollection of the original event is required. Newcombe and Siegal cite recent work on young children's autobiographical memory and their 'theory of mind' to support this notion.

Repeating questions

Another example of the detrimental effects of children's belief that adults 'know' comes from research on the effects of repeating a question. In a 1987 study by Stephen Moston the same questions were asked twice within a single interview session. He found that the number of correct responses to such questions was lower the second time the questions were put, especially for his youngest group (of six year olds). This drop in accuracy he attributed to the children's assumption that by asking the same question on a second occasion the adult questioner was implying that their first answers were incorrect. Poole and White (1991) found a similar effect for 'yes-no' questions but not, we should note, for open-ended questions (repetition of which might merely be taken as a request for more, rather than different, information). (See also Poole and White, 1995; and Memon and

Vartoukian, 1996.) The conclusion from studies of the effects of repeating questions is to avoid using repeated 'yes-no' questions. (Gudjonsson, 1992 uses adults' willingness to alter their responses to 'yes-no' questions as an indicant of their suggestibility.)

A further example of how a misleading/suggestive question might bias a child's reply to it involves questions on matters about which the child has no memory. Again, if the child believes that the adult would only ask a question if it were sensible to do so, children who have been taught at school (or at home) that saying 'don't know' is frowned upon may wish to avoid giving this response (even when it may be correct). Thus if asked 'Was the man's jacket blue or red?' (when in fact it was yellow, this being unknown to the questioner) a child might reply 'blue' rather than with the correct reply 'neither' or with 'don't know'. Young children have been found rarely to respond 'don't know' to misleading questions (Cassell and Bjorklund, 1995), and some investigative interviewers seem rarely to inform children that such responses are acceptable (Warren, Woodall, Hunt and Perry, 1996). A few studies have attempted to increase children's appropriate use of 'don't know' responses but these have not been very successful (e.g. Moston, 1987).

Rapport

The deleterious effect of misleading questions upon replies may well be heightened when a good, warm, respectful relationship exists between the interviewee and interviewer (Vrij and Winkel, 1994). Many of the respected protocols for interviewing child witnesses (e.g. the 1992 Memorandum of Good Practice) quite rightly emphasize the necessity of rapport being established between the interviewer and interviewee before the witness is asked to provide relevant information (see Goodman, Rudy, Bottoms and Aman, 1990). However, the positive atmosphere characteristic of good rapport may increase the likelihood of the child giving incorrect information to the types of misleading/suggestive questions mentioned above. Although this possible interactive effect between rapport and inappropriate questioning has rarely been researched (see Saywitz, Geiselman and Bornstein, 1992 for a small example) interviewers need to be alive to its possibility, though Carter, Bottoms and Levine (1996) found that children interviewed in a warm, supportive manner were more resistant to misleading questions than were those interviewed in an intimidating manner.

Interviewers should try to maintain rapport with the child throughout an interview. However, doing this successfully may not be as easy as it seems. In everyday conversation one main way to maintain (and establish) rapport is to express interest in what the other person says by paying attention and responding appropriately (both verbally and non-verbally). In order to keep a person talking we reward/reinforce their behaviour. In an interview conducted for legal purposes if this delivery of reward/reinforcement is not done appropriately it might bias what the child says. If the interviewer reacts more positively to certain information from the child this could lead (i) by standard 'conditioning' procedures to the child producing (correctly or incorrectly) more of the same behaviour, and/or (ii) to the child working out in his or her own mind what specific types of information the interviewer seems to want to hear and then providing more of this.

Loftus (1979; Loftus and Ketcham, 1991) has established that suggestions put to adults after they witnessed an event can bias their later recall. The kinds of biasing effects found by Loftus could be explained in one of two competing ways. Loftus herself tends towards the view that the suggestive post-event information actually alters or changes somewhat the memory for the original event. Other psychologists (McCloskey and Zaragoza, 1985a and b) explain the results of studies like those of Loftus by positing that both the original event information and the subsequent suggestion are now both stored in the subjects' memory. When the subjects later try to recall, some of them access the memory for the suggestion (which was part of a question previously put to them) rather than the (probably 'nearby') memory for the relevant part of the original event. (See the section below on source monitoring).

Scripts

In addition many people may never have set down in their memory some aspects of the originally witnessed event. The subsequent (inappropriate) suggestion contained in a question put to them may, however, be remembered. Later when asked about the event they remember information contained in the suggestive question but attribute their recall of this information to the original event rather than to the suggestive question. This seems particularly likely to occur if the information incorrectly suggested by the question nevertheless makes sense. If the suggestive/misleading question had been: 'Was the man wearing a barrel eating a sandwich or a cake?' far fewer people would later recall him as wearing a barrel as would those given the suggestive/misleading question containing mention (incorrectly) of a jacket. People's knowledge of the world, of what usually happens will affect the influence of a suggestive/misleading question on later recall. Psychologists refer to people's knowledge of 'what usually happens' as 'scripts'. Children's scripts, their knowledge of 'what usually happens' will affect the influence of suggestive/misleading questions (Snyder, Nathanson and Saywitz, 1993). If children's scripts are not as well developed as are those of adults they may not so easily realize that what is being suggested to them by a skilful misleading question is likely to have happened (even though it didn't). An adult with a well-developed script may be *more* likely to be 'tricked' by a script-consistent (yet incorrect) suggestion.

Another psychological factor which may influence the effects of suggestive/misleading questions upon later recall is called 'source monitoring'.

Source monitoring

Source monitoring (or 'reality monitoring') refers to the extent to which individuals are able to distinguish between their memories of events that they have actually experienced and memories of imagined or suggested events (see Chapter 7). The writings of early psychologists such as Freud and Piaget were taken to imply that children may well have difficulty in discriminating fact from fantasy. However, Freud never conducted any proper experimental studies on this topic, and the children Piaget studied may not have understood his instructions and therefore failed to demonstrate discriminations which they might have been capable of.

In the 1970s researchers at last conducted good empirical studies on this topic and these 'researchers converged on the view that young children were able to distinguish between reality and fantasy' (Ceci and Bruck, 1993, p. 417). However, when the boundary between reality and fantasy is not very clear cut Ceci and Bruck suggest that young children may experience some discrimination difficulties. Steve Lindsay is one of the leading researchers on this topic. His research suggests that when asked to discriminate their memories for actual, real events from their memories of suggested events, children only have greater difficulty than adults when these memories (i.e. actual *v.* suggested events) arise from very similar (or the same) sources (Lindsay, Gonzales and Eso, 1995). In addition, young children have difficulty discriminating between their memories for things they themselves have done and their memories for similar things they have been asked merely to imagine doing. However, they seem to have little difficulty distinguishing their memories of what other people have done from their memories of merely imagining what other people have done. However, research on this topic is still at a relatively early stage and so it would be premature to use it as a way of explaining the results of other types of research on children's suggestibility. Nevertheless, this exciting, complex research on source monitoring clearly indicates that in some circumstances children may be no more suggestible than are adults. Again, whether children are more suggestible seems to depend more on the relevant circumstances than on any general deficit in children.

These circumstances will often be of a social or of a cognitive type. Social circumstances may cause a child to acquiesce (i.e. say 'yes') to a leading question (and therefore produce possibly incorrect recall). Cognitive circumstances would affect whether an incorrect reply would 'carry over' to become part of a child's report on a subsequent occasion. As in much of psychology, human behaviour and the mind, the effects of social circumstances/factors are mediated by cognitive circumstances/factors (and vice versa). More research is needed on the extent to which the effect of each type of circumstance is dependent on the other type of circumstance. Nevertheless, what we can now say is that the more suggestible the interviewing circumstances the more likely it is that biased accounts will be provided by child witnesses, especially if both social and cognitive suggestibility is involved.

Stereotypes

This is exemplified in Steve Ceci's experiment involving 'Sam Stone'. Ceci and Bruck (1993) describe this study (see also Leichtman and Ceci, 1995) in which the character, Sam Stone was described to three- to six-year-old children across a period of one month as a very clumsy man who broke things that weren't his. After this 'stereotype induction procedure' Sam Stone visited the nursery school. He spent two minutes interacting with the children in a friendly way during a class story-telling session but did not break anything or be clumsy. The next day the children were shown a soiled teddy bear and a ripped book, and asked if they knew who had done this. Few of them said that they saw Sam Stone do it, but a quarter said that maybe Sam had done it. Following this the children were interviewed at fortnightly interviews five times in the ensuing 10 weeks. Each interview contained two suggestive questions: 'I wonder whether Sam Stone was wearing long pants or short pants when he ripped the book?', 'I wonder if Sam Stone got the teddy bear dirty on purpose or by accident?'. At the end of the 10 weeks the children were interviewed by another interviewer who said she had not been present during Sam Stone's visit but needed to know everything that had happened. Three-quarters of the three- and four-year-olds indicated that Sam Stone had ruined the book or dirtied the bear, and when asked almost a half of them replied that they had seen Sam Stone do this. Some of these false replies were spontaneously accompanied by (apparently) relevant details. However, only 10 per cent (but still 10 per cent) of the older children (i.e. five- and six-year-olds) indicated that they had seen Sam Stone ruin the book or dirty the bear. Ceci and Bruck (1993) take such findings as indicating that not only can young children (of three and four years of age) form powerful social stereotypes, but also that this information interacts with suggestive questioning to produce false accounts. They echo Sue White's (1990) point that in response to strongly suggestive interviewing children (even young ones) may initially realize that what they say in such an interview may be incorrect recall. However, in subsequent interviews or when testifying, the children may then remember their previous incorrect recall rather than what they initially could remember.

Ceci and Bruck (1995) note that their research (and writings) have been severely criticized by those who advocate that all child witnesses should be believed *and* by those more sceptical about child witnesses. They stated (1995) that: 'There have even been times when representatives on each side have tried to thwart the publication of our ideas by organizing letter-writing campaigns to pressure editors against publishing our work' (p. 4). Such pressure reveals how crucial is the work of psychologists in this area of the law. Pressure of a somewhat similar nature was exerted upon us (i.e. Poole, Lindsay, Memon and Bull, 1995) concerning our surveys of therapists' practices and beliefs concerning adults' possible memories of childhood sexual abuse.

Children can be tricked into providing false information and they can, on occasion, purposely lie. Those who have argued, on the one hand, that children's testimony is less reliable than adults or, on the other hand, that children should more readily be believed than adults, miss the essential point. It is how the witness' testimony is obtained (Bull, 1995a, 1996; Lamb, Sternberg and Esplin, 1994) and the circumstances surrounding this (including the motivation of the witness) which are very much more important than debates (though academically and theoretically important) as to whether children are more suggestible than adults.

Assisting the court

In 1995 the American Psychological Association published a book on child witness suggestibility by Ceci and Bruck. This book not only presents a comprehensive, easy-to-read summary of many of the psychological factors likely to influence children's accounts, it also relates this to five notorious, recent trials which involved child witnesses. In one of these cases the Supreme Court of New Jersey (in the case of State *v.* Kelly Michaels, 1994; the Wee Care Nursery School case) overturned a conviction of multiple child abuse and ruled that a defendant may request a pretrial taint hearing to challenge the adequacy of investigative interviews with child witnesses. This ruling was almost certainly influenced by an amicus brief sent to this court when it was deliberating on the appeal made by Kelly Michaels. This amicus brief (a briefing document submitted by 'friends' of the court) was signed by 45 leading social scientists knowledgeable about factors likely to affect the performance of children in investigative interviews (Bruck and Ceci, 1995). Ceci and Bruck

(1995) end the penultimate chapter of their seminal book (pp. 292–293) with a quotation from this brief, which is:

> The authors of this brief also wish to convey their deep concern over the children in this case. Our concern is that if there were incidents of sexual abuse, the faulty interviewing procedures make it difficult to detect real abuse. But we have further concerns. And these involve the interviewing techniques which we view as abusive in themselves. After reading a number of these interviews, it is difficult to believe that adults charged with the care and protection of young children would be allowed to use the vocabulary that they used in these interviews, that they would be allowed to interact with the children in such sexually explicit ways, or that they would be allowed to bully and frighten their child witnesses in such a shocking manner. No amount of evidence that sexual abuse had actually occurred could ever justify the use of these techniques especially with three- and four-year-old children. Above and beyond the great stress, intimidation, and embarrassment that many of the children so obviously suffered during the interviews, we are deeply concerned about the long-lasting harmful effects of persuading children that they have been horribly sexually and physically abused, when in fact there may have been no abuse until the interviews began. The authors of this brief will be permanently disturbed that children were interviewed in such abusive circumstances regardless of the ultimate innocence or guilt of the accused.
>
> (Ceci and Bruck, 1995, pp. 292–293)

The public's opinion

Even if a child witness/victim is interviewed properly their testimony still faces a number of hurdles to be overcome. Some of these involving laws and legal procedures have been reduced (e.g. see earlier in this chapter) but others remain (e.g. see Cashmore and Bussey, 1996), especially the general public's (e.g. jurors') view, partly supported by weak psychological research earlier this century, that children are inherently unreliable providers of testimony. However, a worthwhile, free narrative, uncontaminated account from a child (as recommended in the 1992 Memorandum of Good Practice) can have a strong effect. For example in 1995 Luus, Wells and Turtle noted that their 'findings suggest that jurors may enter the courtroom with a negative bias against child witnesses. However, qualities of the witness's testimony seem to play a more important role than does the witness's age in judgements of eyewitness credibility'. People's 'preconceived negative views ... may be quickly discarded on actually observing a child testify' (p. 325). Saywitz and Geiselman (1996) overview some recently developed, innovative methods of maximizing the completeness and minimizing the error in child witnesses' accounts, and Hutcheson, Baxter, Telfer and Warden (1995) note that the child's age may well influence which type of question (see Bull, 1996) is most appropriate.

Marxsen, Yuille and Nisbet (1995) made the point: 'That young children are more suggestible than adults is well established. This does not mean that the investigative interviewing of children is impossible, only that it requires skill and care. However, the literature's overemphasis on suggestibility can give the police, the judiciary, the media, and the general public the mistaken impression that children are inherently unreliable' (p. 458).

Psychologists have a duty to inform people (e.g. relevant professionals) of the findings of their research (for more on this issue see Chapter 10).

Assumed unreliability may be even more the case for children who have communicative disability or learning disability (formerly called mental handicap). Unfortunately, such children may be the ones most at risk from abuse (Westcott, 1991, 1992), yet the ones requiring most skill from the interview (Bull, 1995b). Few psychologists have attempted to conduct research concerning the investigative interviewing of these children, though Milne and Bull (1995) found the cognitive interview to be of use (for more on the cognitive interview see Chapter 8).

CONCLUSION

This chapter has tried to present an overview of some of psychology's contribution to the obtaining of information from child witnesses. (For more on investigative interviewing see Chapter 8 on the cognitive interview.) Though much has been discovered through psychologists' research and changes have accordingly been made in the 'real world', there is still more for us to try to comprehend. These are the closing words from Aaron Hoorwitz' 1992 fine book entitled *The Clinical Detective: Techniques in the Evaluation of Sexual Abuse*:

Hoorwitz: 'I guess I'm telling you just to remember that there's more to learn. That you don't know everything'.

Student: 'Is that it? Is that all you're saying?'

Hoorwitz: 'Yes'.

Student: 'Well, guess I know that'.

Hoorwitz: 'If you do, then you know everything you need to know'.

Steward, Bussey, Goodman and Saywitz (1993) concluded their brief overview of several psychological issues relating to investigative interviews with children by stating that 'although we have come a long way, we still have much to learn about interviewing children' (p. 34).

REFERENCES

Binet, A. (1900). *La Suggestibilité*. Paris: Schleicher Freres.
Birch, D. (1992). Children's evidence. *Criminal Law Review*, April, 262–276.
Bottoms, B. and Goodman, G. (eds) (1996). *International Perspectives on Child Abuse and Children's Testimony: Psychological Research and Law*. Thousand Oaks, CA: Sage.
Bruck, M. and Ceci, S. (1995). Brief on behalf of amicus developmental, social and psychological researchers, social scientists and scholars. *Psychology, Public Policy and the Law*, **1**, 1–51.

Bull, R. (1982). Can experimental psychology be applied psychology? In S. Canter and D. Canter (eds), *Psychology in Practice*. Chichester: Wiley.

Bull, R. (1991). Commentary: the issue of relevance . In J. Doris (ed.), *The Suggestibility of Children's Recollections*. Washington, DC: American Psychological Association.

Bull, R. (1992). Obtaining evidence expertly: the reliability of interviews with child witnesses. *Expert Evidence*, **1**, 5–12.

Bull, R. (1995a). Innovative techniques for the questioning of child witnesses, especially those who are young and those with learning disability. In M. Zaragoza, J. Graham, G. Hall, R. Hirschman and Y. Ben-Poroth (eds), *Memory and Testimony in the Child Witness*. Thousand Oaks, CA: Sage.

Bull, R. (1995b). Interviewing people with communicative disabilities. In R. Bull and D. Carson (eds), *Handbook of Psychology in Legal Contexts*. Chichester: Wiley.

Bull, R. (1996). Good practice for video recorded interviews with child witnesses for use in criminal proceedings. In G. Davies, S. Lloyd-Bostock, M. McMurran and C. Wilson (eds), *Psychology, Law and Criminal Justice*. Berlin: deGruyter.

Bull, R. and Clifford, B. (1976). Identification: the Devlin Report. *New Scientist*, 6 May.

Carter, C., Bottoms, B. and Levine, M. (1996). Linguistic and socioemotional influences on the accuracy of children's reports. *Law and Human Behavior*, **20**, 359–374.

Cashmore, J. (1992). The use of closed circuit television for child witnesses in the ACT. Sydney: Australian Law Reform Commission.

Cashmore, J. and Bussey, K. (1996). Judicial perceptions of child witness competence. *Law and Human Behavior*, **20**, 313–334.

Cassell, W. and Bjorklund, D. (1995). Developmental patterns of eyewitness memory and suggestibility. *Law and Human Behavior*, **19**, 507–532.

Ceci, S. (1994). Cognitive and social factors in children's testimony. In B. Sales and G. VandenBos (eds), *Psychology in Litigation and Legislation*. New York: American Psychological Association.

Ceci, S. and Bruck, M. (1993). Suggestibility of the child witness: a historical review and synthesis. *Psychological Bulletin*, **113**, 403–439.

Ceci, S. and Bruck, M. (1995). *Jeopardy in the Courtroom: A Scientific Analysis of Children's Testimony*. Washington, DC: American Psychological Association.

Ceci, S., Ross, D. and Toglia, M. (1987). Age differences in suggestibility: psychological implications. *Journal of Experimental Psychology: General*, **117**, 38–49.

Clyde, J. (1992). The Report of the Inquiry into the Removal of Children from Orkney in February 1991. Edinburgh: Her Majesty's Stationery Office.

Cohen, R. and Harnick, M. (1980). The susceptibility of child witnesses to suggestion. *Law and Human Behavior*, **4**, 201–210.

Davies, G. and Flin, R. (1987). The accuracy and suggestibility of child witnesses. In G. Davies and J. Drinkwater (eds), The child witness: do the courts abuse children? *Issues in Criminological and Legal Psychology*, **13**, Leicester: British Psychological Society.

Davies, G. and Noon, E. (1991). An evaluation of the live link for child witnesses. London: Home Office.

Davies, G., Wilson, C., Mitchell, R. and Milsom, M. (1996). Videotaping children's evidence: an evaluation. London: Home Office.

Dent, H. (1982). The effects of interviewing strategies on the results of interviews with child witnesses. In A. Trankell (ed.), *Reconstructing the Past*. Stockholm: Norstedt.

Devlin, Lord (1976). Report to the Secretary of State for the Home Department of the Departmental Committee on Evidence of Identification In Criminal Cases. London: Her Majesty's Stationery Office.

Donaldson, M. (1978). *Children's Minds*. London: Fontana.

Doris, J. (1991). *The Suggestibility of Children's Recollections: Implications for Eyewitness Testimony*. Washington, DC: American Psychological Association.

Feldman, R. and White, J. (1980). Detecting deception in children. *Journal of Communication*, 30, 121–128.

Feldman, R., Jenkins, L. and Popoola, O. (1979). Detection of deception in adults and children via facial expressions. *Child Development*, 50, 350–355.

Fielding, N. and Conroy, S. (1992). Interviewing child victims: police and social work investigations of child sexual abuse. *Sociology*, 26, 103–124.

Flin, R., Bull, R., Boon, J. and Knox, A. (1993). Child witnesses in Scottish criminal trials. *International Review of Victimology*, 2, 309–329.

Flin, R., Boon, J., Knox, A. and Bull, R. (1992). The effect of a five month delay on children's and adults' eyewitness memory. *British Journal of Psychology*, 83, 323–336.

Flin, R., Davies, G. and Tarrant, A. (1988). The child witness. Final Report to the Scottish Home and Health Department (Grant 95/9290).

Gaffam Walker, A. and Warren, A. (1995). The language of the child abuse interview: asking the questions, understanding the answers. In T. Ney (ed.), *True and False Allegations of Child Sexual Abuse: Assessment and Case Management*. New York: Brunner/Mazel.

Goodman, G. and Reed, R.S. (1986). Age differences in eyewitness testimony. *Law and Human Behavior*, 10, 317–332.

Goodman, G. S., Rudy, L., Bottoms, B. and Aman, C. (1990). Children's concerns and memory: issues of ecological validity in the study of children's eyewitness testimony. In R. Fivush and J Hudson (eds), *Knowing and Remembering in Young Children* (pp. 249–284). New York: Cambridge University Press.

Gudjonsson, G. (1992). *The Psychology of Interrogation, Confessions and Testimony*. Chichester: Wiley.

Hedderman, C. (1987). Children's evidence: the need for corroboration. Research and Planning Unit. Paper 41. London: Home Office.

Heydon, J. (1984). *Evidence, Cases and Materials*. London: Butterworths.

Hoorwitz, A. (1992). *The Clinical Detective*. New York: Norton.

Hughes, M. and Grieve, R. (1980). On asking children bizarre questions. *First Language*, 1, 149–160.

Hutcheson, G., Baxter, J., Telfer, K. and Warden, D. (1995). Child witness statement quality: question type and errors of omission. *Law and Human Behavior*, 6, 631–648.

Johnson, M. and Foley, M. (1984). Differentiating fact from fantasy: the reliability of children's memory. *Journal of Social Issues*, 40, 33–50.

Lamb, M., Sternberg, K. and Esplin, P. (1994). Factors influencing the reliability and validity of statements made by young victims of sexual maltreatment. *Journal of Applied Developmental Psychology*, 15, 255–280.

Lampinen, J. and Smith, V. (1995). The incredible (and sometimes incredulous) child witness: child eyewitnesses' sensitivity to source credibility uses. *Journal of Applied Psychology*, **80**, 621–627.

Leichtman, M. and Ceci, S. (1995). The effects of stereotypes and suggestions on preschoolers' reports. *Developmental Psychology*, **31**, 568–578.

Lepore, S. and Sesco, B. (1994). Distorting children's reports and interpretations of events through suggestion. *Journal of Applied Psychology*, **79**, 108–120.

Lindsay, S., Gonzales, V. and Eso, K. (1995). Aware and unaware uses of memories of post event suggestions. In M. Zaragoza, J. Graham, G. Hall, R. Hirschman and Y. Ben-Porath (eds), *Memory and Testimony in the Child Witness*. Thousand Oaks, CA: Sage.

Loftus, E. (1979). *Eyewitness Testimony*. Cambridge, MA: Harvard University Press.

Loftus, E. and Ketcham, K. (1991). *Witness for the Defense*. New York: St Martin's Press.

Luus, E., Wells, G. and Turtle, J. (1995). Child eyewitnesses: seeing is believing. *Journal of Applied Psychology*, **80**, 317–326.

Marin, B., Holmes, D., Guth, M. and Kovac, P. (1979). The potential of children as eyewitnesses. *Law and Human Behavior*, **3**, 295–305.

Marxsen, D., Yuille, J. and Nisbet, M. (1995). The complexities of eliciting and assessing children's statements. *Psychology, Public Policy and Law*, **1**, 450–460.

McCloskey, M. and Zaragoza, M. (1985a). Misleading post event information and memory for events: arguments and evidence against the memory impairment hypothesis. *Journal of Experimental Psychology: General*, **114**, 381–387.

McCloskey, M. and Zaragoza, M. (1985b). Post event information and memory: reply to Loftus, Schooler and Wagenaar. *Journal of Experimental Psychology: General*, **114**, 381–387.

McGurk, H. and Glachan, M. (1988). Children's conversation with adults. *Children and Society*, **2**, 20–34.

Memon, A. and Vartoukian, R. (1996). The effects of repeated questioning on young children's eyewitness testimony. *British Journal of Psychology*, **87**, 403–415.

Memorandum of good practice on video recorded interviews with child witnesses for criminal proceedings. (1992). London: Her Majesty's Stationery Office.

Menig-Peterson, C. (1975). The modification of communicative behaviour in preschool-aged children as a function of the listener's perspective. *Child Development*, **46**, 1015–1018.

Milne, R. and Bull, R. (1995). Children with mild learning disability: the cognitive interview and suggestibility. Paper presented at the Fifth European Psychology and Law Conference, Budapest.

Montoya, J. (1993). Something not so funny happened on the way to conviction: the pretrial interrogation of child witnesses. *Arizona Law Review*, **35**, 927–987.

Montoya, J. (1995). Lessons from Akiki and Michaels on shielding child witnesses. *Psychology, Public Policy and Law*, **1**, 340–369.

Moston, S. (1987). The suggestibility of children in interview studies. *First Language*, **7**, 67–78.

Mulder, M. and Vrij, A. (1996). Explaining conversation rules to children: an intervention study to facilitate children's accurate responses. *Child Abuse and Neglect*, **7**, 623–631.

Murray, K. (1995). Live television link: an evaluation of its use by child witnesses in Scottish criminal trials. Edinburgh: Scottish Office.

Newcombe, P. and Siegal, M. (1996). Where to look first for suggestibility in children. *Cognition*, **59**, 337–356.

Parker, J., Haverfield, E. and Baker-Thomas, S. (1986). Eyewitness testimony of children. *Journal of Applied Social Psychology*, **16**, 287–302.

Poole, D. and White, L. (1995). Tell me again and again: stability and change in the repeated testimonies of children and adults. In M. Zaragoza, J. Graham, G. Hall, R. Hirschman and Y. Ben-Porath (eds), *Memory and Testimony in the Child Witness*. Thousand Oaks, CA: Sage.

Poole, D. and White, L. (1991). Effects of question repetition on the eyewitness testimony of children and adults. Developmental Psychology, 27, 975–986.

Poole, D.A., Lindsay, D.S., Memon, A. and Bull, R. (1995). Psychotherapy and the recovery of memories of childhood sexual abuse: US and British practitioners' opinions, practices and experiences. *Journal of Consulting and Clinical Psychology,* **63**(3), 426–37.

Pratt, C. (1991). On asking children – and adults – bizarre questions. *First Language*, **10**, 167–175.

Saywitz, K. and Geiselman, E. (1996). Interviewing the child witness: maximizing completeness and minimizing error. In S. Lynn (ed.), *Memory and Truth*. New York: Guilford.

Saywitz, K., Geiselman, R. and Bornstein, G. (1992). Effects of cognitive interviewing, practice, and interview style on children's recall performance. *Journal of Applied Psychology*, **77**, 744–756.

Siegal, M. and Peterson, C. (1995). Memory and suggestibility in conversations with young children. *Australian Journal of Psychology*, **47**, 38–41.

Snyder, L., Nathanson, R. and Saywitz, K. (1993). Children in court: the role of discourse processing and production. *Topics in Language Disorders*, **13**, 39–58.

Spencer, J. and Flin, R. (1993). *The Evidence of Children: The Law and the Psychology*. London: Blackstone.

Spencer, J., Nicholson, G., Flin, R. and Bull, R. (1990). Children's evidence in legal proceedings: an international perspective. Cambridge: Faculty of Law.

Stern, W. (1910). Abstracts of lectures on the psychology of testimony and on the study of individuality. *American Journal of Psychology*, **21**, 270–282.

Steward, M., Bussey, K., Goodman, G. and Saywitz, K. (1993). Implications of developmental research for interviewing children. *Child Abuse and Neglect*, **17**, 25–37.

Tobey, A., Goodman, G., Batterman-Faunce, J., Orcutt, H., and Sachsenmaier, T. (1995). Balancing the rights of children and defendants: effects of closed–circuit television on children's accuracy and jurors' perceptions. In M. Zaragoza, J. Graham, G. Hall, R. Hirschman and Y. Ben-Porath (eds), *Memory and Testimony in the Child Witness*. Thousand Oaks, CA: Sage.

Varendonck, J. (1911). Les temoignages d'enfants dans un proces retentissant [The testimony of children in a famous trial]. *Archives de Psychologie*, **11**, 129–171.

Vrij, A. and Winkel, F.W. (1994). Strategies to detect and reduce false statements in children: a social-psychological approach. *Journal of Police and Criminal Psychology*, **10**, 22–29.

Warren, A., Woodall, C., Hunt, J., and Perry, N. (1996). Do investigative interviews follow guidelines based on memory research? *Child Maltreatment*, (in press).

Westcott, H. (1991). Institutional abuse of children – from research to policy: A Review. London: NSPCC.

Westcott, H. (1992). The disabled child witness. Paper presented at the NATO Advanced Study Institute on The Child Witness in Context, Italy.

White, S. (1990). The investigatory interview with suspected victims of child sexual abuse. In A. La Greca (ed.), *Through the Eyes of a Child*. Boston: Allyn and Bacon.

Yuille, J., Hunter, R., Joffe, R. and Zaparniuk, J. (1993). Interviewing children in sexual abuse cases. In G. Goodman and B. Bottoms (eds), *Child Victims, Child Witnesses: Understanding and Improving Testimony*. New York: Guilford.

EXPERT TESTIMONY

Amina Memon

INTRODUCTION

Nijboer (1995) defines expertise as the possession of special qualities – quantity and reliability – acquired through special education and training. Mental health expertise informs a range of topics such as the connections between mental health and criminal responsibility, child sexual abuse allegations, children's mental health treatment/placement issues, predictions of future danger, defendant and witness competencies to participate in legal proceedings (see O'Connor *et al.*, 1996 for more examples). This chapter will examine the effects of expert knowledge on accuracy and reliability of eyewitness memory. Leippe (1995) defines expert testimony about eyewitness behaviour as follows:

> Expert testimony about eyewitness behaviour occurs when a psychologist admitted by the judge as an expert authority on 'eyewitness testimony' takes the stand in a jury trial and presents information about research and theory concerning memory and the variables known to influence memory and memory reports.
>
> (Leippe, 1995, p. 910)

As indicated in a review by Penrod and colleagues (1995) until recently expert testimony on eyewitness issues was rare. Over the last 20 years the courts have become more responsive to expert testimony on witness issues.

This chapter is divided into two parts. In the first part, the inquisitorial and adversarial modes of presenting expert evidence are described. The criteria that may be used to determine expertise and to assess the scientific validity of evidence are presented next. The important issues with respect to the admissibility of expert evidence are (1) the qualifications of the expert and (2) the relevance and scientific status of the expert's testimony. In the second part of the chapter, the extent to which expert testimony is necessary and helpful will be addressed. The role of expert testimony in three areas will be described: child witness credibility, rape trauma syndrome and repressed memories. The chapter concludes with a description of expert testimony on witness issues in a real trial and a discussion of some of the ethical dilemmas that may arise when serving as an expert witness.

ADMISSIBILITY OF EXPERT TESTIMONY

The standards for determining the admissibility of testimony have always been an issue for the courts. Until the middle of this century it was rare for the courts to hear testimony on mental issues from experts who were not medical doctors (O'Connor *et al.*, 1996). The qualifications an expert is expected to have vary from one legal system to another. In the UK, the 1993 Royal Commission on Criminal Justice recommended that professional bodies assist the court by maintaining a register of members qualified to act as expert witnesses in particular fields (Runciman, 1993). A psychologist practising in the UK is expected to hold chartered status which is endowed by the British Psychological Society on the basis of relevant qualifications and experience in the field in which the psychologist claims expertise. In England and Wales, it is good practice for expert witnesses to give an overview of their qualifications once they are sworn in. In the USA, there are no uniformly adopted standards by which courts operate but there are requirements that have to be met in order for expert testimony to be admissible. The best known criteria on which expert testimony has been judged are Frye and Daubert.

Frye test

Since 1923, research on eyewitness memory has been subject to the Frye test, a legal criterion that scientific testimony is admissible only if it is based on a theory and evidence that is sufficiently established to have gained acceptance in the particular field in which it belongs (Frye *v*. US, 1923). The judge relies on consensus as to the status of the evidence from the relevant scientists, for example that work upon which the expert evidence is based has been documented in a scholarly journal or conference presentation. This approach is limited in several ways. Once an expert's research is deemed credible there may be no further scrutiny of the scientific status of the evidence undertaken by the courts. This problem this can result in is well illustrated by O'Connor *et al.* (1996):

> Once a court deems a particular type of expert testimony as generally accepted it facilitates the introduction of that type of evidence in other courts and may create a cottage industry of experts who can be called into service.
>
> (O'Connor *et al.*, 1996, p. 46)

Another problem with Frye is that it is not clear how the courts should assess mental health testimony based upon clinical opinion. Clinical expert testimony (assessment of mental competency) is not routinely subject to the Frye test (Flanagan *v*. State, 1991) so it seems that there are different standards for evidence based upon clinical judgement and experience versus evidence based upon empirical research. In other words the courts are applying one set of criteria to clinical expertise and another to scientific expertise. This has become an important issue for debate as the number of cases that draw upon evidence for recovered memories increases (see Chapter 7).

Daubert ruling

A supreme court decision taken in 1993 in Daubert *v.* Merril Dow Pharmaceuticals addressed the standards that federal courts use for the admission of scientific evidence. The Daubert case debated the testimony of experts on whether or not the anti-nausea drug Bendectin was responsible for birth defects. Daubert said Frye was not the test of expertise and gave trial judges the task of making a preliminary assessment of the scientific validity of expert evidence (but see Faigman, 1995). Daubert listed four factors which are deemed necessary in testing the validity of expert evidence: these are falsifiability, error rate, peer review and general acceptance. The first is based on Popper's criterion for distinguishing scientific from non-scientific evidence, the principle of refutability or testability. The second factor is the known or potential error rate of the expert's opinion: Faigman (1995) interprets this as a concern about the accuracy of the diagnoses given by the expert. He gives the following as an example: what proportion of rape victims are not likely to fit the category of 'rape trauma syndrome'? A third factor is checking the credibility of an expert's knowledge by looking for evidence of peer review/publication in scholarly journals. Of course, a number of factors other than the quality of the article may determine what gets published in a 'mainstream journal' (Peters and Ceci, 1982). The fourth criteria is general acceptance: this is the standard used under the Frye test but suffers the same problems as peer review and publication, it depends on the standards. However, unlike the Frye test general acceptance is no longer in itself a sufficient criterion for admission under Daubert, what is most important is scientific rigour. To quote Faigman (1995) under Daubert judges must ask 'where are the data?' While it is clear that greater attention is drawn to the science that the scientist proclaims to practise, the scope of Daubert remains unclear, for instance in dealing with the range of mental health testimony some of which is based on clinical judgements (see O'Connor *et al.*, 1996 for a detailed discussion on the problems of relying on clinical opinion in mental health testimony). It is too early to know what impact Daubert will have, it certainly places a lot more weight on the shoulders of the trial judges who will have to undertake the task of determining whether a new scientific theory/procedure is valid.

Adversarial *v.* inquisitorial systems

According to Damaska (1973) it was a deep routed distrust of judges in the UK and the USA that led to the adversarial system. The latter minimized the role of judges and placed the case in the hands of interested parties. In continental Europe (all European countries except the UK) judges have a key role to play. They are the major channel for information and play an active part in the preparation and evaluation of evidence and in the questioning of witnesses. For instance, in Germany and France, the courts routinely appoint experts. The defendant in the trial is questioned largely by the judge while the advocate's role is to object to questions and seek supplementary information (see McEwan, 1995 for a discussion of the merits of the adversarial/inquisitorial systems). In the inquisitorial system, the psychologist could be appointed as an *amicus curiae* or friend of the court to appear in an educational role (taking no sides). Experts have more freedom in the inquisitorial system in how they present their evidence and they are encouraged to reenact scenarios where possible in order to resolve conflict. Evidence may be presented in the form of a brief which provides a summary of relevant literature and conclusions, this can give juries a balanced overview of the research.

In the USA, court-appointed experts are infrequently employed. This seems to be because of the perceived difficulty in accommodating experts in a system that is used to adversarial presentations of evidence (Cecil and Willging, 1993). A survey conducted by the Federal Judicial Center in 1993 showed that the appointment of the court-appointed expert is often seen as a last resort by judges despite the fact that it may have a strong influence on the outcome of a case (Cecil and Willging, 1993). The survey showed that court-appointed experts were most often used to getting information on technical issues. For example in personal injury cases medical experts would be called to assess the nature of the injury and offer a prognosis. This enables jurors to reach a decision from a more informed perspective.

In the UK, the majority of psychologists who have been called in eyewitness testimony cases have played an advisory role only with their activities being limited to consultation with an attorney (usually the defence) and report writing. Clinical psychologists in the UK usually work across a wide variety of areas of mental health and also work with individual clients in clinical settings drawing on their clinical expertise as well as scientific knowledge (Gudjonsson, 1996). Clinical psychologists in the UK are used as expert witnesses primarily in civil cases (for example in connection with the mental state/capabilities of the client or in child custody disputes). In criminal cases, clinical psychologists can be concerned with questions concerning the sanity, competency and potential danger of the accused.

In the Netherlands, the opinions of expert witnesses are taken at face value by the courts. Experts are court appointed and are the court's own witnesses. As such they are expected to be neutral. Also most expert witnesses are drawn from a relatively small pool (Crombag, 1993).

In France the system is again different. The judge controls the expert's investigations or monitors the whole process. As soon as the judge considers it appropriate he or she orders an investigation by an expert and monitors the expert's work.

THE IMPACT OF EXPERT TESTIMONY

One of the central concerns that arise regarding the use of expert testimony in the courtroom is whether or not it poses a danger to the jury. Penrod *et al.* (1995) suggest that there are four grounds on which expert testimony on eyewitness issues may be rejected by the courts. First, there is the scientific basis of the testimony on eyewitness issues namely the lack of explanatory theory, unreliability of research findings and the limited application of laboratory data to the real world. The evidence reviewed in earlier chapters of this book suggests that researchers in the eyewitness field are in a good position to defend this line of attack. Penrod *et al.* predict that experimental psychologists will be increasingly asked to talk about the role of basic scientific concepts and practices in eyewitness research. As a result of Daubert, judges will be in a position to learn more about the principles governing scientific acceptability of research findings. (So far, Daubert has had a minimum impact on the ways in which eyewitness expert testimony decisions are made.) A second basis for rejecting eyewitness evidence concerns its perceived helpfulness to the jury. One of the central questions here is whether or not eyewitness research invades the province of the jury: is it a matter of common sense? Does it have a prejudicial effect? A third basis for excluding eyewitness expert testimony is that safeguards such as the cross-examination of witnesses or judges' instructions may more adequately address the issues. Finally, expert eyewitness testimony may be rejected because the role of the expert is different. Unlike the expert psychiatrist the typical expert on eyewitness memory does not comment on the reliability or credibility of a witness but the likely effect of witnessing conditions. These basis for testimony on eyewitness issues will now be presented drawing on the issues raised by Penrod *et al.*

A large proportion of the debate surrounding expert testimony centres on the empirical question of what, if any, effects expert testimony has on juror judgement and decision making. One of the central questions is whether scientific research goes beyond common sense and helps the jury reach a decision. As Penrod *et al.* argue, these are essentially empirical questions to which there are empirical answers. For example, there have been several surveys of lay beliefs about the factors that influence eyewitness identification (Deffenbacher and Loftus, 1982) and the general finding is that prospective jurors are sensitive to some factors (e.g. the impact of prior photo identifications on accuracy) but not others. There seems to be little agreement in the responses of individual jurors. Moreover, several studies have reported that laypersons cannot discriminate adequately between accurate and inaccurate eyewitnesses (Lindsay, Wells and Rumpel, 1981).

Can expert testimony on eyewitness issues increase juror sensitivity? In other words, are jurors who are informed about the effects of various witnessing conditions on accuracy better able to discriminate accurate from inaccurate witnesses? Are they able to render decisions in accordance with their knowledge? Can such testimony have a prejudicial impact? These questions will be addressed in the remainder of the chapter by looking in detail at three areas where expert testimony on witness issues has been debated.

EXAMPLES OF RESEARCH ON THE IMPACT OF EXPERT TESTIMONY

Child witnesses

One of the fastest growing areas of research in the eyewitness field has been the study of children as witnesses and as a result of this work the courts have shown greater sensitivity to the needs of children (see Chapter 9).

When children come to court to give evidence, they are often the sole eyewitness in an investigation especially in sexual abuse cases. Concerns about the uncorroborated testimony of child witnesses has led to prosecution and defence calling physicians, mental health professionals and social scientists to serve as expert witnesses either to support or discredit a child's testimony (Ceci and Bruck, 1995). Expert witnesses in child abuse cases for instance may be called to educate fact finders on the relevant scientific literature about child witness testimony and interviewing (see Chapter 9). Other experts may be asked to comment on whether or not a particular child's behaviour is consistent with having been abused. Finally some civil courts allow expert witnesses to testify as to whether they believe the child was abused and whether the child's symptom pattern fits (Myers, 1993).

Child witness preparation may increase the likelihood that a child will remain composed and will provide consistent responses when testifying (see Chapter 9 for a review). Children who have been prepared and are more comfortable, appear more confident, composed and credible (see Saywitz and Snyder, 1993 for a review of this literature). They may provide more coherent testimony. On the other hand, it may be that a prepared child who appears calm/composed on the stand is exhibiting behaviour that contradicts behaviour presented by an expert. Kovera, Borgida and Gresham (1996) hypothesized that if expert testimony sensitizes jurors to an abuse victim's typical response than a prepared child should be judged as less credible than an unprepared child. Expert testimony and child witness preparation were manipulated in a trial simulation study. Information about the behaviours that differentiate a prepared from an unprepared witness was obtained by questioning court attorneys and child witness advocates. Child witness preparation was manipulated by videotaping the same child twice. On one occasion the child was requested to appear nervous, hesitant and fidgety during testimony (unprepared version). Another time the child was instructed to appear calm, confident and less upset (prepared version). The format of testimony was also manipulated to see if expert testimony has a greater impact when the expert explicitly links the research findings to the case at hand (concrete testimony). Previous research has suggested that this 'concrete' form of testimony would produce a more informed jury (Schullar, 1992). Kovera et al. (1996) exposed mock jurors to a videotaped trial simulation based on a Minnesota case where the defendant faced charges of criminal sexual conduct. Among the witnesses was the eight-year-old female victim and the expert. Three versions of expert testimony were created: (1) standard testimony where the expert detailed several common fears of child abuse victims; (2) concrete testimony which applied the information covered in the standard testimony to the case at hand; (3) repetitive testimony where after the standard testimony the expert summarized research findings without explicitly linking the research to the case at hand. Mock jurors who saw the standard repetitive testimony in conjunction with a prepared witness were more likely to convict the defendant than those who saw standard repetitive testimony in conjunction with an unprepared child. Concrete testimony appeared to sensitize jurors in that it led to more convictions than standard testimony where the jurors saw the unprepared child on the stand. This is an important practical finding as it suggests a credibility enhancing and stress reduction procedure such as witness preparation may produce a witness who does not fit the stereotype of a sexual abuse victim (see Crowley et al., 1996). The Kovera et al. study illustrates the complex way in which the nature of expert testimony may interact with witness variables.

The impact of expert testimony in adversarial and inquisitorial modes

Crowley, Ball and O'Callaghan (1996) examined expert testimony in a simulated child abuse trial by presenting testimony in adversarial and non-adversarial modes. They were also interested in the following factors:

- The impact of providing mock jurors with knowledge on children's cognitive abilities (the likelihood of delay in disclosure, memory expertise, distinguishing fact from fantasy and suggestibility).

- The characteristic behavioural reactions to sexual abuse (as in the Kovera *et al.* study described above these included symptoms such as withdrawal and anxiety but in this case the psychologist admitted at the outset that children's responses were highly variable between children).

- The presence in the child's account of statement validity or CBCA criteria (see Chapter 1) regarding the evaluation of children's testimony. That is some of the children's answers were expanded so that exemplars of certain CBCA criteria were added to the standard form of the testimony and it was predicted that jurors would regard these features as credibility enhancing.

In an earlier study Crowley *et al.* (1994) had found expert testimony about children's cognitive development to enhance mock jurors' ratings of child witness credibility on the variables addressed by the expert but its impact on verdicts was less clear. The authors suggest that this is possibly because they presented the psychologist as a court-appointed or impartial educator. In the 1996 study, Crowley *et al.* included an adversarial expert (appearing for the prosecution) in some conditions. This enabled them to compare the inquisitorial system of continental Europe with the adversarial system commonplace in the USA and the UK. The mock jurors in the study were all jury-eligible members of the public who completed a questionnaire designed to assess their attitudes and beliefs about child witnesses prior to the simulation. The simulated trial scenario showed a nine-year-old female who alleged that her father had attempted sexual abuse. A videotaped trial was constructed during the course of which the child was interviewed by a female psychologist and evidence was presented to the judge by the mother, doctor, psychologist and defendant. In the court-appointed role, the psychologist was called and questioned by the judge who made it clear that she was court appointed and was not present to support either the prosecution or the defence case. In the adversarial role, the psychologist was called by the prosecuting counsel. The same questions, answers and cross-examination were conducted in both adversarial and non-adversarial scenarios. Measures included jurors' assessments of the child witness testimony (e.g. confidence, reliability, consistency), verdicts before and after deliberating, and evaluations of the expert and expert testimony.

Crowley *et al.* (1996) observed that mock jurors' pretrial attitude towards conviction based solely on the child's testimony was an important predictor of their subsequent verdict ratings. There was an effect of varying the content quality of the child's statement. Jurors who saw the enhanced statement (i.e. a statement that included six of the CBCA criteria) were more likely to vote guilty and those who voted guilty identified more of the CBCA features as being present in the child's testimony although the jurors were not in agreement as to which criteria would increase or diminish credibility. For example only 28 per cent perceived the presence of spontaneous corrections as credibility enhancing and one-third thought this detracted from credibility despite this being one of the confirmed criteria (see Chapter 1). The other effect found for type of testimony was that jurors who heard the testimony on psychological consequences of abuse on children rated the child less confident and degree of harm as greater but this did not impact on verdicts, a finding that is at odds with their 1994 study (Crowley *et al.*, 1994).

Finally there was a tendency for the recall of testimony delivered in the inquisitorial mode to be poorer than the adversarial mode suggesting less scrutiny of facts presented by the non-adversarial expert. The differing role of the experts had no impact on verdicts but this is hardly surprising given that that questioning was identical with both types of expert witness.

EXPERT TESTIMONY IN A RAPE TRIAL: A SOCIO-COGNITIVE ANALYSIS

In rape cases (as in child sexual abuse cases) prosecutors have difficulty in obtaining convictions based solely on a victim's testimony. Moreover, the public hold myths and stereotypes about this type of crime that may influence the victim's credibility (Brekke and Borgida, 1988). Expert testimony may counteract these stereotypes and misconceptions. Adopting a socio-cognitive perspective, Brekke and Borgida (1988), were interested in whether mock jurors would use group probability data (the small number of women who falsely accuse men of rape, the proportion of rapes that involve casual acquaintances, rape is a crime of violence rather than a crime of passion, and so on) in making a decision. Cognitive psychologists have noted that biases in judgements typically occur as a result of the vast amount of information that has to be processed in reaching decisions. One type of bias is known as a base rate fallacy which is a tendency to use group·data in preference to individuating information. Brekke and Borgida were interested in how the base rate fallacy would operate in a jury context. It was hypothesized that jurors would make the most use of group data in the form of expert testimony when presented early in trial proceedings and linked to the case at hand. Participants (jurors) were 208 undergraduates. The type of testimony (standard expert and hypothetical) and timing of it (expert first/last) were varied in a 2-by-2 design with an independent/no expert testimony control. The duration of the trial varied according to the type of expert. All versions included an opening statement from the judge; opening arguments from prosecution/defence, defendant's testimony, cross-examination/closing arguments and the judge's final charges to the jury. In the standard form the expert dispensed testimony in a lecture-type format. In the hypothetical form, jurors listened to standard expert testimony followed by an explicit attempt to point out the connection between expert testimony and the case under consideration.

As expected women were more favourably disposed towards the defendant on a variety of measures and they rendered significantly more guilty verdicts although the sex differences were less pronounced after deliberation. Women attributed less responsibility to the victim and considered it less likely that she had consented. Female jurors also rated the victim as being significantly more credible (consistent with the studies reviewed earlier). Mock jurors exposed to the specific hypothetical expert testimony were significantly more likely to vote for conviction and to recommend harsher sentences than were jurors who received standard expert testimony.

Brekke and Borgida concluded that expert testimony on behalf of the prosecution may counteract the pervasive effect of rape myths and misconceptions on juror judgements in a simulated trial. When such testimony was linked directly to the case by means of a hypothetical example or presented early in the trial, the result was a higher conviction, harsher sentences and more favourable perceptions of the victim. These findings were obtained despite the fact that jurors did not rate expert testimony as being useful in reaching verdicts. Thus it is possible that when expert testimony is linked with details of the case, it may be useful in reaching verdicts. Timing also seems to be important, most use is made when testimony appears early in the trial. This suggests jurors approach the case with an impression set rather than a recall set i.e. rather than store case facts one by one, jurors may try and organize information into a consistent meaningful whole. Expert testimony presented early may serve as a powerful organizing theme for jurors' first impression of a case.

JURY SIMULATION STUDIES OF RECOVERED MEMORIES

When presented with evidence based on a 'recovered' memory in a court of law, psychologists may be called to assess the reliability of that memory. They may wish to ask some questions about the nature of the recovered memory and these are likely to focus on the conditions prevalent at encoding and the processes by which the memory was recovered.

What are the characteristics of jurors, victims, defendant and case that will predict the outcome in a trial based on evidence from a recovered memory? Some of these questions have recently been addressed in jury simulation studies (Loftus *et al.*, 1993; Key *et al.*, 1996; Clark and Nightingale, 1996; Tetford and Schullar, 1996). Typically, it is found that jurors are skeptical about repressed memory claims although the effects may vary with juror gender, victim gender and details of the case such as the conditions under which the memory was recovered. A recent study conducted at Southampton University (Memon, Wedge and Beese, 1996) provides some pilot data on the effects of providing expert evidence on juror beliefs and decisions. In the Memon *et al.* study, expert testimony was presented in the form of an amicus brief, a statement summarizing current scientific knowledge about recovered memories. We presented all our jurors with a definition of recovered memories from the British Psychological Society Report (1995) and the pretrial information group received a simple non-technical summary of the issues to take into consideration in assessing the validity of repressed memories. The summary acknowledged that early memories could be forgotten and later recovered but the mechanisms involved remain unclear. The possibility that such memories could be inaccurate and the suggestibility of techniques such as hypnosis was highlighted. Our participants (56 males and 52 females, age range 18–65 years) were recruited from a local hospital (staff and visitors) and asked to serve as mock jurors. They were presented with a trial summary which presented an allegation of childhood sexual abuse by an adult victim whose memory was recovered after hypnosis in therapy. Dependent variables were juror ratings of believability of the victim, evaluation of victim's testimony (telling the truth, honestly mistaken or deliberately lying), verdict and sentence. Briefly we found that providing pretrial information had no significant effect on victim believability ratings but it significantly reduced the number of guilty verdicts suggesting that it served to make jurors more skeptical of the victim's testimony. There was also a tendency for the information group to believe the victim to be honestly mistaken rather than telling the truth accurately whereas the no-information group were more likely to believe the opposite. Clearly this line of research is worth pursuing using more representative samples of subjects exploring such issues as background of juror (age, race, religion, profession) and the effects of expert evidence and lay beliefs about recovered memories on jury deliberation and decision making.

SUMMARY

Jury simulation studies suggest that expert testimony may have an impact on jury beliefs and decision making. In the examples above, it was shown that scientific information on the abilities of child witnesses, responses of rape victims and reliability of recovered memories may be applied in making judgements about specific individuals in a trial. It has typically been found that females are more lenient than males in cases of sexual abuse and related crimes and regard victims as more credible (but see Epstein and Bottoms, 1996).

In the final section of this chapter we will examine a trial in which psychologists serving on behalf of the prosecution and defence presented scientific evidence. The impact of the Daubert ruling on evidence of this kind will also be discussed.

EXPERT TESTIMONY IN RECOVERED MEMORY CASES

The first murder case to rest heavily on repressed memory was the trial of George Franklin in California, accused by his daughter Eileen of killing Susan Nason in 1969 when both girls were eight years old. The memory supposedly lay buried for some 20 years amidst a history of childhood abuse. At the time of Franklin's arrest, detectives found evidence of paedophile activities. During the course of therapy Eileen recalled her father having sexually abused her and an incident is described where she caught her father molesting her own daughter. There were a number of inconsistencies in the various accounts that Eileen gave of the murder of Susan Nason from the time the memory was recovered right up to the court proceeding (Maclean, 1993). The extent to which Eileen's memory was derived from media reports of the crime was not considered since press cuttings from the time at which the murder occurred were not admitted as evidence in the trial. Expert witnesses were called upon to provide the jury with some information about the effects of trauma on memory. Lenore Terr, a psychiatrist, served as an expert witness for the prosecution in the Franklin case. Terr's evidence on the effects of repeated trauma, based upon her own research and anecdotal observations, was critical in convincing the jury about the validity of Eileen's memory (Terr, 1994). Elizabeth Loftus gave expert testimony for the defence. Loftus cited her studies which show that stress at encoding can impair recall and her extensive work on the malleability of memory under suggestive questioning. Her studies were deemed irrelevant on the basis that they did not manipulate delay between encoding and test sufficiently and do not tap into an unconscious mental process (Maclean, 1993). Loftus (in Loftus and Ketchum, 1994) asks 'how is it possible for a scientist to search for evidence to prove or disprove an unconscious mental process involving a series of internal events that occur spontaneously without warning and with no external signs to indicate what is about to happen or what has already happened' (p. 64). She concludes that her findings only apply to the real and verifiable and not to the unknown and unverifiable.

The jury voted unanimously that there was evidence beyond reasonable doubt that George Franklin was guilty of first degree murder and he was convicted in November, 1990. Readers will be interested to note that Franklin's conviction has recently been overturned. One reason for the reversal of the court's decision was that the defence was not permitted to introduce newspaper accounts of the crime scene which would have shown that Eileen's memories may have been derived from this source. The latter contained details similar to those given by Eileen after she recovered the memories (Bikel, 1995).

Faigman (1995) argues that the Daubert ruling constitutes a major problem for recovered memories: hypotheses are difficult to test, effects difficult to replicate, alternative explanations cannot be ruled out, and of most concern in the legal context is that we cannot distinguish true and false accounts and thus we cannot be sure about the accuracy of recovered memories. However, as argued in Chapter 7 there is a wealth of evidence on the retrieval of information from memory and the processes that may lead to accurate recall and distortions. Where the evidence is lacking is on special mechanisms to support the previous inaccessibility of a memory (and to enable the tolling of the statute of limitations). As pointed out by Faigman (1995) the decision to admit expert testimony rests on the necessity principle. The acceptance or rejection of evidence must be linked to the consequences of giving such testimony. The problem is that legal proceedings need immediate answers and cannot wait for more research to be conducted. 'Science can defer judgment until sufficient data have been collected. When judges look to science and find an incomplete picture they should decide admissibility on the basis of a combination of scientific merit and judiprudential need' (Faigman, 1995, p. 64). The necessity principle thus provides judges with a way of gauging the state of current evidence and to weigh up the risks and benefits of admitting such evidence. Faigman (1995) suggests that the necessity principle seems ideally suited to repressed memory evidence where judges have to consider the complexity of the research and the scarcity of clinical evidence.

The Daubert criteria were applied in a criminal case based on recovered memories of sexual abuse (State v. Hungerford, Hillsborough Country, 1993) where the judge concluded that there was insufficient scientific evidence for repression and the lack of agreement among psychologists about the likelihood of recovery following amnesia. Moreover, the judge criticized the psychotherapy techniques used to recover memories as having failed to satisfy the Frye test and the failure on the part of therapists to corroborate the alleged abuse. The judge also expressed a concern that allowing experts to testify on the accuracy of a compliant's memory (when there was no external corroboration of abuse) would make jurors base their decisions solely on the experts' testimony. The Hungerford case was a criminal one, it is likely that courts will be less stringent in civil cases (Taub, 1996).

ETHICAL ISSUES

The debate concerning the reliability of recovered memories reminds us of the ethical dilemmas that face expert witnesses who give testimony on psychological issues. This will be the final topic of discussion in this chapter.

Advocate or impartial educator?

According to Loftus (1986) the most important ethical issue surrounding the role of experimental psychologists as experts is whether or not the psychologist should assume the role of advocate or impartial educator. Loftus points out that it is very hard to avoid becoming identified with one of the sides since the essence of working in an adversarial system is that one side of the case is presented and challenged by the other. Indeed expert witnesses such as Loftus are accused of being advocates for one side. Moreover, jurors attitudes may be swayed by misperceived bias. It has been found that jurors believe experts are chosen to testify because their opinions favour the party by whom they are called (Vidmar and Schullar, 1989).

Geiselman (1994) has pointed out that it is a difficult task for an expert to play the role of consultant without straying into the advocate role. Ethical dilemmas are most likely to arise in cases where a defendant stands accused of a serious crime. Geiselman (1994) recounts a murder case on which he served as eyewitness expert for the superior court of Los Angeles. An armoured courier was carrying money in a store when he was shot in the back. The assailant fired a second time to make sure the victim died before fleeing. A single witness had a brief view of the assailant and this was used to form a police sketch. The latter was given to the news media and a woman who saw the composite claimed it was the same person who had shot her son some years earlier. The person she referred to was on parole and his photograph was placed in a lineup for the witness to view. The eyewitness to this crime stood to gain 30 000 dollars reward money. This is a crime which may justify the death penalty, the defendant had already been convicted for shooting another person. There is much that an expert could comment on in the case: stress, weapon focus, confidence and so on. One of the concerns that Geiselman had in this case was the possibility that the suspect was innocent. Another was that his feelings about the crime may bias his judgement. For example, one time Geiselman (1994) was asked to take on a case where a gang member stood accused of holding a knife at the throat of a three-month-old baby while he robbed the mother. The only evidence was the husband's identification. Geiselman refused to take on the case given that he could identify strongly with the parents in the case, he had a baby at home also.

Objectivity in child abuse trials

There have been professional concerns about the objectivity of experts in child sexual abuse trials. For example it has been alleged that child advocates may express more opinions in favour of the child (Levy, 1989). Kovera, Borgida, Gresham, Swim and Gray (1993) have expressed the opinion that clinical experts in adversarial roles may hold more polarized beliefs that favour the child witness. Kovera et al. (1993) undertook an empirical study to examine to what extent experts' prochild beliefs would lead them to evaluate a child's evidence favourably. They sampled members of the International Society for Traumatic

Stress, many of whom will be familiar with post-traumatic stress disorder and other responses to child abuse. They sent a questionnaire to members asking for their opinions about various aspects of child sexual abuse, children's capabilities as witnesses, and the prosecution of child sexual abuse. The major finding of the survey was that while the respondents expressed generally favourable beliefs about child witnesses, the background of the experts was likely to predict their beliefs (although the extent to which these beliefs translate to the courtroom situation is unknown). Those respondents who specialize in working with child sexual assault victims expressed more positive beliefs about children's capabilities presumably because they are likely to be more knowledgeable about their capabilities and limitations. The Kovera study provides us with some information on experts beliefs, however, we cannot tell from this study the extent to which beliefs are based on their knowledge of the research, their experiences and so on. Moreover, further research is needed to determine how these beliefs influence decision making in the courts.

CONCLUSIONS

In 1983, McCloskey and Egeth argued that there was not much that a psychologist could tell a jury concerning general eyewitness memory. Ten years later Egeth (1993) admitted that research on eyewitness testimony continues to accumulate and improve in quality. Psychologists working in the forensic psychology field have broadened their focus away from the courts to look at the process of evaluating the impact of variables prior to court appearance (e.g preparation of the witness). They have begun to use more relevant research scenarios including field research, archival data and research designs which take into account the complexity of human behaviour in the real world. A good example is the work on suggestibility of witness memory (see Chapters 7 and 9). This has gone from traditional laboratory studies where subjects are presented with slides of an event to real-life interviews where memories are implanted over a period of time. Similarly, research on techniques for enhancing eyewitness memory have progressed from laboratory studies of factors that influence encoding and retrieval to studies of techniques used by police officers in the field (Chapter 8). As far as our understanding of the variables that impact jury decisions, however, we have a long way to go. Much of the jury simulation research relies on unrepresentative samples (i.e. undergraduate students) and unrealistic scenarios. Future research needs to draw on the processes that govern jury decisions in real trials and the impact of jury deliberation on verdicts.

The increased communication between psychologists and lawyers is well illustrated by the recent publication of *The Handbook of Psychology in Legal Contexts* edited by a lawyer (David Carson) and a psychologist (Ray Bull), a text that has been well received. Indeed, in the USA, the Arizona Supreme Court made a unique decision to overturn a guilty verdict on the grounds that expert testimony on eyewitness behaviour had not been permitted (State *v*. Chapple, 135 Ariz. 281, 660 P.2d 1208, 1983). Expert evidence provides a means whereby scientific knowledge and insight can inform the court's decisions (Carson, 1992). We hope that we have presented you with a clear picture of the many areas of psychological research that may be applied in legal contexts and that this encourages further collaboration between psychologists and legal professionals.

REFERENCES

Bikel, O. (1995). *Memories: A House Divided*. Frontline, Boston: WGBH.

Brekke, N. and Borgida, E. (1988). Expert psychological testimony in rape trial: a social-cognitive analysis. *Journal of Personality and Social Psychology*, (55), 372–386.

Carson, D. (1992). Expert evidence in the courts. *Expert Evidence*, 1(1), 13–18.

Ceci, S.J. and Bruck, M. (1995). *Jeopardy in the Courtroom*. Washington, DC: American Psychological Association.

Cecil, J.S. and Willging, T.E. (1993). Court-appointed experts: defining the role of court-appointed experts under federal rules of evidence 706. Federal Judicial Center.

Clark, H.L. and Nightingale, N.N. (in press). When jurors considered recovered memory cases: effects of victim and juror gender? *Journal of offender rehabilitation: Special issue on jury simulation and eyewitness testimony*.

Crombag, H.F.M. (1993). Expert witnesses as vicarious anchors, *Expert Evidence*, 5, 127–131.

Crowley, M.J., O'Callaghan, M.G. and Ball, P.J. (1994). The judicial impact of psychological expert testimony in a simulated sex abuse trial. *Law and Human Behavior*, 18, 89–105.

Crowley, M.J., Ball, P.J. and O'Callaghan, M.G. (1996). Impact of varying child statement quality and expert testimony in a simulated child sexual abuse trial. Manuscript submitted for publication.

Damaska, M. (1973). Evidentiary barriers to conviction and two models of criminal procedure: a comparative study. *University of Pennsylvania Law Review*, **506**.

Daubert *v.* Merrell Dow Pharmaceuticals, Inc., 113 S CT. 2786 (1993).

Deffenbacher, K.A. and Loftus, E.F. (1982). Do jurors share a common understanding concerning eyewitness behaviour? *Law and Human Behavior*, 6, 15–30.

Egeth, H.E. (1993). What do we not know about eyewitness identification? *American Psychologist*, **48**, 577–580.

Epstein, M.A. and Bottoms, B.L. (1996). Gender differences in child sexual abuse case judgements: what happens after deliberation and why. Paper presented at the March 1996 Biennial meeting of the American Psychology-Law Society, Hilton Head, South Carolina.

Faigman, D.L. (1995). The evidentiary status of social science under Daubert: is it scientific, technical or other knowledge? *Psychology, Public Policy and Law*, 1(4), 960–979.

Frye *v.* United States 293 F.1013 (D.C. Cir. 1923).

Geiselman, R.E. (1994). Providing eyewitness expert testimony in Los Angeles. *Expert Evidence*, 3(1), 9–15.

Gudjonsson, G. (1996). Psychological evidence in court, *The Psychologist*, 9(5), 213–219.

Key, H.G., Warren, A.R. and Ross, D.F. (1996). Perception of repressed memories:aA reappraisal. *Law and Human Behavior*, **20**(5), 555–563.

Kovera, M., Borgida, E., Gresham, A., Swim, J. and Gray, E. (1993). Do child sexual abuse experts hold pro-child beliefs? A survey of the International Society for Traumatic Stress Studies. *Journal of Traumatic Stress*, 6(3), 383–403.

Kovera, M., Borgida, E. and Gresham, A. (1996, March). The impact of child witness preparation and expert testimony on juror decision making. Paper presented at the biennial meeting of the American Psychology-Law Society, Hilton Head.

Leippe, M.R. (1995). The case for expert testimony about eyewitness memory. *Psychology, Public Policy and Law*, 1(4), 909–959.

Levy, R.J. (1989). Using scientific testimony to prove child abuse: the Dorsey and Whitney professorship procedure. *Family Law Quarterly*, 23, 383–409.

Lindsay, R.C.L., Wells, G. and Rumpel, C. (1981). Can people detect eyewitness identification accuracy within and between situations? *Journal of Applied Psychology*, 79–89.

Loftus, E.F. (1986). Experimental psychologist as advocate or impartial educator. *Law and Human Behavior*, 10, 63–78.

Loftus, E. and Ketcham, K. (1994). *The Myth of Repressed Memory*. New York: St Martins Press.

Loftus, E.F., Weingardt, K.R. and Hoffman, H.G. (1993). Sleeping memories on trial: reactions to memories that were previously repressed. *Expert Evidence: International Digest of Human Behavior, Science and the Law*, 2, 51–60 .

Maclean, H. (1993). *Once Upon a Time*. New York: Harper Collins.

McCloskey and Egeth, H. (1983). Eyewitness identification: what can a psychologist tell a jury? *American Psychologist*, 38, 550–563.

McEwan, J. (1995). Adversarial and inquisitorial proceedings. In Bull, R. and Carson, D. (eds), *Handbook of Psychology in Legal Contexts*. Chichester: John Wiley and Sons.

Memon, A., Wedge, G. and Beese, R. (1996, June). Juror perceptions of recovered memories: does prior knowledge influence decision making? Poster presented at the NATO meeting on Recollections of Trauma, France.

Myers, J.E.B. (1993). Expert testimony regarding child sexual abuse. *Child Abuse and Neglect*, 17, 175–185.

Nijboer, H. (1995). Expert evidence. In Bull, R. and Carson, D. (eds), *Handbook of Psychology in Legal Contexts*. Chichester: John Wiley and Sons.

O'Connor, M., Sales, B. and Shuman, D.W. (1996) Mental health professional expertise in the courtroom. In Sales, B. and Shuman, D.W. (eds), *Law, Mental Health and Mental Disorder*. New York: Brooks Cole Publishing Company.

Penrod, S.D., Fulero, S.M., Cutler, B.L. (1995). Expert psychological testimony on eyewitness reliablity before and after Daubert: the state of the law and the science. *Behavioral Sciences and the Law*, 13, 229–259.

Peters, D. and Ceci, S. (1982). Peer review practices of psychological journals: the fate of published articles, submitted again. *Behavioural and Brain Sciences*, 5, 187–255.

Lord Runciman (1993). Report of the Royal Commission on Criminal Justice. Cm 2263. London: HMSO.

Saywitz, K. and Snyder, L. (1993). Improving children's testimony with preparation. In G.S. Bottoms and B.L. Bottoms (eds), *Child Victims, Child Witnesses*. The Guildford Press, New York and London.

Schullar, R.A. (1992). The impact of battered woman syndrome evidence on jury decision processes. *Law and Human Behaviour*, 16, 597–620.

Taub, S. (1996). The legal treatment of recovered memories of child sexual abuse. *Journal of Legal Medicine*, 17, 183–214.

Terr, L. (1994). *Unchained Memories: True Stories of Traumatic Memories, Lost and Found*. New York: Basic Books.

Tetford, I. and Schullar, R.A. (1996). Mock jurors' evaluations of child sexual abuse: the impact of memory recovery and therapeutic intervention. *Behavioural Sciences and the Law*, **14**, 205–218.

Tulving, E. and Thomson, D.M. (1973). Encoding specificity and retrieval processes in episodic memory. *Psychological Review*, **80**, 353–370.

Vidmar, N. and Schuller, R. (1989). Juries and expert evidence: social framework. *Testimony, Law and Contemporary Problems*, **52**, 133–176.

Wells, G. (1986). Expert psychological testimony: empirical and conceptual analysis of effects. *Law and Human Behavior*, **10**, 83–95.

Wells, G.L., Rydell, S.M. and Seelau, E.P. (1993). The selection of distracters for eyewitness lineups. *Journal of Applied Psychology*, **78**(5), 835–844.

SUBJECT INDEX

AUTHOR INDEX